STOCKING UP ON SIN

STOCKING UP ON SIN

How to Crush the Market with Vice-Based Investing

Caroline Waxler

WILEY

John Wiley & Sons, Inc.

Published by John Wiley & Sons, Inc., Hoboken, New Jersey.
Published simultaneously in Canada.

For general information on our other products and services, or technical support, please contact our Customer Care Department within the United States at 800-762-2974, outside the United States at 317-572-3993 or fax 317-572-4002.

Wiley also publishes its books in a variety of electronic formats. Some content that appears in print may not be available in electronic books.

For more information about Wiley products visit our web site at www.wiley.com.

Library of Congress Cataloging-in-Publication Data:

Waxler, Caroline.
  Stocking up on sin : how to crush the market with vice-based investing /
Caroline Waxler.
      p.   cm.
Published simultaneously in Canada.
Includes bibliographical references and index.
    ISBN 0-471-46513-5 (cloth)
1. Investments–Moral and ethical aspects.   I. Title.
HG4515.13 .W39 2004
332.63'22–dc22
                                                            2003021774

Printed in the United States of America.

10 9 8 7 6 5 4 3 2 1

Acknowledgments

I can't express enough thanks to my agents, Greg Dinkin and Frank Scatoni of Venture Literary, for all their incredible hard work, thoughtfulness, example, care, and yenta-ing. They did practically everything but write the book.

Greg teamed me up with the perfect editor, Debra Englander of Wiley, to make this book happen. She had the vision to see the potential in this project and the patience to guide me through the process. I was lucky to collaborate with someone who has such a rare combination of perseverance, diligence, and talent. I am indebted also to her colleague Greg Friedman for all his hard work.

My appreciation to Randy Jones, founder of *Worth* magazine, for assigning the article that spawned this book and to Michael Peltz for patiently editing and shaping that article. Without them this book would not exist.

I am grateful to the people who have helped and generously shared their expertise with me: John Semel, Michael Tew, Anthony Butler, Martin Vostry, Tim McDarrah, Dan Ahrens, Dr. Roderick Pettis, Adam Glickman, and Richard Laermer. I am especially grateful to Webster Stone for coming up with the title of this book, and to Sam Coolik and Gretchen Morgenson, who taught me about investing in the first place.

Thanks to Carter Crum, CFA, for all his helpful research on gambling, drinking, eating, and so forth. He is the savviest money manager I have ever worked with.

Brian Lerner was an enormous help. He was a great partner in making this book possible and a first-rate researcher. And to the fabulous Pan sisters, Amelia and Esther, thanks for being a godsend in times of crunch.

For the daily encouragement, support, and deadline reminders: Ilana Albert, Joey Anuff, Emily Cohen, Sean Gottlieb, Brent Hoff, and Nadine Zylstra. And, for his thoughtful suggestions, not to mention a job that provides inspiration for all things vice, Michael Hirschorn.

Enormous thanks for their encouragement and for keeping me focused: Ali Weiss, Bernadette Durham, Annalise Carol, Sabina Forbes, and Susan Mactavish Best. And, of course, to my family for all your support, particularly Aunt Joan, with her unflagging work ethic and ingenuity, kept me inspired throughout this whole process. Grandma Sylvia, the true writer in the family, would have enjoyed this book more than anyone. The book is dedicated to my mother, Barb, a woman who may not know from vice but, thanks to Miss Finney, knows a thing or two about investing. Luckily, she has passed that knowledge on to me.

Contents

1

Why Vice Is Nice

Sin Never Goes Out of Style

When everything seems to be going badly in your life, do you feel like taking a drink? Pigging out? Having a–gasp–cigarette? Watching a porno? (Well, maybe the last one doesn't apply to everyone, but you get the idea.) Do you also feel like doing these things in good times too? If you do, you're not alone.

Besides having some fun, and having someone else to drink with, what does that mean for you? What does it mean for your wallet?

It turns out that these common impulses mean a lot, according to Tom Galvin, who commissioned a report on vice stocks when he was the chief investment officer of banking powerhouse Credit Suisse First Boston in 2001. What's vice? It can be loosely defined as all those things you're not supposed to do: drink, smoke, and make weapons for the military–what Galvin called the "Vice Squad." This is a longstanding trend, not just a fly-by-night flirtation with sin.

During the past recessions, according to Galvin's research, particularly during the ones in 1982 and 1990–1991, sectors like alcohol, tobacco, and food consumption outperformed the market. At these times industry pricing in all these areas, with the exception of food, rises above the national average. This ability to raise prices is called pricing power (you'll be seeing this term throughout the book). These sectors are classified as a good, safe bet in all markets, their vice aspect aside, but they are at their best during the early parts of recessions.

"The reason we did the Vice Squad report is that there are some sectors that tend to show better business performance during economically weak periods. They are beneficiaries of mere flaws in human character," says Galvin. "It turns out that demand for drinking, smoking, and gambling remain pretty steady and actually increase during economically volatile conditions."

Galvin notes that these stocks significantly outperformed the market over the 18 months before the report's release in March of 2001. What inspired Galvin to write it? The world around him. The week he wrote the Vice Squad report, the Mafiosi-centered series *The Sopranos* was a top-rated show. He notes that at the other end of the spectrum the docudrama *The Kennedys*–showing the Camelot aspect, not the scandals–was one of the lowest-rated shows. He took this to mean that there was steadier demand for vice during times of weak economic conditions.

"It was 2001 and the economy was entering a recession. It was a report on counter-cyclical stocks, defensive plays," says Galvin. "I labeled it Vice Squad because I thought it would be a bit more focused than a defensive oriented fund."

Get Active

Galvin's report was only a guidepost for investors but if you want someone to actively manage your money in a sinful way, the only dedicated fund is something called, appropriately enough, the Vice Fund. Based in Dallas, Texas, this fund focused solely on vice was launched in August of 2002 by the investment company Mutuals .com. The $6 million vice fund was co-founded and is co-run by Dan Ahrens, who is a big believer in the economic power of the not-so-nice things.

The Vice Fund is now your only mutual fund option when it comes to a targeted fund of sin stocks. This book will, however, help arm you as you go about setting up your own mini-sin fund, which you can tailor to your own personal Achilles heel, if that's the way you want to go. Along with an experienced, talented money manager, Carter Crum, CPA, I've put together a Stocking Up on SINDEX (See Appendices II and III) of my favorite vice stocks. Turns out the market liked them, too. The portfolio returned 42% over 5 years while the S&P had a negative return.)

For those seeking a mutual fund, the Vice Fund (VICEX) is a no-load fund. It defines a vice stock as any company that makes at least 25% of its revenues from politically incorrect products in one of four sectors: tobacco, gambling, defense/weapons, and liquor.

As of this writing, the fund's top five holdings were Altria Group (makers of Philip Morris cigarettes), Shuffle Master (automatic card shufflers used in casinos), Anheuser-Busch (Budweiser and other beers), British American Tobacco (Benson & Hedges and other cigarettes), and defense contractor L-3 Communications. About 95% of the holdings are in companies like these—big blue chip defensive players. The remaining 5% is in companies such as Electronic Arts Inc. and THQ Inc., both video game makers. If you're talking sloth, video games are up there. Besides, have you played video games lately? They are pretty much sin central: violence and sex, or at least sex appeal. One of the most popular games is called Vice City.

Ahrens says that the sectors chosen to represent the Vice Fund are easy for the public to understand and largely recession-proof. He expects the fund to adhere to its straightforward sinful mantra. The only categories that really diverge from the obvious sin places are video games and one other big tech company that you might have heard of—Microsoft, which makes up about 2% of the fund's investments. "With everything else we have," Ahrens said, "we had to throw in a little antitrust."[1]

In the short history of the Vice Fund, it has reported some impressive numbers for the sin side of things: three of its four sectors have outperformed the S&P 500 Index in 1- 3-, and 5-year periods (see Figures 1.1–1.12). Using June 30, 2003 as the starting point, the S&P was down 1.55% for 12 months prior, down 33.01% for 3 years prior, and down 14.05% for 5 years prior. In the same period, gaming and casinos returned 24.65%, 66.36%, and 145.13%, respectively.

TABLE 1.1   The Vice Fund's Top Ten Holdings as of 7/31/03

4.91%	Altria Group (Philip Morris)
4.53%	Shuffle Master
4.40%	Anheuser-Busch
4.35%	Constellation Brands
4.35%	L-3 Communications
3.91%	British American Tobbacco
3.79%	Harrah's Entertainment
3.69%	United Technologies
3.48%	Northrop Grumman
3.46%	Lockheed Martin

TABLE 1.2   Top Industry Breakdown as of 7/31/03

26.66%	Gaming
24.47%	Defense
22.37%	Alcohol
17.74%	Tobacco

TABLE 1.3   Full List of Vice Fund Holdings as of August 2003

Multimedia Games, Inc - MGAM	Altria Group Inc - MO
L-3 Communications - ILL	Shuffle Master - SHFL
Constellation Brands - STZ	Anheuser Busch Cos - BUD
British American Tobacco ADR - BTI	
United Technologies Corp - UTX	
Harrah's Entertainment Inc - HET	
Northrop Grumman Corporation - NOC	
Lockheed Martin Corp - LMT	
Harley Davidson Inc - HDI	
MGM Mirage - MGG	
Coors Adolph Co CL B - RKY	
GTECH Hldgs Corp - GTK	

TABLE 1.3 (*Continued*)

Diageo ADR - DEO

ManTech International Corp - MANT

Electronic Arts Inc - ERTS

General Dynamics Corp - GD

Imperial Tob Group PLC ADR - ITY

Scientific Games - SGMS

Microsoft Corp - MSFT

Ameristar Casinos Inc - ASCA

Central European Distribution - CEDC

Fortune Brands Inc - FO

Alliance Gaming Co - AGI

United Defense Inds Inc - UDI

UST Inc - UST

Fomento Economico Mexicano S A - FMX

Chicago Pizza & Brewery - CHGO

Companhia de Bebidas PR ADR - ABV

Penn National Gaming Inc -PENN

Universal Corp VA - UVV

Kerzner International Ltd - KZL

Reynolds RJ Tobacco Holdings - RJR

Carolina Group - CG

THQ Inc - THQI

MTR Gaming Group Inc - MNTG

Curtis Wright - CW

Honeywell - HON

Heineken NV ADR - HINKY

DRS Technologies Inc - DRS

Standard Commercial Corp - STW

Swedish Match ADR -SWMAY

Rockwell Collins Inc - COL

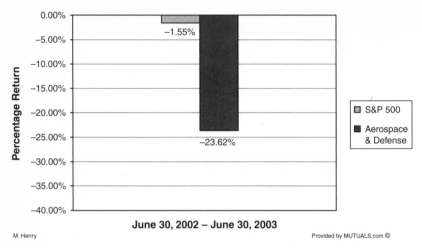

M. Henry   Provided by MUTUALS.com ©

FIGURE 1.1*   **1-Year Return: Aerospace and Defense vs. S&P 500**

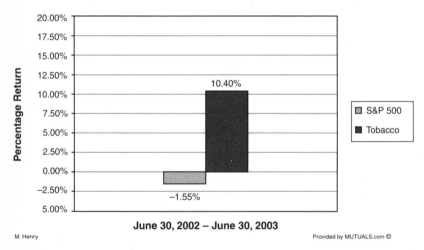

M. Henry   Provided by MUTUALS.com ©

FIGURE 1.2*   **1-Year Return: Tobacco vs. S&P 500**

*The S&P 500 Index includes 500 common stocks, most of which are listed on the New York Stock Exchange. The Index is a market capitalization-weighted index representing approximately two-thirds of the total market value of all domestic stocks. It is compared to a smaller group of stocks from particular industries.

Data is based on a study of all alcohol, tobacco, defense, gaming, and casino industries with the exception of those companies with a market capitalization of less than $50 million, conducted by MUTUALS.com. The historical sector data was provided by Commodity Systems, Inc. (CSI) and screened by MUTUALS. com to eliminate companies with a market capitalization less than $50 million. The sectors are then capitalization-weighted by their individual components. All data is adjusted for splits and dividends. Data and information is provided for informational purposes only and is not intended for trading purposes or to imply any future performance.

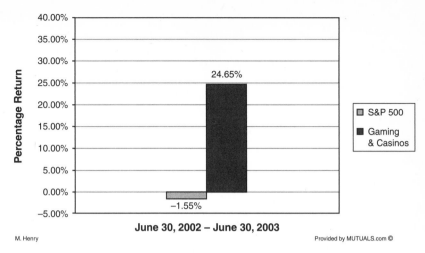

M. Henry   Provided by MUTUALS.com ©

FIGURE 1.3   1-Year Return: Gaming and Casinos vs. S&P 500

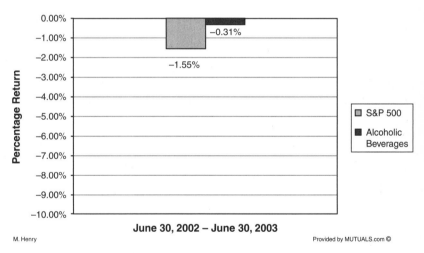

M. Henry   Provided by MUTUALS.com ©

FIGURE 1.4   1-Year Return: Alcoholic Beverages vs. S&P 500

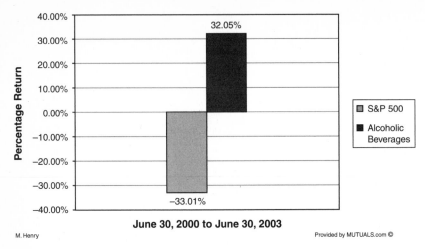

M. Henry   Provided by MUTUALS.com ©

FIGURE 1.5   3-Year Return: Alcoholic Beverages vs. S&P 500

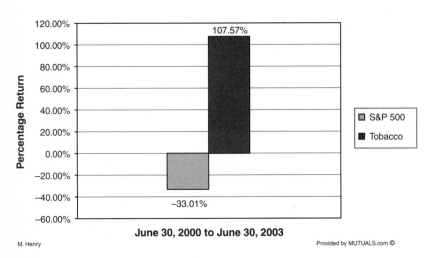

M. Henry   Provided by MUTUALS.com ©

FIGURE 1.6   3-Year Return: Tobacco vs. S&P 500

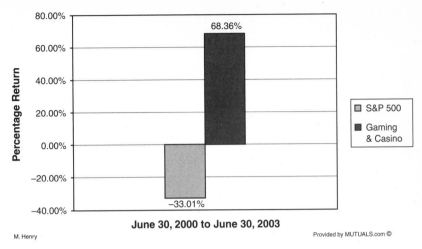

M. Henry   Provided by MUTUALS.com ©

FIGURE 1.7   **3-Year Return: Gaming and Casinos vs. S&P 500**

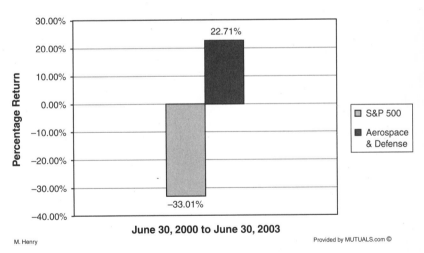

M. Henry   Provided by MUTUALS.com ©

FIGURE 1.8   **3-Year Return: Aerospace and Defense vs. S&P 500**

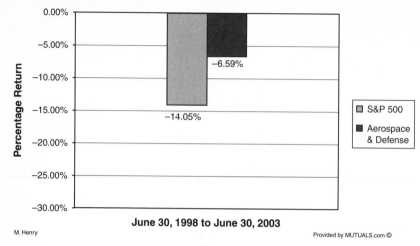

FIGURE 1.9   5-Year Return: Aerospace and Defense vs. S&P 500

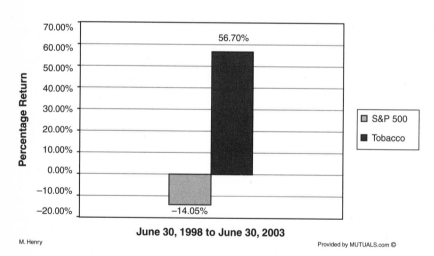

FIGURE 1.10   5-Year Return: Tobacco vs. S&P 500

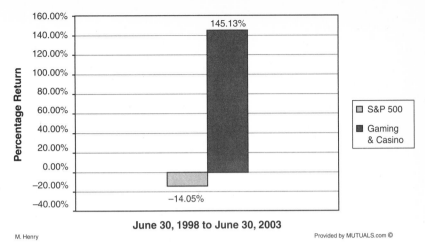

FIGURE 1.11   **5-Year Return: Gaming and Casino vs. S&P 500**

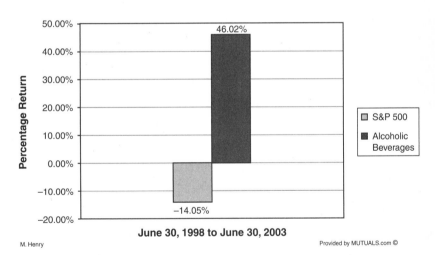

FIGURE 1.12   **5-Year Return: Alcoholic Beverages vs. S&P 500**

Alcohol was down 0.31%, up 32.05%, and up 46.02%. Tobacco was up 10.40%, 10.57%, and 56.70%. The only disappointing sector was aerospace and defense: down 23.62%, up 22.71%, and down 6.59%.

Of course, as in any other industry, these stocks have their down times. During the fourth quarter of 2002 there was a rally led by telecom and technology stocks. Since those stocks (except for Microsoft) aren't in the sin portfolio, the holdings of the Vice Fund weren't exactly on the winning side of the equation.

Quasi Sin Funds

The Vice Fund isn't completely *sui generis*; there are some distant relatives. Let's look at how its kin, more mainstream investment vehicles, such as the Invesco Leisure Fund and Fidelity Select Food & Agriculture Fund, which incorporates hotels, cable, chocolate, and fast food, have done for comparable periods. Invesco returned 5.21% for June 30, 2002 to June 30, 2003; down 1.09% for June 30, 2000 to June 30, 2003; year-to-date June 30, 2003, it was up 12.19%. The Fidelity Fund was down 9.03%, up 4.92%, and up 2.91% for the same periods.

The only other somewhat naughty fund in the industry's 8,000-plus mutual funds was something called Morgan FunShares, Inc. It was started as Morgan Sin Shares in 1979 by Burton D. Morgan, who put together an investment partnership for family members with the money he made from manufacturing adhesives–what he calls "sticky paper." The idea was that he would invest only in stocks involved in vices, such as smoking, gambling, drinking, and sex. It included stocks like Philip Morris Cos., Harrah's Entertainment Inc., Seagram Co., and Carter-Wallace Inc., (at that time makers of Trojan condoms). Four years later, he took the fund public under the name Morgan Funshares. (Why the name change? Big-time investor Sir John Templeton, a friend of Morgan's and a very conservative religious man, told Morgan that he didn't like the word *sin*.)

Morgan, who described himself to me as an 86-year-old farmer in Hudson, Ohio, said about the fund, "I just do this as a lark." He didn't actively manage the fund ("We never sell."). Indeed, his mantra was: "Buy low and never sell," he told me. "That's the key. I'm sorry I waited so long in life to find this out."

Considering his buy-and-hold strategy, it's no wonder that the fund had mixed results. While the good intentions were there, the market didn't respond so well to a fund whose portfolio rarely changed. Over its lifetime, to November 10, 2003, the fund returned 6.23% on an annualized basis. In March of 2003, the zestful Burt Morgan passed away, and in August the president, Robert Pincus, announced that he would be shutting it down by the end of the year. It seems that the closed-end fund, with its $8 million in assets, would have been too expensive to keep running. Morgan owned 49.3% of the fund's outstanding common shares and at the time of his death planned to exercise rights to acquire $1 million more. (Such an undertaking would have been costly, so the fund withdrew the registration for the rights offering in April.) Plus, it was trading at a discount to its underlying asset value, which often happens when demand is low.

In this case, it was a great concept, but with its strict holding strategy this was more one man's hobby than appropriate for the general public consumption. Since it was a "fun" fund, not a vice fund, holdings were pretty broad; the third largest holding was Wm. Wrigley Jr., the gum maker. But hey, the owner had a good time—"a lark"—before he died.

The Nay Sayers

Vice stocks have their appeal, the same sex appeal of their holdings. That, of course, attracts attention. Then there's the interest stemming from the backlash against political correctness.

Meir Statman, professor of finance at the Leavey School of Business, Santa Clara University in California, thinks vice funds are attractive because investors are, in his words, sick of "goody-goodies." "People who want to single out tobacco and alcohol companies may do it to express exasperation with those who want to reduce the amount of smoking," he says. The vice funds appeal to people's inner contrarian, although Statman and other gurus dismiss them as a something of a gimmick: "Vice funds seem to be a gag. It's a fun idea and has novelty value."[2] But can a gimmick with such nice returns be such a bad thing? (That's a gimmick I would take.) Because of its tiny size Ahrens' Vice Fund isn't so cheap: It has an annual expense ratio of 1.75%, whereas the average expense ratio of all equity funds is 1.61%.

Though some may charge that Ahrens is the polar opposite of socially responsible, he begs to differ. "We believe another level of social responsibility is that there are a lot of good corporate citizens in the sin stock industries," he says. "These are solid corporations with believable financials. We don't think there are any accounting scandals going on in tobacco, alcohol, gaming, or defense right now."[3] Hard to argue with him considering how closely scrutinized those industries are.

Politically Correct

Now that you've heard about the vice camp, what of the opposition? What about the funds that are so politically correct? If that's your bag—and if it is, you're only reading this book for sermon fodder, no doubt—you are not alone. According to calculations that Martin Vostry at the investment research firm Lipper, put together for this book (see Appendix I), there is $19,598 billion (!) invested in socially responsible funds. And it's estimated all total socially responsible investing (SRI) represents more than $2 trillion in professionally managed assets. If you want to choose a mutual fund, there are certainly enough of these funds to choose from. Lipper research analyst Martin Vostry calculates that there are 153 different classes of socially responsible funds and 76 unique portfolios.

So what constitutes a socially responsible investment? (See Table 1.4 for how two Wharton professors define it.) Essentially the fund managers won't touch anything on the wrong side of ethics with a 10-foot pole. Different funds categorize bad things differently. Funds from religious organizations and other institutions that call themselves socially responsible leave on the table any company that makes things like weapons, alcohol, or cigarettes, or are involved in gaming. Others won't touch anything that profits from war. Many of them shy away from companies that use sweatshop labor. So, bye-bye, Nike. Also off some funds' lists is Wal-Mart, not just because it sells guns, but also because its superstore nature has made life difficult for mom-and-pop shops. Other funds go deeper and invest in companies involved in shareholder activism.

TABLE 1.4   Screens Employed by Socially Responsible Mutual Funds

We categorize the screens typically employed by SRI funds using 20 classifications. Some funds employ only one of these positive or negative screens, but most employ one or more. Negative screens represent the types of firms that managers of socially responsible mutual funds may eschew. Positive screens characterize firms that socially responsible funds may hold as investments.

A. NEGATIVE SCREENS

Screens	Definitions
Alcohol	Firms that produce, market, or otherwise promote the consumption of alcoholic beverages
Tobacco	Manufacturers of tobacco products
Gambling	Casinos and suppliers of gambling equipment
Nuclear Power	Manufacturers of nuclear reactors and related equipment and companies that operate nuclear power plants
Firearms	Companies producing firearms for personal use
Defense Contracting (Military) Weapons	Production of weapons for domestic or foreign militaries
Irresponsible Foreign Operations	Investment in oppressive regimes such as Burma or China and mistreatment of indigenous peoples
Abortion/Birth Control	Abortion providers, drug manufacturers that manufacture and distribute abortifacients, insurance companies that pay for elective abortions (where not mandated by law), or companies that provide financial support to Planned Parenthood, manufacturers of birth control products
Usury	Predatory lending, bonds, fixed income securities
Pornography	Pornographic magazines, production studios that produce offensive video and audio tapes, companies that are major sponsors of graphic sex and violence on television

(continues)

TABLE 1.4 *(Continued)*

B. POSITIVE OR NEGATIVE SCREENS

Screens	Definitions
Products/Services	Strong investment in R&D, quality assurance, product safety; avoidance of antitrust violations,consumer fraud, and marketing scandals
Animal Rights	Seek promotion of humane treatment of animals; avoid animal testing, hunting/trapping equipment, and the use of animals in end products
Labor Relations and Workplace Conditions	Avoids worker exploitation and sweatshops; seek strong union relationships, employee empowerment, and/or profit sharing
Diversity	Minorities, women, gays/lesbians, and/or disabled persons recruited and represented among senior management and the board of directors
Environment	Avoid companies that pollute, produce toxic products, and contribute to global warming; seek proactive involvement in recycling, waste reduction, and environmental cleanup
Human Rights	Avoid companies directly or indirectly complicit in human rights violations; seek companies promoting human rights standards

From "Investing in Socially Responsible Mutual Funds" a Wharton Study by Professors Christopher Geczy and Robert Stambaugh and graduate student David Levin, May 26, 2003.

Oddly enough, many of the SRI funds, especially in the 1990s, were heavily invested in technology, actually more so than the mutual fund averages. Considering how many of those kinds of companies imploded because of makeshift financials, it is questionable how "socially responsible" that asset allocation was. But that's a question for another chapter (Chapter 2).

The bottom line is how have socially responsible funds performed? According to Lipper's analysis for the beginning of 2003 to June 30, 2003, (see Appendix I) they've returned 11.04%, versus the S&P at 11.76% and what analyst Vostry describes as Non-Social Criteria Funds (in other words, everything else) at 12.41%. For the year preceding June 30, 2003, those figures are –1.67%, –0.25% and –0.54% respectively. For the 3 years preceding, the numbers are –10.42%, –11.2% and –9.05%. For the 5 years preceding: –0.83%, 1.61%, and 0.04%. For 10 years: up 7.53%, 10.04% and 7.6%. Not such hot numbers, comparatively.

The leader of the socially responsible pack and arguably, the movement, is Amy Domini. She has spent the last couple of decades building up her politically correct empire of investing called Domini Social Investments, which has $1.5 billion in assets. She is best known for her Domini 400 Social Index, which is kind of like a little more responsible S&P 500, and her Domini Social Equity Fund (Mutual Fund: DSEFX) that manages it. For the time periods used above the index fund, DSEFX returned 10.96%, 0.2%, –12.49, and –2.11%, and 9.53. Not so hot.

So, it may not pay to be good. The only question is how to look yourself in the mirror. Keep reading.

So, if you want to sin, you've got some choices. You can look into the Vice Fund by using the ideas in this book, and you can construct your own. Furthermore, in Appendices II and III there is an example sin portfolio that you can adopt called Stocking Up on SINDEX, formuated especially for readers of this book. It will be routinely updated with relevant company news and proprietary research posted on the Web site www.stockinguponsin.com.

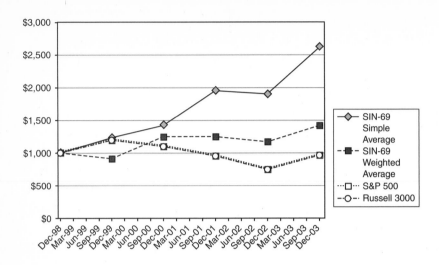

Source: Carter Crum, CFA, and Caroline Waxler.

Value of $1,000 Invested Over Five Years

Vice is nice: Our 69 stocks have handily outperformed both the S&P 500 and the Russell 3000 stock indexes over the last one, three, and five year periods. The weighted Stocking Up on SINDEX average outperformed the S&P 500 and the Russell indexes in four out of the last five years. It returned on average 7.23% per year while the rest of the market was collapsing. The unweighted average crushed the S&P and Russell in *all five* of each the last five years. The unweighted SINDEX average returned 21.45% per year. From a total return vantage, $10,000 invested in the SINDEX on January 1, 1999 would be worth $14,180 by January 1 of 2004. In the S&P 500, $10,000 would have declined to $9,720 over the same 5 year period, and would have deflated to $9,600 in the Russell 3000. At the same time, the SINDEX also had a very low correlation to the S&P 500 and the Russell 3000, with a correlation coefficient of 0.03 to the S&P and 0.13 to the Russell. Remember as an investor, if we add asset classes to our portfolio which have a less than perfect correlation (less than 1.00) with existing asset classes then risk will go down. In this case adding the SINDEX to a portfolio over the last five years would have decreased total risk while increasing total return. Investors should ignore sin stocks at their peril! (For more information about this graph see *www.stockinguponsin.com*)

CHAPTER 2

The Ethical Dilemma and Asset Allocation

If I Invest in *Playboy*, Am I Going to Hell?

You now know that there's money to be made in the more exciting part of town. That's not up for debate. But after you've made your cash, will you be so guilt-ridden that your days will be spent making trips back and forth to church worrying about whether it was ethical to have made a couple of bucks by investing in Pfizer, the company that makes Viagra? I hope not. However, if you're someone who needs to rationalize an investment in anything other than children's daycare centers, keep reading.

Let's go through the vice-ridden world of investing and assuage that overactive conscience of yours. Or at least we'll try. If you still feel guilty, take your profits and donate to charity. It wouldn't be the first time that a wealthy person has given back some of that wealth that perhaps he or she loses a little sleep over. Ever hear of the Gates Foundation? Andrew Carnegie was the pioneer of this strategy (we'll learn more about him later on). If it's any consolation, the fundraising department at the local nursing home or the Red Cross is not likely to have any issues accepting money made through a spike in Anheuser-Busch shares.

But of course all this is within reason. I'm not saying that you should knock off your spouse for the money left to you in the will, donate half of that to your favorite charity, and all will be forgiven. The ethics of sin investing should be kept in perspective by people on both sides of the argument.

Lining Mrs. Smith's Pockets

Vice, as defined in the Merriam-Webster dictionary is **a:** moral depravity or corruption: WICKEDNESS **b:** a moral fault or failing **c:** a habitual and usually trivial defect or shortcoming: FOIBLE.[1]

You get the idea. Vice investing is profiting from the moral depravity or corruption of others, their moral faults—it's not participating in the act. If you make money on *Playboy* stock, are you *making* young women remove their clothes for tens of thousands of dollars? (Hint: It's the tens of thousands that are the incentive.)

Many people avoid investing in vice stocks because of the stigma and fear for their reputations. They think that if anyone catches wind that they've invested in something morally questionable, they'll be looked down on. But you're more likely to be laughed at if you lose all your money in a "proper" company that goes down the tubes. Money has a certain way of buying respectability.

If you're a devout Christian or someone who is morally opposed to profiting from nudity, for example, you wouldn't be investing in *Playboy*, but maybe that means you shouldn't be investing at all. After all, isn't investing in the stock market just betting dressed up?

Unless it's an initial public offering or a secondary offering, such as a bond sale, when you buy shares put on the market by the company or its employees, you are not putting money directly into the company. You are not adding to its revenues or profits. Most likely you'll be buying stock on the open market. In other words, when you buy shares of *Playboy* on the stock exchange, you are buying them from Mrs. Smith, let's call her. She makes the profit. Period. It does not go to Hugh Hefner to buy another silk pajama set, or to the breast implant foundation for his girlfriends.

However, one thing to consider is that Hef probably owns a lot of shares. If there are more people out there who want to buy shares than sell them, the price of the stock will go up. When the stock price goes up, Hef gets richer. So, if you don't want Hef to earn money alongside you, that's a valid argument not to invest in *Playboy*. Of course, bear in mind that the reason people want to buy shares is because prospects for that business look better than investing your hard-earned cash into the shares of some other company.

This is a concept that seems to elude many people. They equate buying stock with buying a company's product. The only time that's the same is either when a company's business is actively buying and selling stock—which makes it a brokerage—or when a company funds itself by continually doing the aforementioned offerings in which it sells stock to the public. Companies like these are often startups, nowadays usually biotech companies that rely on the public market for funding, almost in lieu of a venture capital investment. Except for the tech debacle, many of the companies seeking funding this way are usually striving to discover drugs to improve our health or create things to make our lives easier.

In most cases, you are merely lining Mrs. Smith's pockets when you buy a share, and you hope to be lining your own when you sell the shares or collect dividends. The process of investing is really the process of speculation.

To speculate, as defined by many a trusty dictionary, is to assume a business risk in hope of gain; especially to buy or sell in expectation of profiting from market fluctuations.

It should be noted that companies paying dividends do pay investors based on the company's earnings, so, while you'll be profiting from sales of vice products, you won't be contributing to them.

One Man's Vice Is Another Woman's Virtue

Socially responsible funds have different levels of prudishness and purity through which they screen stocks. But let's take a quick peek at the top twenty-five holdings of the Domini Social Equity Fund—arguably the most famous of all the socially responsible investments—that corresponds with the performance of the Domini Social Index, which consists of approximately 400 companies. (See Tables 2.1 and 2.2.) Some of these holdings may appeal to vice investors as well.

TABLE 2.1   The 400 Stocks of the Domini Social Index

Name	Weight (%)
Microsoft Corp.	5.64
Intel Corp.	3.66
American International Group Inc.	3.10
Johnson & Johnson	2.93
Cisco Systems Inc.	2.68
Bank of America Corp.	2.33
Procter & Gamble Co.	2.25
Merck & Co. Inc.	2.25
Coca-Cola Co.	2.17
Verizon Communications	1.92
Wells Fargo & Co.	1.67
Amgen Inc.	1.67
Dell Inc.	1.64
PepsiCo Inc.	1.53
SBC Communications Inc.	1.50
Home Depot Inc.	1.49
AOL Time Warner Inc.	1.37
J.P. Morgan Chase & Co.	1.36
Fannie Mae	1.24
Medtronic Inc.	1.22
Hewlett-Packard Co.	1.20
American Express Co.	1.16

Name	Weight (%)
Wachovia Corp.	1.14
3M Co.	1.11
Merrill Lynch & Co. Inc.	0.97
BellSouth Corp.	0.94
Bank One Corp.	0.91
U.S. Bankcorp	0.91
Walt Disney Co.	0.85
Lowe's Cos.	0.84
Texas Instruments Inc.	0.80
Comcast Corp.	0.80
Freddie Mac	0.73
Target Corp.	0.72
Washington Mutual.	0.71
Applied Materials Inc.	0.71
eBay Inc.	0.69
Fifth Third Bancorp	0.67
Gillette Co.	0.66
Walgreen Co.	0.65
United Parcel Service Inc.	0.65
QUALCOMM Inc.	0.64
Colgate-Palmolive Co.	0.60
MBNA Corp.	0.59
McDonald's Corp.	0.58
EMC Corp.	0.55
Marsh & McLennan Cos.	0.54
Kimberly-Clark Corp.	0.52
Boston Scientific Corp.	0.52
Automatic Data Processing Inc.	0.48
Emerson Electric Co.	0.46
AT&T Wireless Services Inc.	0.45
Illinois Tool Works Inc.	0.44

(continues)

TABLE 2.1   (Continued)

Name	Weight (%)
Sysco Corp.	0.41
FedEx Corp.	0.39
National City Corp.	0.39
Yahoo! Inc.	0.39
SLM Corp.	0.37
Gap Inc.	0.36
SunTrust Banks Inc.	0.34
General Mills Inc.	0.34
AT&T Corp.	0.34
Forest Laboratories Inc.	0.34
AFLAC Inc.	0.33
Baxter International Inc.	0.33
Guidant Corp.	0.31
Progressive Corp.	0.30
Harley-Davidson Inc.	0.30
Stryker Corp.	0.30
Analog Devices Inc.	0.30
Avon Products Inc.	0.30
Costco Wholesale Corp.	0.29
Charles Schwab Corp.	0.29
State Street Corp.	0.29
Kroger Co.	0.29
Omnicom Group Inc.	0.29
Tribune Co.	0.28
Sears Roebuck & Co.	0.28
Hartford Financial Services Group Inc.	0.27
Kellogg Co.	0.27
Mellon Financial Corp.	0.27
Paychex Inc.	0.27
PNC Financial Services Group Inc.	0.27

Name	Weight (%)
Deere & Co.	0.27
Golden West Financial Corp.	0.27
Southwest Airlines Co.	0.26
Sprint Corp. (FON Group)	0.26
CVS Corp.	0.25
Electronic Arts Inc.	0.25
Masco Corp.	0.24
Sun Microsystems Inc.	0.24
Capital One Financial Corp.	0.24
McGraw-Hill Cos.	0.23
Devon Energy Corp.	0.23
Chubb Corp.	0.23
Staples Inc.	0.23
KeyCorp	0.23
H.J. Heinz Co.	0.23
TJX Cos.	0.22
Franklin Resources Inc.	0.22
Apache Corp.	0.22
Safeway Inc.	0.21
Air Products & Chemicals Inc.	0.21
Anadarko Petroleum Corp.	0.21
Starbucks Corp.	0.21
Allergan Inc.	0.21
Electronic Data Systems Corp.	0.21
Praxair Inc.	0.20
Xilinx Inc.	0.20
Zimmer Holdings Inc.	0.20
Campbell Soup Co.	0.20
WM. Wrigley Jr. Co.	0.19
McKesson Corp.	0.19
Clorox Co.	0.19

(continues)

TABLE 2.1   (Continued)

Name	Weight (%)
Becton Dickinson & Co.	0.19
St. Jude Medical Inc.	0.19
Northern Trust Corp.	0.18
Pitney Bowes Inc.	0.18
Limited Brands Inc.	0.18
MedImmune Inc.	0.17
Micron Technology Inc.	0.17
Comerica Inc.	0.17
Mattel Inc.	0.17
Lexmark International Inc.	0.17
MBIA Inc.	0.16
AutoZone Inc.	0.16
Symantec Corp.	0.16
Albertson's Inc.	0.16
Rohm & Haas Co.	0.16
May Department Stores Co.	0.16
Moody's Corp.	0.16
Lucent Technologies Inc.	0.16
St. Paul Cos.	0.15
Apple Computer Inc.	0.15
Biomet Inc.	0.15
Xerox Corp.	0.15
AmSouth Bancorp	0.15
Dollar General Corp.	0.15
Hershey Foods Corp.	0.15
Synovus Financial Corp.	0.15
Charter One Financial Inc.	0.14
AON Corp.	0.14
Family Dollar Stores Inc.	0.14
CIGNA Corp.	0.13

Name	Weight (%)
Ecolab Inc.	0.13
Cintas Corp.	0.13
New York Times Co.	0.13
Mylan Laboratories Inc.	0.13
Kinder Morgan Inc.	0.13
Cincinnati Financial Corp.	0.13
Jefferson-Pilot Corp.	0.13
Newell Rubbermaid Inc.	0.13
Lincoln National Corp.	0.12
Avery Dennison Corp.	0.12
Univision Communications Inc.	0.12
Biogen Inc.	0.11
MGIC Investment Corp.	0.11
Genuine Parts Co.	0.11
J.C. Penny Co. Inc.	0.11
PeopleSoft Inc.	0.11
KeySpan Corp.	0.11
Washington Post Co.	0.10
National Semiconductor Corp.	0.10
First Tennessee National Corp.	0.10
MeadWestvaco Corp.	0.10
NiSource Inc.	0.10
Scientific-Atlanta Inc.	0.10
RadioShack Corp.	0.10
GreenPoint Financial Corp.	0.10
SAFECO Corp.	0.10
Solectron Corp.	0.10
Delphi Corp.	0.09
EOG Resources Inc.	0.09
Centex Corp.	0.09
Whirlpool Corp.	0.09

(continues)

TABLE 2.1 *(Continued)*

Name	Weight (%)
IMS Health Inc.	0.09
Cooper Industries Inc.	0.09
Williams Cos.	0.09
W.W. Grainger Inc.	0.09
D.R. Horton Inc.	0.09
Leggett & Platt Inc.	0.09
Watson Pharmaceuticals Inc.	0.09
Estée Lauder Cos.	0.08
VF Corp.	0.08
CDW Corp.	0.08
LSI Logic Corp.	0.08
Janus Capital Group Inc.	0.08
UnumProvident Corp.	0.08
Sealed Air Corp.	0.08
Pulte Homes Inc.	0.08
NuCor Corp.	0.08
Sigma-Aldrich Corp.	0.08
Waters Corp.	0.08
Thermo Electron Corp.	0.08
SPX Corp.	0.08
Liz Claiborne Inc.	0.07
Pixar	0.07
Robert Half International Inc.	0.07
Darden Restaurants Inc.	0.07
Wendy's International Inc.	0.07
Engelhard Corp.	0.07
Advanced Micro Devices Inc.	0.07
C.R. Bard Inc.	0.07
Rouse Co.	0.07
American Power Conversion Corp.	0.07

Name	Weight (%)
JetBlue Airways Corp.	0.07
Nordstrom Inc.	0.07
King Pharmaceuticals Inc.	0.07
Black & Decker Corp.	0.07
BMC Software Inc.	0.07
Hillenbrand Industries Inc.	0.07
Whole Foods Market Inc.	0.06
Citizens Communications Co.	0.06
Oxford Health Plans Inc.	0.06
SUPERVALU Inc.	0.06
Harman International Industries Inc.	0.06
Sunoco Inc.	0.06
Fastenal Co.	0.06
Pepco Holdings Inc.	0.06
Providian Financial Corp.	0.06
Telephone & Data Systems Inc.	0.06
Invitrogen Corp.	0.06
A.G. Edwards Inc.	0.06
Ceridian Corp.	0.06
Humana Inc.	0.06
Toys "Я" Us Inc.	0.06
Molex Inc.	0.06
Allied Capital Corp.	0.05
R.R. Donnelley & Sons Co.	0.05
KB Home	0.05
Manor Care Inc.	0.05
Stanley Works	0.05
Deluxe Corp.	0.05
Cooper Cameron Corp.	0.05
Tellabs Inc.	0.05
Questar Corp.	0.05

(*continues*)

TABLE 2.1   *(Continued)*

Name	Weight (%)
Dow Jones & Co. Inc.	0.05
Equitable Resources Inc.	0.05
Bemis Co. Inc.	0.05
Foot Locker Inc.	0.05
Wesco Financial Corp.	0.05
Dana Corp.	0.05
Rowan Cos. Inc.	0.04
Donaldson Co. Inc.	0.04
Bausch & Lomb Inc.	0.04
Noble Energy Inc.	0.04
Sonoco Products Co.	0.04
Millipore Corp.	0.04
Hon Industries Inc.	0.04
Circuit City Stores Inc.	0.04
Compuware Corp.	0.04
3Com Corp.	0.04
PepsiAmericas Inc.	0.04
Reebox International Ltd.	0.04
Cummins Inc.	0.04
Maytag Corp.	0.04
Tektronix Inc.	0.04
J.M. Smucker Co.	0.04
Autodesk Inc.	0.04
Hubbell Inc.	0.04
Arrow Electronics Inc.	0.04
Graco Inc.	0.04
Meredith Corp.	0.04
Alberto-Culver Co.	0.04
National Fuel Gas Co.	0.04
Novell Inc.	0.04

Name	Weight (%)
ADC Telecommunications Inc.	0.04
Ryder System Inc.	0.04
DeVry Inc.	0.04
AGL Resources Inc.	0.03
Herman Miller Inc.	0.03
Lubrizol Corp.	0.03
Snap-On Inc.	0.03
OGE Energy Corp.	0.03
Quintiles Transnational Corp.	0.03
Cabot Corp.	0.03
AMR Corp.	0.03
Claire's Stores Inc.	0.03
Nicor Inc.	0.03
Delta Air Lines Inc.	0.03
Ruby Tuesday Inc.	0.03
Helmerich & Payne Inc.	0.03
Peoples Energy Corp.	0.03
Timberland Co.	0.03
Media General Inc.	0.03
Airgas Inc.	0.03
Lee Enterprises Inc.	0.03
WGL Holdings Inc.	0.03
Worthington Industries Inc.	0.02
Cooper Tire and Rubber Co.	0.02
Church & Dwight Co.	0.02
Imation Corp.	0.02
Dillard's Inc.	0.02
Energen Corp.	0.02
Andrew Corp.	0.02
Crown Holdings Inc.	0.02
Toro Co.	0.02

(continues)

TABLE 2.1   (Continued)

Name	Weight (%)
Men's Wearhouse Inc.	0.02
Invacare Corp.	0.02
American Greetings Corp.	0.02
Plantronics Inc.	0.02
Airborne Inc.	0.02
Tootsie Roll Industries Inc.	0.02
IKON Office Solutions Inc.	0.02
Scholastic Corp.	0.02
CLARCOR Inc.	0.02
Minerals Technologies Inc.	0.02
GATX Corp.	0.02
Thomas & Betts Corp.	0.02
Southern Union Co.	0.02
Bob Evans Farms Inc.	0.02
Emmis Communications Corp.	0.02
Lincoln Electric Holdings Inc.	0.02
Tupperware Corp.	0.02
Chittenden Corp.	0.02
Pep Boys-Manny Moe & Jack	0.02
Roadway Corp.	0.02
IDACORP Inc.	0.02
Banta Corp.	0.02
Cathay Bancorp Inc.	0.02
Longs Drug Stores Corp.	0.02
Visteon Corp.	0.02
Dionex Corp.	0.02
Nordson Corp.	0.02
Kelly Services Inc.	0.02
Yellow Corp.	0.02
Modine Manufacturing Co.	0.02

Name	Weight (%)
Granite Construction Inc.	0.02
Hutchinson Technology Inc.	0.02
Baldor Electric Co.	0.01
Brady Corp.	0.01
Borland Software Corp.	0.01
H.B. Fuller Co.	0.01
Kansas City Southern	0.01
Cleco Corp.	0.01
John H. Harland Co.	0.01
Adaptec Inc.	0.01
Northwest Natural Gas Co.	0.01
Alaska Air Group Inc.	0.01
A.O. Smith Corp.	0.01
FirstFed Financial Corp.	0.01
Charming Shoppes Inc.	0.01
Hain Celestial Group Inc.	0.01
Russell Corp.	0.01
Rock-Tenn Co.	0.01
United Natural Foods Inc.	0.01
MGE Energy Inc.	0.01
Advent Software Inc.	0.01
Trex Co. Inc.	0.01
Palm Inc.	0.01
Value Line Inc.	0.01
Cross Country Healthcare Inc.	0.01
Bright Horizons Family Solutions Inc.	0.01
Steelcase Inc.	0.01
Stride Rite Corp.	0.01
Thomas Industries Inc.	0.01
Phillips-Van Heusen Corp.	0.01
Sapient Corp.	0.01

(continues)

TABLE 2.1   (*Continued*)

Name	Weight (%)
New England Business Service Inc.	0.01
Standard Register Co.	0.01
Fleetwood Enterprises Inc.	0.01
Ionics Inc.	0.01
Radio One Inc.	0.01
Tennant Co.	0.01
Champion Enterprises Inc.	0.01
Apogee Enterprises Inc.	0.01
Bandag Inc.	0.01
Wild Oats Markets Inc.	0.01
Stillwater Mining Co.	0.01
Lawson Products Inc.	0.01
Interface Inc.	0.01
Wellman Inc.	0.01
Oshkosh B'Gosh Inc.	0.00
Caraustar Industries Inc.	0.00
Horizon Organic Holding Corp.	0.00
Calgon Carbon Corp.	0.00
Cascade Natural Gas Corp.	0.00
Mirant Corp.	0.00
Merix Corp.	0.00
Angelica Corp.	0.00
Gerber Scientific Inc.	0.00
Bassett Furniture Industries Inc.	0.00
Green Mountain Coffee Roasters Inc.	0.00
Nature's Sunshine Products Inc.	0.00
CPI Corp.	0.00
QRS Corp.	0.00
Hartmarx Corp.	0.00
IMCO Recycling Inc.	0.00

Name	Weight (%)
Spartan Motors Inc.	0.00
Oneida Ltd.	0.00
A.T. Cross Co.	0.00
Milacron Inc.	0.00
Lillian Vernon Corp.	0.00
Luby's Inc.	0.00
Gaiam Inc.	0.00
Isco Inc.	0.00
AstroPower Inc.	0.00
Northwestern Corp.	0.00
Ault Inc.	0.00
Total	100.00

Portfolio Date: 6/30/03
Source: Lipper, a Reuters company

TABLE 2.2   The Top 25 Stocks of the Domini Social Index

Name	Weight (%)
Microsoft Corp.	5.64
Intel Corp.	3.66
American International Group Inc.	3.10
Johnson & Johnson	2.93
Cisco Systems Inc.	2.68
Bank of America Corp.	2.33
Procter & Gamble Co.	2.25
Merck & Co. Inc.	2.25
Coca-Cola Co.	2.17
Verizon Communications	1.92
Wells Fargo & Co.	1.67
Amgen Inc.	1.67
Dell Inc.	1.64
PepsiCo Inc.	1.53

(continues)

TABLE 2.2   (*Continued*)

Name	Weight (%)
SBC Communications Inc.	1.50
Home Depot Inc.	1.49
AOL Time Warner Inc.	1.37
J.P. Morgan Chase & Co.	1.36
Fannie Mae	1.24
Medtronic Inc.	1.22
Hewlett-Packard Co.	1.20
American Express Co.	1.16
Wachovia Corp.	1.14
3M Co.	1.11
Merrill Lynch & Co. Inc.	0.97

Portfolio Date: 6/30/03
Source: Lipper, a Reuters company

The fund's largest holding, Microsoft, may raise some eyebrows. Though the company has donated computers, Bill Gates isn't exactly universally revered as a good guy. Just ask the Department of Justice. Antitrust suit, anyone? Funny enough, the Social Equity Fund shares this investment with the Vice Fund. But I guess one man's vice is another woman's virtue.

The fourth largest holding is Johnson & Johnson, which, considering that among their products is K-Y jelly, it's something a vice investor would consider. Then there's Verizon, which in 2003 was in the middle of a public relations war with its unionized employees.

Holier Than Thou's Bank Account

For all their holier-than-thou-ness, socially responsible funds do have a good mantra. Who can argue with funds that want to support and vote with their money in companies that have business practices they admire? Many people feel these are good places to put their money.

Another positive thing socially responsible funds do is use their voting power to encourage companies not to employ sweatshop labor, for example. But some of their other practices, smack of bullying such as insisting on recycling or meddling in corporate governance. Who's to say that all companies should have to listen to what these fund managers want? It seems that these funds sometimes buy shares so they can put their own political agenda on the proxy statements. Are they really interested in owning stock in the company? Their proposals don't often pass, but they can be distracting to management as well as to other mutual funds, which are required to vote for everything on the proxy. One move by Domini Social Investments, with $1.5 billion in assets under management, was challenging Nordstrom on its international labor standards. The press release trumpets the result: Nordstrom announced that it would be adding "freedom of association" to its global code of conduct.

Just a thought, but maybe fund managers should be paying more attention to the balance sheet than to lobbying.

But that may not be good enough. Some money managers think that managers who put their clients in SRI funds are doing their clients a huge disservice. Managers who screen out anything that they find suspect can handicap their clients. They may very well be missing out on key investments. Money managers who oversee pensions may find that in some cases going with a strict SRI way of doing things might actually violate their fiduciary duty as dictated by the Employee Retirement Income Security Act (ERISA).

Two Wharton finance professors, Christopher Geczy and Robert Stambaugh, along with graduate student David Levin, are not big SRI fans. Their 2003 study on investing in socially responsible mutual funds from 1963 to 2001 showed that since these funds cost so much—the average expense ratio is 1.36% a year versus 1.1%—that they underperform conventional funds by at least 3.5% a year.

One reason this is dangerous is that many funds, such as The California Public Employees' Retirement System (Calpers), the largest U.S. pension fund, follow the SRI way. In March of 2002, the fund announced that it would not invest in countries that aren't up to its ethical standards, no matter the financial loss. I guess that's just too bad for the teacher in Fresno who wants to make a profit by investing his money in the emerging markets of India, Russia, Thailand, and Venezuela. These four countries are verboten by Calpers.

Easily Dismissed

These funds often dismiss other investing styles—read vice—as abhorrent. According to Terry Halbert, a professor of legal studies who teaches business ethics at the Fox School of Business at Temple University, tobacco and liquor companies prey on vulnerable consumers such as teenagers. Halbert said, "Putting money into their stocks is participating in that activity. These vice businesses are exploiting vulnerable populations of our society. I would feel that I was living on tainted money, and I would not feel like I should retire more comfortably, or buy a house at the shore, on their backs." This is my favorite observation of hers. She also says, "I would say it is more unethical participating [directly] in [tobacco and liquor stocks] than in, say, putting your money into a big mutual fund and finding a few tobacco companies in it."[2] And then leaving your money in there? Hmm.

As you might imagine, the Vice Fund isn't exactly too popular with SRI followers. "This is a marketing-driven fund," observes Burt Greenwald, a Philadelphia-based industry consultant. "I don't think it appeals to anybody who wants to see their money grow."[3]

Now that's just silly. And, in fact, many of the sin investors are very financially responsible.

In fact, many of the sin stock industries are very closely controlled. The gambling industry is regulated within an inch of its life. The owners know they'll be closely scrutinized, so they are hyperaware of tripping over a regulation that applies to their own industry, let alone having the will or the means to cover up any book-cooking. There would be nowhere to hide.

It's the non-sin companies that some of these SRI funds need to be worried about. Some people were so caught up in worrying about pollution and the like that their morality screens missed the Enron problems. These companies may not be selling thongs to tweens, á la Abercrombie, but their executives were spending a little too much time in strip clubs, billing it to the company. Was that socially responsible?

Many of the socially responsible funds were invested in Enron. Steve Schueth, a director of The Social Investment Forum, a Washington, D.C.-based industry group that includes money managers, brokers, and financial planners has had to address that. According to Schueth, there wasn't much pollution that could be attributed to Enron, and the company said all the right things. "The fact that the Enron debacle happened," Schueth said, "is a good lesson. Just because they're recycling paper and doing a lot of other wonderful things . . . doesn't mean at the same time they're not . . . lying to investors."[4]

SRI funds say that they have been schooled, and the managers are being more careful in screening for companies that may have executive-level mismanagement.

The Bad Can Do Good

There is little room for doubt that cigarette companies have done evil things over the years, such as targeting children and minorities. However, we must remember that a lot of informed, consenting adults love their cigarettes–could there have been a bigger outcry in New York when smoking was banned from bars?–and smoking is still legal. Plus, tax dollars from cigarettes help buttress the economies of many states and keep jobs around.

It seems the tobacco companies are trying to make amends. As an industry, they've given generously to charities. Altria, née Philip Morris, has given $1 billion in cash and food donations in the past decade. Their dollars have helped hundreds of organizations like the AIDS Resource Center of Wisconsin, Battered Women, Inc., Boat People SOS, Inc., and the Queens Museum of Art keep going.

Your Inner Andrew

If you're still feeling guilty, channel your inner Andrew Carnegie (the philanthropist, not the robber baron).

Carnegie, the nineteenth-century steel magnate, was part of an exclusive club that became known as robber barons. That is, they rob society by monopolizing an industry or by taking advantage of others. Along with his fellow industrialists John Rockefeller and J.P. Morgan, Carnegie would do whatever it took to make his business profitable: Dishonesty and monopolizing their respective markets were pretty hot game plans.

Carnegie's area of monopoly and dishonesty was the steel industry, through his Carnegie Steel Company. He intimidated competitors and paid his workers very low wages. When employees went on strike, the results were dreadful: A strike at the company's Homestead steel mill escalated into violence and deaths after Pinkerton security guards were called in.

Not such a great guy, right? You'd think. But Carnegie changed his ways later in life and is now remembered in pretty glowing terms. In his retirement, he became devoted to charity, something he didn't really practice so much beforehand. In fact, it's said that he did it just to make himself more popular.

No matter. He is remembered as a patron of the arts, education, and culture through his public works and foundations, something that his wealth allowed for on a massive scale. In 1901, he sold his steel company to J.P. Morgan for $480 million, making Carnegie the richest man in the world.

In his book, *The Gospel of Wealth*, Carnegie threw down the gauntlet to his wealthy business peers, saying they should be ashamed to die wealthy. They should give their money away while they're still alive. He went so far as to advocate big estate taxes so that the state could really show the "condemnation of the selfish millionaire's unworthy life." His philosophy was that of social Darwinism: Help the poor by giving them a chance to work or educate themselves out of poverty instead of giving them handouts. To that end the poured his money into places like colleges, hospitals, parks, and libraries.

In fact, his money built 3,000 libraries. He concentrated on giving his fortune away to what he called "ladders upon which aspiring people can rise," places that he felt would even out the "temporary unequal distribution of wealth."

He also provided private pensions for many folks, everyone from his childhood pals to the famous, such as Rudyard Kipling and Booker T. Washington. He set up the Carnegie Teachers Pension Fund with $10 million and did the same with $10 million to the Carnegie Endowment "to hasten the abolition of war." He also used $125 million to establish the Carnegie Corporation "to promote the advancement and diffusion of knowledge among the people of the United States." In all, he spent $350 million on philanthropic causes.

"Maybe with the giving away of his money," said his late biographer Joseph Wall, "he would justify what he had done to get that money."[5]

If you want to try another way, do as CNBC columnist Timothy Middleton points out: A better approach to feeling good about your investment than the SRI route might be to try a portfolio manager who cares more for his responsibility to his investors than being P.C. Middleton likes John Montgomery of the Bridgeway mutual funds. This manager has done quite well but pays himself little compared to his peers and donates half his profits to charity. Another example is hardcore Mormon Don Yacktman, of the Yacktman Fund, which has nabbed the top spot in the midcap value category for three years. One of his big holdings is Altria, the old Philip Morris. He described the company to Middleton as "an ATM machine you don't need a card for."[6]

Vice Is in the Eye of the Stockholder

Sin stocks are all in how you interpret them, sort of like tea leaves. I'll call Pfizer a sin stock because it makes Viagra. That blue pill isn't a lifesaving medicine for anyone, as far as I know, but purely a recreational drug. Other investors may see Pfizer as a socially responsible stock because it is developing Macugen, a drug to treat age-related blindness. Other people may not want to touch gambling stocks because people can become addicted to gambling and it is viewed as a sin. The flip side is that gambling is legal and people do it by choice, and it can help state economies. What about bankrupt and/or scandal ridden companies like Enron? Sin stocks, in my book.

Of course, there are limits. Some people may go so far as to try to find companies that are Mafia owned and invest in them because they'll have the muscle to get their way. Same for other companies whose stocks are being manipulated–although this one is a bit, um, illegal. Then there's the possibility of investing in companies that produce drugs that are being misused, like oxycontin, or trying to profit from heroin sales in Afghanistan or even from companies in the Middle East with suspected ties to terrorists. I don't think I'll touch any of those. But what of Saddam Hussein? It's said that he owned 8%, or $90 million, of French media conglomerate Lagardere, parent of Hachette Filipacchi, which publishes *Elle* and *Car & Driver*. If you bought Lagadere wouldn't you be making the pre-captured Saddam richer? Vice is in the eye of the stockholder.

Allocate This

You want sin, but how much to allow in your portfolio?

Since this is a quick section on allocation we can't personalize your portfolio here. Everyone has different factors to consider and weigh differently: income, risk tolerance, tax bill, tuition bill, and so on. To get a very detailed individual portfolio, it's best to consult a financial planner. But here's a back-of-the-envelope guideline on how to diversify your portfolio, courtesy of some very smart professional portfolio managers I know.

   10–15% international stocks
   10% real estate/REITS
   10% bonds
   10% hedge funds (there are mutual funds that you can invest in
      for this)

5% managed futures (precious metals, pork bellies and the like, think Hillary Clinton's windfall; again there are mutual funds to deal with this)

5% cash/money market (useful in case a good investment opportunity pops up)

The rest in U.S. stocks, about 60% value and 40% growth, depending on how risk-averse you are (more growth = more risk).

Different people define growth and value differently, but I find it easiest to think of it like this: Growth stocks generally have a price-to-earning (P/E) ratio of 20 or above and value stocks have a P/E of 17 or below (17–20 is a gray area). P/E is defined as the rate of the share price divided by the earnings per share. It's also known as a *multiple*, as in how much investors will pay for each dollar of earnings. Know your P/E: It's a key criteria to evaluating picking stocks. (See Box 2.1 for that and other markers.)

BOX 2.1

Picking the stock should not be a hasty decision. Investors should put as much research and legwork into it as they do when buying a new car or house. After all, you are buying a *company*. This concept seems to elude most investors.

I've put together a checklist that you should consider a starting point when selecting a stock. When I was screening stocks for my picks in the "Streetwalker" investing column in *Forbes*, this was my first line of defense (offense?) in choosing candidates to highlight in the column. Whether we liked it or not, shares often moved on what I wrote—meaning that many people followed my advice. So, I had to be sure as I could that what I was recommending was indeed a good investment. *Would I put my money in it?*

This checklist below is by no means the be-all-and-end-all, but it's a good start.

■ *P/E ratio*. That's the current share price divided by earnings per share. Both numbers, and the P/E ratio, can be found on Yahoo Finance. The value of a share is a multiple of what the company earns. So, a P/E of

(continues)

10 means that the shares are trading at 10 times earnings. Depending on the industry, of course, I like to stick to companies that are trading somewhere around 20 at most.

- *52-week price range.* What have the shares done over the past year? Past five years? If they've taken a dive at some point I look at the news during that time period (easily searchable on services like Yahoo) to see what happened. Was the whole industry in a slump, or was it company specific? Is it fixable? Right now are the shares on the way up or down?
- *Earnings and sales.* It practically goes without saying, but check out the direction of earnings and sales. Are they moving north? At a faster rate than the year before?
- *Who's running the ship? What is the manager's background?* Find out what the CEO did before this. Is he a successful turnaround artist, who has revived bankrupt companies, or is he simply the founder's no-good son?
- *Who else has their money in this company?* When I was at *Forbes* I was up on who the "smart money" was, as they say. (That is, who are the most well-respected money managers who are making money for their clients?) Read the business press to keep tabs on who they are; *Barron's* is practically built on information like this. From there cross-reference whether any of these folks have thrown their lot in with your company. (You can see the list of institutional investors who are the largest shareholders in a company by going through Yahoo Finance and also through the company filings. Those I consider a good sign to be investing alongside: FMR Corporation (Fidelity Management & Research Corp), Soros, Tweedy Browne, and JP Morgan Asset Management.

  On the flip side, when I was looking for short candidates I would consider it a "check" if I saw the same group of momentum investors that would ride a stock sky high and then dump it. To update who is the latest in momentum investors, keep up to date on your finance industry mags or do a Google search for "momentum investing." One momentum name that I used to look for: Pilgrim Baxter funds (PBHG). Best to think long-term; these funds just ride the wave. So, if you're investing—and not shorting—you'd do well to give these companies a good going over if the momentum firms are fellow investors.
- *Research.* Do these new headlines have a lot of analysts suddenly upgrading their opinions of the stock? Downgrading it?
- *News.* Read the news stories. Is the company coming up against a significant event or riding a trend? Does it look like it is employing a new—successful—strategy? Is there a catalyst in its future?

The different sectors are known for being different types of stocks. For example, tobacco is a value stock, and retail is growth, but some names, such as J.C. Penney, will be value. Alcohol: mostly value. Defense: value. Gaming: growth. Pharmaceuticals: growth. Of course, none of that is set in stone; rather they are generalizations.

The reason you need diversification, even among growth and value stocks, is so that the investments have a low correlation to each other. In other words, when one asset class takes a dive, if all is working correctly, another should go up. Correlating the stock classes to each other is a good way to accurately calculate risk; it's not how many stocks you own but instead their correlation to each other that's important. There are different ways to measure the level, such as Sharpe and the beta ratio, which you might want to look into. (See Box 2.2.) But again, in very general terms, the allocation list presented in Box 2.1 is a good starting point.

BOX 2.2

The Sharpe ratio tries to measure the *total risk* of a portfolio. It is the return of the portfolio divided by the standard deviation—a statistical measure of how widely returns have varied over a certain time period. It is often used to predict future volatility in the share price. Essentially it's the amount of return per unit of risk.

For example, anyone can say I had a 50% gain—or make that anyone who is quite fortunate!—but for good portfolio managers it's really meaningless if they can't tell you how much risk they took to get that. Say you had a standard deviation of 20% and were able to get a 30% return. Start by subtracting out what you could have gotten just by buying risk-free treasury bonds, say 5%, so that 30% is now 25%. Now, divide that by .20–.25 minus .20. The total is 1.25. The average Sharpe ratio of the S&P is around .21; the higher the Sharpe ratio, the better.

Now say your neighbor was able to get a 50% return, but his portfolio had a standard deviation of 75% because he took out a lot of leverage. His Sharpe ratio would have been .60. So, you had a superior performance than your neighbor.

Calculating all this is tricky. And it just gets trickier with the more stocks you own.

(continues)

Another measure of risk is beta, which is a ratio to determine how the moves of one stock's share price relates to that of the entire stock market. It's a very simple concept. The stock market has a beta of one and if your beta is higher than one, it carries more risk than the market. If your portfolio has a beta of 1.1, when the market goes up 10%, the portfolio goes up 11%. If the stock market goes down 10%, the portfolio goes down 11%. A really good portfolio has a beta of less than 1 but has a return more than the stock market. The armchair investor can find a listing for beta at http://finance.yahoo.com. To get the beta of your entire portfolio, do a weighted average of the betas of the stocks in it. To learn more about the beta and the Sharpe ratio check out www.stockinguponsin.com.

However, between the different classes of stocks, even among the general groupings of value and growth, it's best to vary the different industries included. In other words, if you have all tech holdings across the sectors—international, bonds, domestic, and so forth—then any big disaster in the industry can knock all the shares down, be they value or growth. (According to Mark Hulbert, editor of *The Hulbert Financial Digest* newsletter, "In the five years preceding May 2002, according to Shanna Zimmerman, a fund analyst at Morningstar, the average SRI equity fund devoted 23% of its portfolio to the technology and telecommunications sectors versus an average of 14.5% for all other funds."[7])

So when oil zigs, tech should zag. And, if this system is working correctly, international stocks should perform completely differently. Above all, you want stocks to add a level of diversification, and even within asset classes you should mix not only industries, but also small and large caps. It may happen that large cap stocks will be in favor, for example, which would depress small caps.

The easiest way to measure a particular stock's risk, in terms of correlation to the other stocks, is its beta (see Box 2.2), a number that is generally printed on Yahoo! finance.

And, you should note that research for the Stocking Up on SIN-DEX-69 portfolio (see Appendix II) shows that vice stocks have a very low correlation to both the S&P and the Russell.

If you like vice, then that theme could be played out across your portfolio—in growth, value, international—to make it about 15% of your total holdings.

Since you likely already own mutual funds, be sure to comb through the current holdings to see what's there. Be sure you are up to date on your information because fund managers change their minds and their portfolios frequently. In other words, you want to know that you aren't duplicating stocks across several funds and your own individual stocks. I've heard stories about people who didn't realize that half of their portfolio was made up of Pfizer, thanks to a few like-minded mutual fund managers.

There are no rules when it comes to deciding what's a vice stock. That's your call. In light of what had come out in the news, if you wanted to call televangelist Jim Bakker's PTL Club a vice stock (provided it was a public company), you wouldn't have many arguments. There are more than seven ways to interpret the seven deadly sins of greed, sloth, gluttony, pride, anger (violence), and lust. Just make sure you've spread the vice around—in your portfolio, that is.

CHAPTER 3

This Is Research?

Pantyhose and the ADA

Research. The very word connotes the dullest aspects of scientific labor or an image of someone poring over technical charts to see which blips are blipping just a little higher.

As you might imagine, doing research on vice stocks isn't quite as dry. Since most of the companies make consumer-friendly products, it is a lot of buying what you see others buying.

I admit it . . . I'm following the Peter Lynch principles of picking stocks. This basically boils down to keeping your eyes open for trends. Once you've got a trend in your sights, do your homework to make sure it's not a fluke and to find the winners in a category. Lynch must have gotten something right. He ran Fidelity's Magellan Fund for 13 years (1977–1990). In that period, Magellan was up over 2700%. He is the most successful money manager in America.

His stock picking process has entered into the mythology of the American investor. Think of the L'eggs pick. In the 1970s, when he noticed his wife Carolyn bringing L'eggs pantyhose home from the supermarket, his Fidelity Magellan fund bought stock in Hanes. The value of its shares rose nearly 600%.

This is how Lynch tells it on a 1998 PBS and WGBH/Frontline interview.

> I had a great luck company called Hanes. They test marketed a product called L'eggs in Boston and I think in Columbus, Ohio, maybe three or four markets. And Carolyn, ah, brought this product home and she said, "It's great." And she's almost got a black belt in shopping—she's a very good shopper. If we hadn't had these three kids, she now—when Beth finally goes off to college, I think we'll be able to resume her training. But she's a very good shopper and she would buy these things. She said, "They're really great." And I did a little bit of research. I found out the average woman goes to the supermarket or a drugstore once a week. And they go to a woman's specialty store or department store once every six weeks. And all the good hosiery, all the good pantyhose are being sold in department stores. They were selling junk in the supermarkets. They were selling junk in the drugstores. So this company came up with a product. They rack-jobbed it, they had all the sizes, all the fits, a down they never advertised price. They just advertised "This fits. You'll enjoy it." And it was a huge success and it became my biggest position and I always worried somebody'd come out with a competitive product. About a year-and-a-half [after] they [came] on the market another large company called Kaiser-Roth came out with a product called No Nonsense. They put it right next to L'eggs in the supermarket, right next to L'eggs in the drugstore. I said, "Wow, I gotta figure this one out." So I bought 48 different pairs at the supermarket, colors, shapes, and sizes. They must have wondered what kind of house I had when I got to the register. They just let me buy it. So I brought it into the office. I gave it to everybody. I said, "Try this out and come back and see what's the story with No Nonsense." And people came back to me in a couple weeks and said, "It's not as good." That's what fundamental research is. So I held onto Hanes and it was a huge stock and it was bought out by Consolidated Foods, which is now called Sara Lee, and it's been a great division of that company. It might have been a 30-bagger instead of a 10-bagger, if it hadn't been bought out.[1]

How can you find a L'eggs of your own? And since this is a vice book, how to make it of the fishnet variety?

Look at Web sites like the American Decency Association www.americandecency.org to see what they're railing against, watch TV, read magazines, and be as observant as possible.

Keep a Notepad Handy . . . Always

Even in the movies. Sounds silly, right? This behavior probably would scare off your date, but you don't have to use it until you're waiting on the line to the restrooms later. You never know what can come out of it.

There are the obvious trends spawned by movies for example, Ray Bans in *Risky Business*, one shoulder sweatshirts in *Flashdance*.

But there are more subtle ones that become popular as the by-product of appearing in movies or maybe just having appeared in the movies is an indicator of what's big on college campuses. Now of course one may argue that it's merely a case of product place-ment. While quite often that is the case, I don't consider that a problem. Product placement isn't cheap—it can range from $2,500 to $40,000—and can signify a larger marketing plan with lots of money behind it. Although many of the most successful trends start organically, many of them need a little push.

In one scene in the popular movie *Old School*, an 89-year-old, Social-Security collecting fraternity brother suffers a fatal heart attack in a baby pool of K-Y jelly while getting set for a wrestling match with two topless college girls—a millennial twist on the Jell-O fight.

Whether that's a product placement or the rearing head of a new trend, there's a huge marketing push by the K-Y folks. The product, which came out in 1917, is a lubricant used for sex—and doctor's visits—yet it has a medical image. The marketing folks are trying to change that. They're expanding the line to include some-thing called K-Y Ultra Gel, which dispenses like soap, and some-thing naughty called Warming Liquid that gets hot on contact.

K-Y's marketing folks are trying to make the brand more mainstream. Already, it owns its own domain: The brand has a 52% market share in America, more than three times that of its closest competitor, Private Label. "We're taking a little bit of the taboo off the brand. We're trying to have more fun with it," says Danielle Devine the brand's spokesperson.[2] To that end, it's publicizing different uses for the brand, including lip gloss and hair gel. The company is also publishing a booklet, *The Modern Girl's Guide*, with dozens of other uses, like shoe polish.

Whether this will catch on remains to be seen. It could enjoy a widespread appeal like Avon's Skin-So-Soft, which was originally a skin softener but found use as a product to ward off insects, but these are the sorts of trends you should be looking for. Or even that of Arm & Hammer, née baking soda, is now used for everything from mouthwash to silver polish.

How Can I Profit from This?

Okay, now that crucial question. A little hunting around on the Web turns up that K-Y jelly is made by a division within a division of monolith Johnson & Johnson, which has had trailing 12-month revenues of $36.30 billion. K-Y revenues wouldn't even make a dent in that. So, it won't make much of a difference really in this kind of company, which makes Tylenol, a nearly $2 billion-sales product. Right now that is the case, but who knows what will happen in the future? Although one product does not a company make, it often is a sign of something larger—and quite possibly innovative—that's going on in a company.

Sharper Image

The same notepad and observant eye you bring to the theaters should be with you when you're watching TV at home. Besides the bigger picture of the kinds of programming–more on that later– the content of programs can be an indicator.

In a memorable episode of "Sex and the City" Samantha goes to the electronics and gadgets store The Sharper Image to return her broken vibrator. However, considering it's officially a neck massager, the $49.95 AcuVibe, the clerk gives her a hard time. Nonetheless, she is able to return it and give some advice to eavesdropping female shoppers who are shopping for their own vibrators/neck massagers.

"Sales made a huge jump" as a direct result of the show, said Sharper Image spokeswoman Mollee Madrigal in a September 2002 *San Francisco Chronicle* interview. She didn't specify how much sales of that product affected the company's bottom line, but the fact is that for the month during which the show aired, store sales went up 15%.[3] The stock crept up for the next few months while the market went lower. It's hard to attribute that increase to Samantha . . . but still.

Another company spokeswoman, Maggie Pattengill, recently told me, "The Sharper Image has been featured in many television shows and movies. Any time we get a product placement or mention like we did on "Sex in the City," "Friends," or "Will and Grace," it has a beneficial effect on our business. Our massage products have always been a popular category of our business and we continue to offer new, innovative, and high-quality products to our broad customer base."

Sometimes these vice products are just harbingers of what could be a good company or investment that may actually have nothing to do with porn. For example, I can't imagine that other Sharper Image products have multiple uses that intersect with vice. So, is the Sharper Image one such investment?

I wouldn't bet on it. The stock, however, looks just fantastic on a cursory glance: For the 12 months ending April 30, 2003, Sharper Image's sales were up 30% to $549 million, while the company had more than tripled its earnings to $16.4 million. Since the beginning of the year, the company's shares have soared 61.3%, still trading at just 20 times its projected fiscal 2003 earnings, only a slight premium to slower-growing retailers.

However, if history repeats itself, this company could be a victim. Its current big-time product is something called Ionic Breeze, which purifies air. For all of 2001, that product made up 16% of company sales, up from 7% the previous year. The company didn't break out 2002 numbers, but one money manager estimated that it was over 30%. That's not a good thing because it means that should something happen to the popularity of that product, the sales for the whole company will be down. Coincidentally, a big competitor, Homedics, is coming out with a cheaper version around the beginning of 2004; it sells its products through big chains like Target and Walgreens.

That could very well be a problem. The last time Sharper Image had a killer product was in 2000 with the Razor Scooter. Remember those? Sharper Image shareholders sure do. In 2000, company revenues were 38% on sales of $405.9 million; $70 million of that was due to Razors, which accounted for 62% of the growth. The following year's results were pathetic in comparison: Only $4.7 million in Razors sold. Stock was down 30%, although some of that was September 11 and recession related, *but still* you get the point.

Sharper Image might be a better candidate to consider shorting.

But How Can I Find This Out?

You say, "Okay, it's easy enough to sit back and watch TV and catch trends, but how do I do a little digging myself?" The answer is simpler than you'd believe: Just ask.

But who? Don't bother asking the companies directly. They won't reveal a thing–assuming you do get someone on the phone, and that's unlikely because most investor relations calls go to voice mail. Even if you do get a call back, the companies won't tell you a thing that's not printed because of new regulations that prevent such disclosures. And chances are that they'll think you're a professional money manager or short seller so they'll definitely keep mum.

Do contact them, however, to get annual reports. Phone numbers, e-mail, and street addresses can be found on Yahoo.com's finance section, if the company is public. Or you can search for the contact information on Google.com. (Typing in the company name and contact and investor relations usually does the trick.) Get a copy of a company's annual report, which is much easier to read than the downloadable 10Ks and other filings on line, although you should get those reports, too, to decipher information. (To figure out how to search through these and through the financial numbers see Box 3.1.)

Beyond requesting reports, the kind of research I'm advocating involves amateur journalism. Make a habit of getting out to stores and being inquisitive. If you're shy, this may be difficult, but get over it: This is about your money. The goal is to get good at chatting up people to find out what's selling. Very simple.

BOX 3.1

Quick Primer on What to Look Out for in Financial Documents

This should just be a handy primer—or refresher—of what to zero in on to see how a company is faring. Use it when combing through 10Ks (yearly company reports), annual reports (the glossy version that the company sends out to shareholders), and 10Qs (quarterly reports).

As with all these terms and their results it's crucial to compare them to the results in previous years/quarters to get the context of the numbers.

BALANCE SHEET

Assets: What the company actually owns.

Cash and cash equivalents: The money that a company can lay its hands on immediately.

Receivables: IOUs to the company. Look at the day's receivable portion to see how long it's taking the company to get paid. If it's getting longer and is significantly higher than say, this time last year, there may be a problem.

(continues)

Liabilities: What the company owes.

Long-term debt: The company's debt over the long haul. It's good when this gets paid down (just like your credit cards!) and bad when it keeps piling up and cash is depleting.

STATEMENT OF INCOME

Net sales: Sales, also known as the top line.

Cost of sales: How much the company paid for the widgets it's selling. Do the math between cost of sales and sales and you'll be able to get the profit margin picture.

Operating, selling, and general and administrative expenses: The company's overhead expenses.

Income before . . . : Sometimes known as cash flow. Often just referred to as "Ebitda" (Earnings Before Interest, Taxes, Depreciation, and Amortization) or a variation, depending on what factors are included or excluded.

Net income: Also important. This is earnings with taxes and so on taken out.

CASH FLOW

Increase in inventories: Watch this. If it spikes for no good reason, it means that the product is languishing in the warehouse.

Net income: As listed above.

It's simple *and* lucrative. You'd be floored to find out how much professional investors are willing to pay for the kind of knowledge that this information gathering brings in. The people who do the information gathering don't do too badly themselves. I was once paid $50 an hour to do research for a company that sold its market research to money managers; the information-gathering part of the job amounted to little more than telemarketing, which is how I thought of it. One of my projects consisted of calling a lot of publicly traded health food stores and their wholesalers to ask innocent-sounding questions about the industry. I also did the same thing to stores that sold cigarettes.

You'd be surprised at how easily people will give you information. (In case you're curious, from my "telemarketing" gig I found out that more people are getting prepared meals at health food stores and that cigarette companies are doing more promotions.) This kind of information alone is not enough on which to base an investment, but when it's part of a larger dossier that includes data points on how sales fared year after year, it makes sense. Consider it a game of connect the dots (of information).

Getting people to open up over the phone can be exceedingly difficult, but with practice it can be done. The key is to make your questions sound as innocent as possible and work them into a conversation. If you come out and say, "I'd like to know how Marlboro Reds are selling," the only answer you'll get is a dial tone. A better way to approach it is asking, "Do you have X number of packs left? I'd like to buy a bunch." And from there, depending on the answer you can probe further. These are the types of things that years of interviewing reluctant subjects will teach you.

Note that many people in managerial positions—especially if they work for publicly traded companies—are warned about giving information out over the phone. Professional money managers are calling stores and doing check-ups—or at least they should be if they are doing their jobs. Lower-level employees, especially those who stock shelves, are not usually given this lecture, which is why it's often good to go into stores and chat them up. (It's not always the highest person on the corporate ladder who knows the most. Anyone who has spent time in an office realizes that the most observant and knowledgeable people on the staff are the secretaries and office managers.)

Gumshoe Investing

When I was writing the stock market column for *Forbes*, I was particularly impressed with a few retail analysts who would regularly visit malls in different parts of the country to do spot checks on how things are selling. Talk about a fun job! People tend to be a lot more trusting if they can see you rather than speak to you on the phone. If you happen to be somewhat young looking asking too many questions will only elicit the push back of "Is this a project for college?" (How to answer? You can ignore and change the subject or say that it's part of some other research you're doing.)

Learning to talk to sales clerks is easy. Start by asking, "What is your best-selling product?" Repeat after me, "What is your best-selling product?" It's not so tough.

That kind of trend spotting has become so second nature to me that I find myself chatting up sales clerks constantly. Unfortunately, much of the information can't be acted on because the companies are private, but it could be useful for something in the future.

For example, a recent gift-buying excursion to a Sephora store gave me an excuse to talk to the clerk. "What's your best-selling product?" I asked. "J.Lo's Glow perfume." Good to know. Though J.Lo, Inc., as it were, isn't public, but should a big luxury goods corporation like LVMH buy it, that kind of info is valuable.

Another basic question you should ask is something like "Are you always this busy?" or "What's your busiest time?" Or, if it's around the holidays, "were you this busy last Christmas?"

Store workers are usually outgoing people, which is why they're in that line of work. They enjoy talking to people and will not be put off by these questions. In fact, one question often elicits more information. The clerk at the Sephora store in Times Square (Sephora, by the way, is owned by LVMH) told me that J.Lo perfume is the best seller in all the stores. Information about other regions is important—many salespeople are told about how products sell elsewhere in the country—to get a big picture. He also told me something he'd been briefed on about upcoming products: Jennifer Lopez was coming out with a new scent. Very interesting!

Besides, shopworkers also chat up other customers. If you see people buying an Ionic Breeze, ask them how they heard about the product and what prompted them to buy it. If they offer up that all their neighbors and friends are buying them, that's a key piece of information.

Much More Fun Than Visiting
Technology Warehouses . . .

Since vice is what you're after—investing-wise, of course—go to where vice lives. If you're invested in Rick's Cabaret, the strip club, by all means go there. Chat up the strippers (aka workers), since they are the front lines. If your wife doesn't believe that I've advocated this, please highlight the preceding sentence. If you really like your local strip club and think business is booming, ask the manager if it's traded on the stock market. (I suggest avoiding companies, however, that are traded over the counter; see Chapter 8 for more details.)

Take trips to Las Vegas, Atlantic City, and regional casinos. Are the lines long out at the airport? (See Chapter 5.) When I was in Vegas the line was two hours to get a cab. Again, talk to people. If you're visiting a resort or gambling destination and there are not a lot of people at the airport, ask the baggage handlers if the airport has been busy. If it's a resort that people drive to, just chat up the guards at the front gate when you drive in. Before you book your reservation, check out the occupancy rate. See how big the discounts are on the Internet Web sites, like expedia.com and hotels.com. Too much availability and flexibility is not a good sign for investors. It's good for bargain hunters who want to negotiate a lower room rate. A full house doesn't take a bargain, and investors look for a full house.

This stuff is all about common sense and the mundane kind of intelligence gathering that helps put a puzzle together. What do you think our CIA operatives do?

Next time you're at a dance club, ask what the best-selling drink is. If shouting above the din during a raucous night out isn't your thing, go earlier, when things are slow, and engage the bartender. Would it be the first time that someone has spoken to a bored bartender? I don't think so. Information like this would help reveal that, say, Red Bull is the best selling drink at many bars and that some malternatives, like Zima, aren't.

Think Like the CIA Secret Agent

Visit sections of town that you otherwise wouldn't. For a newspaper story I once interviewed a bodega owner in Harlem to see how cigarette taxes were affecting his business. He told me exactly how much his margins would be squeezed and what promotions and discounts the cigarette companies would be offering. Of course, I was a reporter on site for a story. However, with this kind of situation, the way you present yourself will get the information you need. If a clerk or owner asks why you want to know, be honest and say that you are a potential investor in cigarette stocks. He may be sympathetic and talk to you about what's going on in his store. In fact, he may relish the opportunity to vent. If they trust you, the folks you speak with once could turn into your long-term sources, just like with a journalist. After they've seen you enough and are comfortable, they may offer up information about what's going on. Remember, people love to talk about themselves—it's everyone's favorite subject—and, by extension, their businesses. If it's their own business, they're proud. If they're disgruntled, they may want to sell out their boss. (If there are shenanigans going on, often people throughout the company have heard rumors.)

What if they ask to get paid for info? Well, that's your call. I wouldn't even think about it. That gets you into a whole other area beyond a casual conversation. As a journalist I'd never do it, but taking a source out to a free dinner and drinks never hurt. But, hmmm, do you really want to be lunching with the salesperson from Condomtown?

Getting in touch with the suppliers is more difficult than calling a store or walking into a bar. First of all you need to identify them. That can be as easy as looking on a corporate Web site. Sometimes they're listed. But it may require a trip to the store to get the names of the products. Once you have the name of the product, you can call up the makers. Just say it makes widgets for XYZ chain store. Once you've identified the maker of the product, call that company and ask who handles the XYZ account. More often than not you will be given a name or patched through. Should a secretary ask you what you're doing, you can say that you're doing personal research. If she asks for what, go ahead and tell her that you're an investor or potential investor in XYZ. Now since suppliers don't really get calls like that—money managers and analysts are too busy/lazy to do this kind of legwork—you'd be surprised at how many "hits" you could get. If you get the right person on the phone, especially outside of cities like New York/LA/San Francisco, people might enjoy the novelty and be willing to chat. Just by asking, I've gotten people to tell me that XYZ chain has upped their order.

Your take-away from that? Depending on what your potential investment is, of course, the info could be useful. If your target is XYZ, maybe the widget seller is the Sharper Image's equivalent of the Ionic Breeze. If the target is the widget maker, then it's interesting to note that orders are going up. Either way, this kind of information goes to underscore the old saying that knowledge is power.

The same kind of technique could be used to find distributors. In this case, as with finding suppliers, you could also try to ask the store manager. If the manager asks why, just say that you are doing research on the main ABC industry distributors.

If you're really entrepreneurial, you could attend industry events. And since this book is on vice, well, the porn industry, for one, has a ton of them. Though I'm not quite sure how you'd explain it to your family, it wouldn't hurt to be in Las Vegas during the annual Adult Video Awards—sort of like that industry's Oscars. To find exact dates, check the avn.com Web site, which also tells you about other industry events. Though you may not be allowed in to the awards show, it won't be too difficult to figure out who in the industry to pop a few questions to.

Web sites in general are a treasure trove of information. Going to chat rooms enables visitors to eavesdrop on what people familiar with a particular industry are saying. Of course, smart marketers from the companies in question often go onto sites anonymously to pump their own products. The film, *The Blair Witch Project,* procured amazing buzz, and ticket sales, just from online efforts done by the marketing department of the film's distributor, Artisan.

Chat It Up

Analyst Tony Butler, who directs coverage of pharmaceutical companies, says that there is a lot to be gleaned from chat rooms. For those suffering from erectile dysfunction, any news of Viagra and its competitors is of interest. They want to know about side effects, benefits, and activation time. Investors want to know what they think. Their opinions are an early indication of what products could gain widespread popularity. They also are a center for rumors and news. What drug is catching on in Europe? What drug is giving users headaches? If you want to be part of the discussion then search on Google to find the latest room to join.

Looking on the Web is a good idea for many pharmaceutical areas. People with various ailments tend to seek out Web sites and chat rooms so that they can discuss their problem—and potential cures—with other folks who have the same thing. Depression and anxiety is another area with a lot of online chat and informational Web sites. (That area falls under vice as far as I'm concerned because many people feel like these drugs are a crutch and addictive.) See Box 3.2 for some Web sites.

Besides chat rooms, you should use the Internet to sign up for industry newsletters and e-mails. I've found these especially useful for finding out what teenagers and people in their early twenties are wearing and buying. My favorite is www.trendcentral.com. This is the place to find out that Abercrombie & Fitch is selling thongs to 10-year-olds and they are flying off the shelves. Another newsletter that is useful is something called Popdirt.com. It's written in the United Kingdom. Although not directly about what's selling, it's good for hearing about trends while they're happening. These are things that newspapers will pick up on 10 months later.

On the Web you should also be reading weblogs, called blogs, to find out what's happening. These are akin to columnists writing about subjects they feel strongly about, but they're so personal that they're like diaries. So, if someone has a bridal blog about wedding preparations she will talk about which kinds of wedding products she and her friends love. Hunt around to find ones that are writing about what you're interested in investing in. Google pulls up blogs, so just type in words like, say, "Abercrombie" and "thong" and "blog" and you may get people talking about seeing them in a store. Voila! Someone may have saved you a trip to the store to do research! Plus, blogs put you in touch with "spies/sources" in other parts of the country, and you can ask them about their experiences with a particular product or store that they have written, er, blogged about.

There are also various industry blogs done in a more professional, organized way. One blog I look at is www.gawker.com (for more, see Box 3.2) to find out about general trends.

BOX 3.2

Some Useful URLs to Keep on Top of Your Research

www.google.com The search engine. You can find anything in here and it's free. Just type in the terms you're interested in and *something* useful will come up. Type in "World's bestselling cigarette" and you'll find that it's Marlboro. From there, find the producer and you're on your way (In this case, it's Philip Morris, now known as Altria), investing-wise.

www.yahoo.com From here click on the "Finance" icon. From there type in the stock symbol where it says to do so (if you don't know it, click on the area that allows you to look it up). Next, click on the choice for "profile." This, for me, is the money page, with all sorts of useful information about what the stock has done in the past year, market cap, recent headlines. It also has the company in question's phone number and Web site, along with a link to its SEC filings. When checking out a potential investment this should be your first stop.

www.dailycandy.com The place to check out what's hot right now in NYC, LA, and well, everywhere. Free Web site, free e-mail newsletter. If it's in here, it's worth noting. Also, there's a version dedicated to the kid market.

www.popdirt.com This U.K. Web site has tidbits about international pop culture. Read it often enough and you'll decipher the trends. Sign up for their free e-mail newsletter—that's where the juicy stuff is.

www.trendcentral.com It's name doesn't deceive. Read the site and/or get the free e-mail newsletter to learn what intrigues the trendsetting types. It's reported by professional, highly paid trend-spotting consultants.

(continues)

www.gawker.com A fun takedown on New York figures and trends. Go here to learn about what trends are being over hyped in NYC—and so will be coming to a mall near you.

www.thekicker.nymetro.com *New York Magazine* blog about "all things New York," put together by former Gawker editor Elizabeth Spiers.

www.fleshbot.com This webmagazine showcasing trends in the porn industry is put out by the same folks who publish Gawker and is widely read by the New York media.

* * *

Depression Web sites to learn about concerns, benefits, etc.

* * *

www.the body.com/nimh/ Provides information on different mental disorders through a search engine.

www.psycom.net/depression.central Information on various types of depression; sponsored by the Mayo Clinic.

What Do I Know?

One of Peter Lynch's ideas is that you should invest in what you see taking off around you—things that are generating excitement. Like the L'eggs that his wife was snapping up. Look at what you and those around you are buying. What are they talking about? Wearing? (See Box 3.3.)

For me, in the heart of Manhattan, a simple look around reveals an investment that I wish I could make—in the rap company Roc-a-Fella. This company puts out such a diverse product line: movies, music, vodka, and clothing. The latter are sold under the name Roca-wear. Those clothes—really casual rapper wear with oversized, athletic-team style T-shirts and the like and clothes befitting the dancing gals in the back of the videos sipping from magnums of Cristal champagne. Revenues have gone from zero to $300 million in 4 years. Too bad, I can't invest in that company. Even though it's a private company, the management still releases revenue figures. A quick Google search can turn them up as well as what publicly-traded stores carry Roc-a-Fella clothing. Of course you can't bet on company sales alone, but it's just a flag that you should explore the company further.

BOX 3.3

In the late 1980s, you'd have been hard pressed to find a label hotter than L.A. Gear. The company made its name on high-topped aerobic shoes. Pink and other "L.A." colors were their M.O. So, you can imagine that when aerobics was hot, cheesy colors à la Miami Vice were hot, and fitness was the thing (remember Jane Fonda, pre-Ted and post-Hanoi?) these were in the nexus of the trend. Unfortunately, it turned out to be a one-trick pony in a perfect storm. (Ouch, sorry, about all those cliches, but I couldn't resist.)

In 1986, this hot little shoemaker went public and started trading at $3, with respectable sales of $36 million. Sales shot straight up to a peak of nearly a billion ($820 million to be exact) in 1990, making L.A. Gear the third largest sneaker company, behind monoliths Nike and Reebok. Shares jumped to $50. In 1989, *BusinessWeek* dubbed it "the best stock of 1989."

The magazine also had this to say about the company—the last part has scary echoes of what's going on today:

L.A. Gear focused on selling spangled sneakers in ice cream colors to the 80% of buyers who rarely set foot on a tennis or basketball court. They sold sex and sizzle, from ads of scantily clad blondes to trade shows where tanned teens jiggled to a disco beat. (Business-Week, June 19, 1989, Kathleen Kerwin—in Los Angeles) "L.A. Gear is going where the boys are."

It wasn't long before shares hit the skids, dropping to $10 in 1991. The snazzy shoes, featuring extras like sequins, were losing their steam. It became discount city for the shoes the decline had accelerated, and strategies like eating the shipping costs didn't help either. To make matters worse, when the company tried to enter the sports world—with all due respect to John Travolta and Jamie Lee Curtis in their star turns in the movie *Perfect*, aerobics ain't athletics—it was a disaster. There was the foray into men's athletic shoes, but unfortunately a pair fell apart midplay in a college hoops game. Game over. And, oh, did I mention the endorsement by that paragon of athleticism, Michael Jackson?

Shareholders sued in 1990, something about being given bad info that pumped up the shares. The settlement was $54 million. But that's nothing compared to how the short-sellers did. Ask any veteran short-seller and L.A. Gear is in their top 10 list of best shorts.

Beware the company that peaks on a trend. This was one was bleeding money—to the tune of $66 million—only one year after its most successful point. It's great to be on top of what's hot, but without good management and second acts, your money is only as good as the product's 15 minutes.

Think about what is generating excitement near you. What product are people generally always happy to see? What brand do people travel to buy? What store opening generally gets people to line up at the store and launches a thousand press mentions?

Starbucks was a contender, except for the last sentence. Know anyone who camps out in front of a Starbucks franchise? But you probably do know someone who has traveled to and waited in a long line outside of Krispy Kreme (KKD).

The doughnut company began in the mid-1930s as a strictly Southern company—Elvis was a fan—and has grown to 300 stores across the country at last count, making 7.5 million doughnuts a day. International stores are being rolled out toward the end of 2003. Though competitor Dunkin' Donuts has 3,600 outlets in just the U.S., Krispy Kreme has $492 million in sales and earnings of $33 million. The company's stock has more than quadrupled since its inital public offering (IPO) in April of 2000; the market has dropped about 30% during the same period. According to data compiled by Dealogic, Krispy has been the best-performing initial public offering in the time since it has begun trading. And, yes, it's what I'd call a vice stock. Gluttony, anyone?

This is one of those stocks that just seems to keep chugging along. And those kinds of situations engender warning flags to many people. The stock has gone up and up, but that's no reason to dismiss it outright as one that has gone up enough and can't go up more. Naysayers charge that shares of KKD have a high P/E. On estimated 2004 earnings it has a P/E of 32. Starbucks, however, isn't that far off, with a 30 P/E, yet Krispy's earnings are growing more quickly. Customers are not the only ones who are plump: Operating margins are 16% and getting bigger. Those who keep saying that the stock is too expensive keep getting burned when it goes up further.

Okay, the stock and the company can't keep getting fatter forever. It'll pop and fall back down to earth. But that doesn't look like it's happening anytime soon.

Here's the glazed doughnut, er, acid test. Impress your co-workers by bringing in a box of Krispy Kremes. When you stop being the most popular guy in the office, short the stock. But better yet go to the next, most assuredly well-publicized store opening.

(It's well-publicized, in part, because Krispy sends reams of boxes to local reporters to whet their appetites for the story.) If you see a line before the opening bell, you've still got yourself a winner that might be worth socking even more money into.

SHOPPING BAG

Krispy Kreme Doughnuts, Inc.—KKD (NYSE)
www.krispykreme.com

Krispy Kreme Doughnuts, Inc. owns and franchises doughnut stores.

Price as of November 7:	$44.17
Price/Earnings:	34.70
52-Week Price Range:	$26.42–$49.74
Market Capitalization:	$2.09 billion
Trailing 12-Month Revenue:	$491.55 million

4

Tobacco

User Loyalty

When someone's favorite brand of perfume, jeans, or aftershave goes up in price or gets slapped with a tax hike, it may be frustrating, but you rarely see protests or a black market. If you're no longer allowed to use these products in a restaurant, you don't see people spritzing themselves with Chanel Number 5 outside the front door. These are not necessities.

But try making rules about cigarettes. They may not rate among food, water, and air as necessities, but to those who love them that's up for debate. Beyond an emotional connection, it's an addiction.

There's no arguing that what tobacco companies produce is addictive and harmful and can be fatal. In 1999, smokers spent $730 million to stop smoking, yet 3.5 million people die each year because of smoking, according to Tara Parker-Pope's book, *Cigarettes*. Americans spend $50 billion annually for all their medical troubles related to smoking.[1] Even with such well-publicized cautions about the harmful effects of tobacco, there are people who still love their cigarettes.

Nobody is forcing anyone else to smoke. What you may consider dangerous is a panacea to someone else, who may well consider your form of relaxation horrible.

Law and Order

That said, let's consider tobacco as an investment.

Unless you've been living under a rock, you realize that this is one litigious industry. Lawsuits against tobacco companies abound, and they are not for nominal amounts either. Billions of dollars are at stake. Even if the rewards don't come out favoring the plaintiffs, the idea of all these lawsuits has made investors skittish (and made tobacco companies change their names).

The truth of the matter is that the tobacco industry is a powerful group with a powerful Washington lobby. Of all the trials related to smokers since 1996, the industry has won 75% of them (see Table 4.1).

There are exceptions, of course. One notable one was the 1996 Carter case in Florida, in which Grady Carter, a lifetime smoker who had contracted lung cancer, was awarded $750,000 in damages from the Brown & Williamson Tobacco Corp. a subsidiary of British American Tobacco. Meanwhile, the U.S. Justice Department is trying to make the industry pay some $289 billion for lying about the risks of smoking over the last 50 years. Then there is the record-setting $100 billion that Philip Morris (MO) was ordered to pay as a consequence of the 1998 settlement with 46 states to recoup smoking-related health costs. At the time this book was being written, Altria (née Philip Morris) was ordered to pay $10.1 billion, and before could it appeal it was ordered to pay $12 billion in an appeal bond. However, in September 2003, the Illinois Supreme Court cut that $12 billion figure in half and gave the okay to hear the appeal.

The suits aren't going away, but it seems that the capital markets overestimate the importance of jury verdicts. The large awards are not necessarily what the final numbers are—appeals by the tobacco companies have managed to get the decisions thrown out or substantially lowered (see Table 11.1). When they lose, the companies get a long period of time in which to pay out the monetary award. In the $100 billion case, it will be paid out over decades.

Individual suits seem to be the most successful. A lot of what has undermined the class action cases, according to Morgan Stanley's

TABLE 4.1   Success Rate of 75% in Post-1996 Tobacco Claims

Case	Date	Outcome
Carter (FL)	9/96	Industry loss; upheld by Florida Supreme Court ($0.75 million)
Rogers (IN)	8/96	Industry win
Connor (FL)	5/97	Industry win
Kabriwynk (FL)	10/97	Industry win
Wiley (IN)	3/98	Industry win; (ETS)
Widdick (FL)	6/98	Industry trial loss; verdict reversed and dismissed on appeal
Henley (CA)	2/99	Industry loss; on appeal ($26.5 million)
Williams-Branch (OR)	3/99	Industry loss; on appeal ($80.3 million)
Settle (TN)	3/99	Industry win (Directed Verdict)
Ohio Iron Workers (OH)	3/99	Industry win
Karney (TN)	5/99	Industry win
Newcomb (TN)	5/99	Industry win
McDaniel (TN)	5/99	Industry win
Steele (MO)	5/99	Industry win
Butler (MS)	6/99	Industry win; (ETS)
Gilboy (LA)	7/99	Industry win
Whiteley (CA)	3/00	Industry loss; on appeal ($21.7 million)
Farnan/Engle (FL)	4/00	Industry loss; reversed on appeal ($2.9 million in Engle compensatory damages)
Amodeo/Engle (FL)	4/00	Industry loss; reversed on appeal ($5.8 million in Engle compensatory damages)
Della Vecchia/Engle (FL)	4/00	Industry loss; reversed on appeal ($4.0 million in Engle compensatory damages)

(continues)

TABLE 4.1   (Continued)

Case	Date	Outcome
Anderson (NY)	6/00	Industry win
Nunnally (MS)	7/00	Industry win
Jones (FL)	10/00	Industry loss; retrial ordered and upheld on appeal
Apostolou (NY)	1/01	Industry win (despite jury's determination that smoking caused plaintiff's lung cancer)
Little (SC)	2/01	Industry win
Grinnell (TX)	3/01	Industry win
Fontana (FL)	4/01	Industry win; (ETS)
Mehlman (NJ)	5/01	Industry win
Empire (NY)	6/01	Industry loss; on appeal ($17.9 million)
Boeken (CA)	6/01	Industry loss; on appeal ($105.5 million)
Tompkins (OH)	9/01	Industry win
DuJack (CT)	11/01	Industry win (Directed Verdict)
Blankenship (WV)	11/01	Industry win (Medical Monitoring class action).
Kenyon (FL)	12/01	Industry loss; on appeal ($0.165 million)
Burton (KS)	2/02	Industry loss; on appeal ($15.20 million)
Hyde (RI)	3/02	Industry win
Schwarz (OR)	3/02	Industry loss; on appeal ($100.17 million)
Tune (FL)	5/02	Industry win
French (FL)	6/02	Industry loss on appeal (ETS) ($5.5 million; award reduced by trial judge to $0.5 million)

Case	Date	Outcome
Luckacs/Engle (FL)	6/02	Industry loss on appeal and should be overturned following Engle ruling ($37.5 million; award reduced by Circuit court to $25.1 million on the loss of consortium claim.)
Janoff (FL)	9/02	Industry win (ETS)
Bullock (CA)	9/02	Industry loss; loss on appeal ($28.09 million)
Vargas (PR)	9/02	Industry loss, but industry prevails on a post-verdict directed verdict in one claim and a new trial was ordered in the second claim
Tucker (FL)	10/02	Industry win (ETS)
Conley (CA)	1/03	Industry win (Directed Verdict)
Carter (PA)	1/03	Industry win
Lucier (CA)	2/03	Industry win
Seal (FL)	2/03	Industry win (ETS)
Inzerilla (NY)	2/03	Industry win
Allen (FL)	2/03	Industry win
Miles (IL)	3/03	Industry loss; on appeal ($10.1 billion)
Eastman (FL)	4/03	Industry loss; on appeal ($6.5 million; award reduced by the trial judge to $3.25 million due to comparative fault.)
Boerner (AR)	5/03	Industry loss; on appeal ($19 million)
Welch (MO)	6/03	Industry win
Scott (LA)	7/03	Industry win (on medical monitoring)
Reller (CA)	7/03	Industry win
Eiser (PA)	8/03	Industry win

David Adelman, Tobacco Analyst, *September Legal Timeline, Analysis and Observations.* August 20, 2003.

tobacco analyst David Adelman, is the undefined nature of the alleged class—smokers who want to participate in the program that may raise independent constitutional issues. In addition, allowing the plaintiffs to base their claims on an "idealized," nonexistent plaintiff who heard and relied on every alleged fraudulent industry statement raises other independent constitutional issues.

Some analysts think the litigation risk is receding. After all, it has been going on in one form or another for 40 years. Witness a recent punitive damage award reduced from $28 billion to $28 million. Another example is the recent overturning of the biggest award, $145 billion, in a Florida class action suit in 2003. On appeal the award was termed unconstitutional.

Even when the cases do stick—for example, a $105 million award for a single smoker in a California case—the earnings aren't destroyed. The legal costs are transferred into price increases. More on that in a second.

The legalities and complexities of every case are different. There's no doubt that the cases will continue, but should things continue as they are it seems that the effects will be manageable for the companies.

Complications

The tobacco industry is no longer the predictable safe haven it once was. In 1998 the industry shipped 461 billion cigarettes in America. It is estimated that that number will drop to 372 billion in 2003. Going forward, that number should decline by 3% a year. Besides cigarette makers upping their own prices, state governments added an average of 73 cents in taxes to each pack since 1998. On average, the price of a pack of top cigarettes in the United States was up 90% in the five years following 1997. In Massachusetts, a pack of Marlboros goes for a minimum of $4.66 at nonchain stores. Put those numbers together and it becomes easy to see how the raised prices take a chunk out of smoker's incomes, especially considering that smokers have an average household income of about $35,000.

The result of all this price inflation is opportunities. People are crossing state lines, buying from Native American reservations, and going to online sites to get cigarettes. And in cigarette buyers' clubs, "You can make money by simply referring your smoking friends to the club. You can get paid for helping them save money!"[2] When people buy on line, they're going to cheaper brands, which have jumped in market share from a little over 10% in 1997 a tenth of the U.S. market today. Such brands often sell at about half the average price of Marlboro.

The major brands are watching their market share get chiseled. In a Salomon Smith Barney survey of 107,000 retail and wholesale locations nationwide, analysts discovered that inventory levels for deep-discount brands rose, while inventories of premium labels stayed flat or declined. According to the survey, more cigarette smokers are willing to give up their regular brand in order to save an average of over $14 per carton by switching to a deep-discount brand.

In response, the big companies are pushing their own cheaper brands, or looking into developing them. Though this may help them make up some ground in volume, the cheaper brands don't have the high profit margins of the premium ones. As a result, the big tobacco companies have also resorted to promotion after promotion, like two-for-one deals, mainly for their premium brands. Massive marketing is costing hundreds of millions of dollars, but the companies have little choice as they're defending their turf. Marketing in general is so important for tobacco companies that they spend $5 billion per year in advertising to sell $53 billion in cigarettes in this country alone. It's working. In the U.S. market, Philip Morris's retail share increased to 48.5% in the second quarter of 2003 from 48.3% in the first quarter of 2003. The marketing takes it toll, however: Altria's—Philip Morris's parent company— second-quarter 2003 profits fell 6.6%, from shelling out so much money on promotions to help brands like Marlboro compete with discount smokes.

In addition to doing promotions for cigarette sales, many companies are fighting back with PR. "Last year, New York City hiked its tax to $1.50 per pack. Along with the $1.50 per pack already levied by the state, a pack of cigarettes now eclipses $7 in New York City—more than an ounce of silver," said Steve Watson, Lorillard's (LTR) vice president of external affairs. "Mayor Mike Bloomberg touted the tax increase as a way to cut consumption and boost city revenues. However, his administration has quickly learned that higher cigarette taxes lead to increased crime, more smuggling—and in fact, have not been nearly the budget panacea that was predicted. Furthermore, New Yorkers are resilient. Instead of quitting in droves, they are quickly finding ways to subvert the taxes and enjoy cheaper alternatives."[3]

Lorillard is also taking the tack that the higher taxes hurt shop owners and increase crime. According to a study by the Washington D.C.-based Small Business Survival Committee, between 2002 and 2003, small businesses in New York City lost $127 million in profits and have had to slice more than 10,000 jobs to survive. Not only that, but legal cigarette sales in New York City have dropped by nearly 50%.[4]

I saw firsthand what the taxes did. I interviewed Spanish Harlem bodega owner Ramon Murphy, who told me that Bloomberg's proposed cigarette tax would cut his income in half. Cigarettes are an impulse purchase, he said, and when people come in for cigarettes they end up leaving with a lot more. If people didn't come in for a pack, then they also wouldn't pick up a gallon of milk and trashbags.

Branded

As much as these the taxes scare the tobacco companies, the big brands still have a loyal base, slightly eroding as it may be. Names like Marlboro, the world's best selling cigarette, and Virginia Slims, for example, have long dominated the American market. In fact, a whopping 38% of all premium cigarettes sold in the U.S. are Marlboros. Numbers like that gave the tobacco companies the confidence to keep hiking the prices themselves. They have pricing power—to an extent.

"The companies that dominate have excellent franchises," one big-time portfolio manager for a major investment bank told me. "The brands that emerge from such price hikes are strong ones."

Apparently brands don't apply to company names. Or maybe they do. Amid controversy and bad press Philip Morris changed its parent company's official name to Altria. The official party line was corporate speak about brand identity, but clearly this was a smart move to attract investors. After all, the company isn't just about cigarettes; it is one of the largest food companies. It owns 84% of Kraft, which acquired Nabisco in 2000. Up until 2002 it was a really vice-laden company, being the owner of Miller beer (since sold off to South African Breweries, now called SABMiller, of which Altria owns 36%).

Broaden Your Thinking

Keep in mind that problems faced by cigarette makers, especially the lawsuits, seem to be purely a U.S. concern and that tobacco companies have sales all over the world. Says British American Tobacco: "Despite attempted imitation elsewhere litigation is largely confined to the U.S.A. because of the unique characteristics of the U.S. judicial system. The industry has a strong record of winning cases in the U.S. and we–along with many analysts–see an encouraging trend in U.S. litigation in favour of the tobacco industry."[5]

Europe seems to be much more accepting of tobacco companies than the U.S. U.K.-based financial publishing and data company Citywire compiled a table of the top-rated companies in the FTSE-350. It revealed that fund managers' stock pickers from 24 major companies across Europe have chosen tobacco as one of their safe havens.[6]

The top three favorites were British American Tobacco–BTI (Lucky Strike, Pall Mall, Kent, Dunhill, and Rothmans), Imperial Tobacco Group–ITY (Embassy Regal, Lambert & Butler, and Drum, also the distributor of Marlboro in the U.K.), and Gallaher Group–GLIA (brands include Benson & Hedges and Silk Cut).

The best tobacco investments have been in the U.K. where the sector has outstripped the rest of the market. Between 2001 and 2003, Gallaher shares have risen 47%, Imperial Tobacco by 32%, and BAT 18%. Gallaher, the largest producer in Britain, with 39% of the market, has no exposure in America. Imperial Tobacco, with no U.S. exposure as well, actually gained 0.8% in the wake of bad news for Philip Morris, namely, the possibility of having to put up a $12 billion bond.

Though U.S. companies have a lot going for them, a great way to play the tobacco stocks is to invest overseas. They offer the same stable earnings that have been the hallmark of tobacco companies for years but don't face the problems that U.S. companies do.

The stocks to really consider are those in which the smart British money managers are putting their money. BAT, the second largest cigarette company in world, saw its four major brands–Kent, Dunhill, Pall Mall, and Lucky Strike–improve sales 17% in the first half of 2003. Unfortunately, its profits were eaten into, down 25% on a pretax basis for the same period, as it is facing many of the same problems as in the U.S., with lower-priced competition. An area of growth for the company, however, is Russia, where sales volumes are up 18%; the company can't even meet demand.

Philip Morris, um, I mean Altria, should be on anyone's shopping list who's buying cigarette stocks. Two-thirds of its profits come from tobacco, but the rest are from Kraft Foods (which has some of the world's best-known brands, including Oreo, Jell-O, Maxwell House, and Oscar Mayer).

David Dreman, a brilliant conservative money manager, says that since the company is divided into two businesses, you are essentially buying the tobacco component of the company for just under five times earnings, when the S&P is going for 15.6 times earnings. Plus, the tobacco business accounts for only 29% of Altria's profit and the foreign part of the business is increasing at a 10% growth rate for the foreseeable future, according to Dreman. For those who think dividends matter, the company has increased its dividend every year since the postwar era.[7] The current yield is 6.4%.

Not bad, but then again this industry is known for its fat yields. RJR has a 7.30% yield! The industry average is 6.4%, versus 2.5% for consumer noncyclicals and 2% for the S&P. Though their products are about as far from home and hearth as you can get, their dividends certainly are not.

As to the litigation, tax increases, and general bad news, analysts say that these issues have been priced into shares. Altria, for example, is cheap, with a forward price-to-earnings ratio of just 10.27. It has traded at an average discount of 40.1%, according to Adelman. He thinks that gap could close to 30% giving it a $62 price target. (It's now trading at $49.51.)

Nonetheless, R.J. Reynolds (RJR) isn't where I would first go running with my investment money. Adleman, for one, is not a fan. "As we have outlined over time, RJR has the industry's lowest profit margin structure." He says that it faces the group's most significant competitive challenges: "Relative to the group, in our view, the shares appear overvalued."

Despite R.J. Reynolds's announced merger in October 2003 with BAT, the parent company of Brown & Williamson, that would combine the second and third largest tobacco companies into a challenger to Philip Morris's United States dominance, the deal isn't a done thing. These kinds of deals take a while to close, and, as with any merger, it's never certain that it will be accomplished.

However, if it does go through, R.J. Reynolds—or the new company Reynolds American—it will be something to think strongly about buying. It will have earned revenues of $10 billion and over a 30% share of U.S. cigarette sales.

The Wrap

Tobacco investments are worth considering. They have what every product should have: customer loyalty and a recurring stream of revenue. The financials are really very strong, and this group is part of those beloved consumer nondurables and staples, which throw off a lot of cash. Figures 1.2, 1.6, and 1.10 in Chapter 1 show how tobacco stocks outperform the S&P over time, according to research compiled by the vice fund.

It appears that the legal risks in the U.S. are on the wane. Cash strapped states are finding that it is in their best financial interests to make sure that the tobacco companies don't go bankrupt.

According to various estimates States are making about $19.6 billion a year for settlement payments and taxes. To keep the gravy train rolling, state governments have run interference on behalf of the tobacco companies on a few occasions, one of which was to put caps on appeal bonds (the money a defendant must put up in order to appeal) in some 25 states.

Tobacco stocks have very solid fundamentals and pricing power. To boot, they do have influence and power over the distributors, wholesalers, and retailers, says Adelman. In other words they don't have to haggle with the shopkeeper about shelf space–premium shelf space, at that. They can call the shots.

According to Adelman: "Invest carefully; go for the companies with the brands that are the most ingrained and beloved by smokers. When it comes to companies that will survive–and thrive to the extent they can–big brands offer more security."

No matter where you choose to put your money in this sector, however, you must have a stomach for the lurches that may come with each lawsuit–or what one money manager I know dismisses as "noise." It will be worth it.

LESSONS

- The word *lawsuit* scares most people. Don't let it scare you. In fact, it causes investors to overreact, therefore creating buying opportunities.
- Don't just look in your backyard. Tobacco is a worldwide indulgence, and many of the strongest growing markets are overseas. Look for companies, either foreign or domestic, with a presence abroad. Bonus: These countries don't have the litigious culture America does.
- Tobacco companies are just boring value stocks in drag. They pay large dividends and throw off lots of free cash—something very important to note when picking stocks.

■ When evaluating companies, note the ones that have a large customer base built in. Many tobacco companies fit the bill, especially the ones that have customers loyal to their brands. Even though taxes may go up, the consumer will do anything to smoke. The latest nightlife trend in New York? Luxury buses that can be rented out just so partygoers can have a place to light up.

SHOPPING BAG

Altria Group, Inc.—MO (NYSE)

www.altria.com

Altria Group, Inc., formerly Philip Morris Companies Inc., is the parent company of Philip Companies Inc., composed of cigarette manufacturers Philip Morris USA Inc. and Philip Morris International Inc., as well as its majority-owned (84.2%) subsidiary, Kraft Foods Inc., home to brands like Oreo and Jell-O.

Price as of Nov. 7:	$49.51
Price/Earnings:	10.27
52-Week Price Range:	$27.20–$49.51
Market Capitalization:	$100.5 billion
Trailing 12-Month Revenue:	80.41 billion

UST Inc.—UST (NYSE)

www.ustinc.com

UST Inc. makes and markets smokeless tobacco products, like Copenhagen and Skoal, and sells table and sparkling wines.

Price as of Nov. 7:	$34.97
Price/Earnings:	11.24
52-Week Price Range:	$26.73–$37.79
Market Capitalization:	$5.79 billion
Trailing 12-Month Revenue:	1.648 billion

R.J. Reynolds Tobacco Holdings Inc.—RJR (NYSE)
www.rjrholdings.com

R.J. Reynolds Tobacco Holdings Inc. is a cigarette manufacturer whose brands include Camel, Winston, Salem, and Doral.

Price as of Nov. 7:	$49.96
Price/Earnings:	10.87
52-Week Price Range:	$27.52–51.05
Market Capitalization:	$101.4 billion
Trailing 12-Month Revenue:	$6.21 billion

Loews Corp.—LTR (NYSE)
www.loews.com

Loews Corporation is a diversified holding company whose subsidiaries include property, casualty and life insurance; of cigarette business through Lorillard, Inc.; Loews Hotels Holding Corporation; Diamond Offshore Drilling, Inc., and the time watch and clock company, Bulova Corporation.

Price as of Nov. 7:	$38.99
Price/Earnings:	7.45
52-Week Price Range:	$38.23–$49.18
Market Capitalization:	$107.23 billion
Trailing 12-Month Revenue:	N/A

British American Tobacco PLC—AMEX (BTI)
www.bat.com

British American Tobacco is an international cigarette manufacturer whose brands include Dunhill, Lucky Strike, Kent, Rothmans, Benson & Hedges, Kool, Pall Mall, Viceroy, Winfield, and John Player Gold Leaf. The shares trade as American Depository Receipts.

Price as of Nov. 7:	$23.93
Price/Earnings:	10.02
52-Week Price Range:	$17.54–$24.95
Market Capitalization:	$24.99 billion
Trailing 12-Month Revenue:	N/A

CHAPTER

Gambling

The Games Must Go On

As bombs were falling over Baghdad in March 2003, I was crawling along in a line. Waiting and waiting and waiting some more. Was I working as an embedded journalist queuing up for supplies and interviews in war-torn Iraq?

Not exactly. I was fighting a different battle. My overstuffed luggage and I were in the human maze outside of Las Vegas' Mc-Carran International Airport waiting for a taxi. If I didn't know when I was fighting for elbow room on my overcrowded flight in, I now knew it was going to be a long night.

Two hours and three gray hairs later, I was checking into my $350-a-night room at the 2,700-room Venetian hotel—one that I was lucky to be able to book, considering that the hotel was at nearly 100% occupancy that weekend. Not long after that I was staring at a $150 dinner bill for two at one of the hotel's restaurants. The food was okay, maybe a step or two above Olive Garden quality, but the place was packed. A wedding reception dinner was being held right next to us.

I didn't even bother to brave the ten-deep crowd waiting to get into the nightclub Light at the Bellagio.

The next day the lines didn't end either. It was another half-hour wait to get a cab to the Hard Rock Hotel, where a friend was staying. (This was one of about five friends from across the country who by chance were in Las Vegas that weekend for bachelor and bachelorette parties.) My companions and I had to arrive early to grab a beach chair at the pool, called "Beach & Cabanas" since it was a Tahitian-style setting with real sand and real $125 cabanas. It was packed with (presumably) employed yuppies who had no problem paying to fill up the seats at the three swim-up blackjack tables.

Was it a big-time conference, like Comdex, the annual computer and technology industry trade show, that brought so many people out to sin city? Nope. Maybe you could say that it was Spring Break for colleges during that time. Maybe you could blame it on the betting opportunities for basketball season's March Madness games. Or maybe you could say that it was an average weekend in Las Vegas, during a recession, in the middle of a war.

A Rich History

Welcome to Las Vegas. One of the fastest-growing cities in the world comprises one of the most stable industries in the world. No matter what the economy is doing, people are betting that their own personal economy will be doing better. All told, gambling, including Vegas, tracks, Native American casinos, and the rest, is a multibillion dollar industry. An industry that not only is not going away but is growing. In the U.S. more and more states are looking to increase gaming as a way to fill their state's coffers.

Gaming is not an invention of the saloons in the wild west. Anthropologists and archaeologists believe that gambling was happening in ancient China (2300 B.C.), India, Egypt, and Rome in ancient times. A set of ivory dice dating from before 1500 B.C. were recovered from the ruins of Egypt's ancient capitol, Thebes.[1]

In America, gambling has long been a way to fill our government's pockets. In 1776, the founding fathers in Philadelphia actually used the proceeds from gambling to fund our nation's early activities.[2]

While gambling has been around for ages in various forms in the U.S., such as horse racing, Vegas, the U.S. gambling epicenter, took shape as we know it only fairly recently. But it does have an interesting past.

The region that is now Las Vegas was originally discovered by a Mexican group in 1829 when they were passing through en route to LA. They made a Christmas pit stop along the Spanish Trail and stumbled on springs. Cut to Mormons moving in 20 years later to protect the LA to Salt Lake City mail route. Besides multiple wives, the Mormons brought farming to the area, with vegetables and fruit trees. Indian raids soon sent them packing.

Next up were railroad developers, attracted by the watery desert oasis, who envisioned a town and a train stop. That first train left the station in January of 1905, heading to California (with hungover passengers heading home?). And with that a town was born—on May 15, 1905.

From the beginning, the townspeople were gamblers. Even when the federal government tried to put a stop to it, outlawing gambling in any form in 1910, Nevada was the last state to succumb. Nonetheless, the citizens only laid off the bets for a whole three weeks before they took their games underground, speakeasy-style.

Finally, in 1931, legislators gave in, realizing that people in Las Vegas were going to gamble so they might as well make money from it. And make money they did, for most of the last century. In shades of what's happening today all across the country, Nevada legalized gambling as a means to raise taxes. (In this case it was to help a public school.) Despite a depression hitting everywhere else, Las Vegas was insulated because of its growth due to gambling, the railroad, and the Hoover Dam construction.

Other hotels sprang up quickly, the most famous being Bugsy Siegel's Flamingo, in December 1946 (now the Flamingo Hilton). Others, with famous names like the Dunes, the Sands, and the Riviera, weren't far behind. And Las Vegas being Las Vegas, clothing went by the wayside. The Dunes hotel offered up Minsky's Follies in 1957, marking the premiere of topless girls performing in Sin City.

Disneyland in the Desert

The semiclad girls kept dancing and the slots kept jangling at full speed until things slowed down in the late 1980s. By the early 1990s, gambling revenues were dropping fast, by almost half a billion dollars in 1992. Casinos owners, seeing their properties go through a lull and concerned about competition from Atlantic City, and later from riverboats and Native American casinos, thought it might be a smart marketing plan to encourage parents to bring the kids. So, in a breathless building spree, they filled the Strip with resort-y, Disneyland-style properties, each with its own theme. Practically every casino on the four-mile Las Vegas strip was rebuilt, at a total cost of $12 billion.

First, up went the 3,039-room Mirage Hotel-Casino in 1989. Cost: $630 million. The Mirage was Steve Wynn's first venture on the Las Vegas Strip. Its shtick: a fire-spewing volcano. Soon after, Wynn added the Treasure Island and the Bellagio to his holdings on the Strip, as well as casinos in Atlantic City and around the country.

Before being awarded his gaming license for the Mirage, Wynn was questioned by the Gaming Control Board about his 12-year relationship with Michael Milken, who helped finance the Mirage by selling $525 million in mortgage bonds. (Milken, a high-flying corporate takeover guru in the 1980s, was indicted in 1989 for insider trading and racketeering. He pled guilty to securities fraud in 1990 and was sentenced to 10 years in prison, of which he served two, plus three years probation.)

But pretty soon 3,000 rooms and a volcano weren't enough anymore. The 4,008-room, Medieval-themed Excalibur appeared, with court jesters and horseback jousting. Then the Egyptian-themed Luxor, built at a cost of $375 million, featuring a full-scale reproduction of King Tut's Tomb and the world's most powerful beam of light shining from the top of the pyramid. Circus Circus, the trailblazer with its decades old circus-tent–shaped casino complete with games and rides for kids, decided to accessorize, too. It added an adjoining $90 million water theme park, Grand Slam Canyon. And so on, and so on.

The most mega of all the resorts, however, was the MGM Grand—a 112-acre resort hotel, with 5,005 rooms, a casino, and a 33-acre theme park that cost $1 billion. It was built by MGM Grand, Inc., with billionaire developer and entrepreneur Kirk Kerkorian as its principal owner. In 2000, he bought Mirage Resorts from Steve Wynn. Kerkorian now owns MGM Grand, Bellagio, T.I., the Mirage, New York-New York, and the Golden Nugget downtown.

But all the focus on families and mega-expansion started to seem a bit too much. The business models, of course, have changed many times in the casino world. It used to be that they gave everything away—rooms, food, and cigs—to lure people in, because all the revenue was in gambling. However, with more families and convention business, the average room occupants (kids) weren't spending time in the casinos. Neither were their parents. Considering that these people were losing less, the business model changed.

"Families are not great customers," says Jason Ader, former Bear Stearns gaming analyst. "The kids distracted the parents and were occupying the rooms." Echoes *Las Vegas Sun* columnist Tim McDarrah, "Obviously people drinking Shirley Temples aren't the ones dropping C-notes into the slots. Children can't gamble and this is a city based on gambling. Rides were just a bubblehead move by MGM."

Roller Coasters Give Way to Erotic Revues

The restaurants changed from all-you-can-eat proletarian buffets to fancy, brand-name chefs heading up 5-star establishments. Also out were tacky, sequin-filled stores; and in came Tiffany and Versace. (Well, okay, so there was a tacky, sequin-filled store. Mi dispiace, Donatella.) What this did was to change the game plan but diversify the revenue stream.

Down came the roller coasters and the bras, up went the erotic revues and the skirts. As Las Vegas mayor Oscar Goodman explained to the *Los Angeles Times* in 2001, "When folks visit us, they expect to partake in the glitter and glamour of old Las Vegas. This is a return to yesteryear."[3]

In an interview with "20/20" Goodman said, "We want people to feel free. We want them to think that this is the place they can come to and not have any inhibitions."[4] There's even talk of legalizing brothels in downtown Vegas.

Fortunately, when the infrastructure is in place, makeovers are easier. Witness what's happening over at T.I. (formerly Treasure Island). Gone is the British-versus-Buccaneer battle. In its place: "Sirens of T.I." featuring scantily dressed lovelies re-enacting scenes that were never in my history books.

Recently opening was the $30 million dollar Sapphire Gentlemen's Club. At 21,000 square feet, it's the world's largest strip club. Sapphire even has enough demand to have 13 V.I.P. skyboxes(!) People will be able to profit if this strip club—or one of the other mega strip clubs opening there—goes public, or if a publicly-traded hotel buys the club. However, in the meantime, what it does is provide another incentive for people to stay in the city.

There are enough partially nude showgirls dancing today to make the wild Vegas of the 1970s pale in comparison. Here's a recent topless lineup: The MGM Grand has La Femme; Harrah's has Skintight; the Riviera has Splash and Crazy Girls; and the Rio has Showgirls. And what boils down to an X-rated show, Zumanity, at the hotel New York-New York.

Should all this nudity inspire you, some hotels are providing topless sun bathing areas. According to McDarrah, MGM has opened a "European" tanning section, Caesar's has toplessness going on at its Venus pool, Harrah's looks the other way, and Mandalay Bay has quietly opened an official topless bathing area called Moorea Beach Club. Day beds for four go for $125 there.

The city even has a new ad campaign: "What happens here, stays here."

The shift from G to XXX helped Vegas tremendously. John Quinones of "20/20" summed it up well. In a segment about the abandonment of Las Vegas's family image on April 24, 2002: "Las

Vegas's new persona is paying off in a big way. In less than a decade, the number of visitors here has more than doubled to 37 million. And the new, more erotic city of sin is raking in $9.5 billion a year. For the first time ever, entertainment revenues are matching gambling profits."[5]

This has more than a little to do with people coming to Vegas to forget their troubles. "Vegas allows them to escape the misery of their pathetic lives. They can forget about co-workers, children, the stock market, the recession, and the high gas prices," said McDarrah. "They can come to the grown-up Disneyland."

And show up they do. Vegas has emerged as the strongest hotel market in the U.S. "Pricing may be down 5 to 10 percent, but the volume is strong," Ader told me. "Vegas is doing great."

Pack light!

Pickaxe Providers

Cliches can be annoying, but there's a reason they stick around. So, indulge me: Who got rich in the Gold Rush of 1849 (besides some lucky miners whose names are now streets in San Francisco)? That would be the owners of the pickaxe companies, that is, the businesses that sold the necessary tools to make panning for gold a possibility. In this case, it was literally pickaxes. But it was also companies like Levi's, which provided jeans to the miners.

How about the ones who backed a particular miner or mining company? Maybe they won, maybe they lost—it was a crapshoot. But the pickaxe companies rarely lost.

Some investment strategies have a way of staying in style. Instead of jeans or axes, the prize pickaxe in gambling today is slot machines. "The slot machine business will be one of the best in the American economy," according to Jason Ader.[6]

As it is, casinos replace about 15–20% of their slots each year. With an installed base of 600,000 slots, that amounts to around 100,000 replacement machines each year. Slots make up some 75%

of total gaming revenues, and they are highly profitable because of low labor costs.

Goldman Sachs' survey of slot managers came up with results that underscore the trend for slots becoming newer, better, more plentiful, younger, faster, (shinier?), and all sorts of other adverbs.

- More than half of their slot machines are more than 5 years old, compared with 41% in 2001.
- In 2003, 38% of slot managers said they were going to replace 15% of their games, vs. 24% 2 years ago.
- Forty-one percent of casinos said they planned to install more slot machines next year, up 3% from 2002.
- Twelve percent said they were downsizing their table sections to make room for more slots, up from 5% last year.

The slots replacement cycle is speeding up because the coins are losing their jingle. Slot machines are going cashless–meaning that instead of a plastic cup full of quarters the machine basically spits out an IOU instead. Sure, there are the coins jangling, but, sadly for us nostalgics, they're purely sound effects. This IOU/smart card more than makes up for it in convenience, however. It lets gamblers track their tab from machine to machine–as any grandmother in Atlantic City can tell you, machines get lucky at different times–and there are no pulled muscles from carrying around quarters. These so-called cashless slots save casinos money in labor costs and increase playing because they speed things up. In Missouri, for example, there was an 18% increase in money parted with by gamblers compared with the year before. The culprit? More cashless slots.

Right now fewer than 10% of slot machines are cashless, but that number is rising quickly. On average, slot machines are replaced every 7–9 years, but that time is estimated to speed up to 4–6 years because of cashless slots.

Part of the motivation for a wholesale machine replacement is that the current one-armed bandit can't be reconfigured to become cashless; the old machine won't accommodate the new technology. Operators say the costs of the cashless slot machines are more than offset by the reduced expense of coin handling, additional revenue earned by machines that stay in service longer, and increased customer satisfaction because hopper-fill delays are eliminated. In May 2003, Mandalay Bay Resort and Casino (MBG), announced a deal with International Gaming Technology (IGT), to install 2,000–3,000 slot machines that use tickets instead of coins.

Rod Smith of the *Las Vegas Review-Journal* estimates that with the trend away from coin machines, new slot machine sales could jump to $250,000 per year from 2002's approximately $100,000 per year.[7]

Cashless machines aren't the only technical advance on the horizon. Although the Nevada Gaming Commission recently put the kibosh on fitting slots with debit card devices—easy access to cash might mean new gambling addicts—the technology exists to implement such a thing. It's really only a matter of time before it gets installed, at which point the machines will become even more profitable.

Let the Cashless Revolution Begin

MGM Mirage (MGG) has committed to converting all of its casinos to cashless slot machines. Park Place Entertainment Corp. (PPE) completed the conversion of nearly all of its slot machines at its Paris Las Vegas and Bally's Las Vegas to cashless. By the end of the year, Park Place expects to have completely converted Caesar's Palace, with nearly 1,900 slots, and the Flamingo, with more than 1,700 slots. Steve Wynn has said that his fancy new Las Vegas hotel, Wynn Las Vegas (formerly known as Le Reve), set to open in 2005, will be 100% cashless slots. Already, the Borgata Hotel, the new $1 billion property in Atlantic City, jointly owned by MGM Mirage and Boyd Entertainment (BYD), opened July 2003 with 100% cashless slots.

Harrah's (HET) recently announced plans to replace about one-third of its slots with the cashless version this year alone. But, instead of *buying* the souped-up slots, it will make them in-house. The customized system will be designed to work with the company's other software, already in place.

What that ultimately means for Harrah's is more sales. All this technology "talking" to other technology helps to gather information about the customers–tracking their gambling habits–which ultimately personalizes the whole experience. Harrah's can customize its sales pitch to each gambler.

With all the new legislation allowing for gaming expansion, including reservation casinos, racetracks, and so on, Bear Stearns estimates the total market for new slots in these states could top 100,000 units (see Box 5.1). At the rate things are going the number of slot machines should rise by 50% in the next few years. And that's just domestically. Keep in mind that gambling is expanding overseas as well. Macau, for example, will be the home of casinos from Wynn and MGM Mirage Resorts.

BOX 5.1

Legislation

As much as the rumors persist that the mobsters run the Vegas henhouse, it just isn't true. Gaming is one of the most closely regulated industries around.

Since this industry is so tightly watched, as an investor you need to watch, too. You need to keep abreast of what's going on with the constant changes in legislation. Little laws have big effects on these stocks, and legislators are not likely to turn a blind eye to gambling revenues in tough times.

During a House debate on Internet gambling in March 2003, Rep. Jim Leach (R-Iowa), said wagers placed at offshore gambling sites cost the U.S. economy between $4 billion and $10 billion a year. "Gambling . . . on the Internet is the ideal methodology for money laundering, for narco traffickers, and for terrorists," he said.

Political pressure has taken its toll on the casinos. MGM Mirage shut down its online casino venture on June 30, 2003 due to legal ambiguity and political opposition to Internet gambling. Chairman and CEO Terry Lanni said that laws preventing U.S. residents and citizens of other key nations from legally participating in online gambling made it too difficult for MGM Mirage to continue its online casino. "Unfortunately, even in light of a successful working model, the legal and political climate in the US and several countries around the world remains unclear," he said in a statement. "We simply have to wait for the political climate to change and reality to set in."[8]

But the pressure to shut down online gambling is more than equaled by the temptation for states to get a piece of the action. More than 35 states are facing a budget shortfall, and nearly one-third have looked at allowing gambling or expanding or raising gambling taxes. That's not surprising considering that gambling adds $20 billion a year to state and local coffers, more than 4% of all domestic casinos' total revenue.

However, to casino owners and investors, taxes are a big problem. In 2002, Illinois and Indiana, with their riverboat gambling operations, were among states jacking up the tax rates. Indiana upped its tax rates from 20% to 35% and Illinois took its taxes from 35% to 50%, making its rates the highest in the country. But apparently that wasn't enough: The governor of Illinois signed a bill that raised the tax to 70% in 2003.

Considering that this affects the bottom line of casino operators, it's no surprise that the tax increases aren't exactly popular with owners and investors. Deutsche Bank gaming analyst Andrew Zarnett called the Illinois tax policy "Stalinist," and Harrah's CEO Gary Loveman said, "It would make a Scandinavian quiver."[9]

LIBERTARIANS PROVED RIGHT

As any good high school physics student can tell you, for every action there is an equal and opposite reaction. Consider what happened last year when the governor raised the rate to 50%: Argosy Gaming company (AGC) scaled down a new barge-based gambling hall, and Harrah's put a $40 million hotel project on hold at its casino. Both ventures were set in towns in the Chicago market. Heavy taxes also affected the value of bids on gaming licenses: MGM Mirage put the kibosh on a $615 million offer for a license near Chicago because tax increases lowered the value of the license. As of this writing no one has snapped up that license, which is estimated to be worth only two-thirds of MGM's bid.

The Midwest isn't alone in overtaxing the casinos to the point of driving them away. Take a big guess what happened when the New Jersey governor proposed a 25% increase in New Jersey's 8% casino tax rate, up 2 percentage points to 10%, plus a 7% tax on "comps," such as hotel rooms, drinks, and food. (The comp tax is an especially significant problem because some two-thirds of hotel rooms in Atlantic City are comped.)

(continues)

In the wake of this proposal, companies with Atlantic City casinos lost $700 million in market value in 2 days. Companies that were choosing where to do business chose to do so elsewhere. Park Place Entertainment, the largest operator in Atlantic City, halted plans for a parking garage and hotel tower at Caesar's. The company is moving ahead, however, with plans to develop a $500 million casino with the St. Regis Mohawk Tribe in the Catskills. MGM Mirage, which owns the bulk of the land that can be developed in Atlantic City—150 acres in the Marina—put off plans last year for a $1.5 billion casino. Instead, it decided to build in New York State. Said MGM's chairman and chief executive, Terry Lanni, of Atlantic City, "It's not as good of an investment as it would have been."[10]

Wall Street analysts, for example, think that the government legislation could reduce earnings by 10% for companies with major Atlantic City interests, such as Harrah's and Park Place. Yet, while some companies, like MGM, may be able to take their business elsewhere and/or be able to make up the tax hit in one area with revenues in another, companies tied into the particular area doing the tax hikes may not be the safest investment. As with anything, diversity is the way to go.

Consider companies with interests in areas less likely to get slammed by taxes. Nevada is such a place. Station Casinos (STN), whose outlets cater to a local market, is one to consider.

However, new properties also, always generate excitement. Atlantic City's swank Borgata hotel, co-owned by Boyd Entertainment and MGM Mirage, opened in July 2003, and is expected to have $63 million in revenues by 2006.

So, who makes these pickaxes?

There are several slotmakers, such as Gtech Holdings (GTH), Alliance Gaming Corp. (AGI), and Australian firm Aristocrat Leisure Ltd, but the 800-pound gorilla of the industry is Reno-based International Game Technology, with a market share of 70% domestically of the 725,000 installed base of gaming systems. IGT is expected to maintain its leading position because of its research and development budget of $80 million, compared with $28 million for its largest competitor, Gtech. In a recent earnings quarter the company said that growth of gaming and the push to cashless slots helped it record a 70% increase in profit. It currently has 13 consecutive quarters of year-over-year earnings increases.

"Nobody wants to walk up to a machine with $50 worth of nickels. Nobody wants to be weighed down with a bucket," IGT's director of investor relations, Rich Baldwin, told me. Instead, he says, players will warm to the new cashless technology. Although it hasn't been fully implemented, Baldwin is optimistic that his company will be riding the trend. "As it gets implemented we will be selling a lot of slot machines along the way."

Another nice thing about IGT's business is all the cool technology it is developing–the company is essentially a tech company. For example, casinos have player loyalty programs, which allow the casinos to evaluate and treat the $100 players differently than they do the $100,000 players. IGT sells those systems.

The company knows that Native American reservations launching casinos may not be the most cash rich. One way around that is to extend credit in advance of opening new markets. This type of ingenuity is what helped the company pull in $1.34 billion in 2001 revenue and outperform the S&P in the past 5 years by 300%. That winning streak is expected to continue. The industry overall is beating the S&P 500 as based on a study conducted by mutuals.com, parent of the Vice Fund. In Chapter 1 see Figures 1.3, 1.7, and 1.11.

If You Build It, They Will Gamble

Another key part to the legislation is the expansion of venues to gamble in. The more places to gamble, the more places Uncle Sam can collect money. Deutsche Bank analyst Marc Falcone estimates that Americans spent about $47 billion on casino gambling in 2001, up from $11.5 billion in 1991. A lot of that can be attributed to easy access. Back in the old days, you'd have to go Vegas or A.C. to get your game on. Nowadays, more likely than not, you can gamble to your heart's content in your very own state.

Riverboats are one such growing area. Among the companies providing riverboat gaming, my favorite is Argosy. It operates riverboat casinos on the Missouri and Mississippi rivers to support the drinking, smoking, and gambling vices of all those nice folks in

Illinois, Missouri, Kansas, and Louisiana. Get this: 10% of their revenues come from bar and cigarette sales. That's vice multitasking! It's estimated that Argosy will likely bring in more than a billion dollars next year and has really started to stand out in its niche.

Then there are more than 300 Native American casinos in the country. They're spreading so rapidly that in California alone, such gaming is estimated to be a $5 billion-a-year business.

But, uh, how will *you* make money on it? A good start is Multimedia Games (MGAM), the top supplier of gambling technology to Native American casinos. Its stock increased 44% in 2003.

Another way to profit from the legislation expanding Native American casinos is through Shuffle Master, which makes automatic shuffling devices for gaming tables. Shuffle Master (SHFL) develops, manufactures, and markets technology-based products such as automatic card-shuffling equipment, table games, slot game software, and slot operating system software for the gaming industry. In 2003 it was ranked one of America's 100 Fastest-Growing Small Companies by *Fortune* magazine for the second straight year. And, in the past five years that stock has been a ten-bagger—that is, it has gone up ten-fold.

The reservations are big fans of the tables. Why? Revenues from slots are taxed and the money goes to the states; money from tables doesn't. As a result, tables are expanding quickly on the reservations.

Horse Racing Has Become More of a Gamble

Six states have slot machines at racetracks and ten have video poker machines there now, but this business of trackside gambling-racinos is taking off. New York, for example, legalized racetrack gambling in October of 2001 to compensate for the budget deficits in part caused by the terrorist attacks of September 11. So far eight racetracks in the state allow slot machines. Of the racinos one company to note in particular is Penn National (PENN), which has the lock on the racing scene in Pennsylvania, one of the states debating putting slots at racetracks. The Pennsylvania House of Representatives has proposed that racetrack slot machines produce $1 billion in revenue, up from the $400 million projected for this fiscal year in legislation approved by the state Senate.

Considering that Penn National had watched its numbers dwindle over the years, with the addition of slots it's very likely that attendance and revenue will spike, just as they have in other states that have done the same.

Another way states are trying to cut costs and raise money is with lotteries. States are ramping up their marketing campaigns, which in turn is increasing sales notes former Bear Stearn's gaming analyst Michael Tew. As a result the lottery business is growing faster now than it has for the past 10 years. The big beneficiary in that business is a company called Scientific Games, which produces instant lottery tickets and management services for state-run lotteries. Scientific Games (SGMS) works with 28 of the 39 states that allow lotteries using instant tickets and another seven states with online lotteries.

With all this gaming expansion a natural fear is that Vegas will lose business. After all, isn't it much easier to pile in the car to go to Chief Halftown's Slot World than to drive or fly to Vegas? Yes, but who cares? Vegas is still Vegas and people will make an effort to go there as well. No matter how swank the riverboats or the Indian casinos are, I sincerely doubt that they sport $125 tanning day beds for four at topless pools and skyboxes at strip clubs. Gamblers will still come to the Mecca of gambling; local venues will only introduce newbies to the pleasures (and pitfalls) of gambling.

"The same people who drive 30 blocks out of the way to save money on groceries or gas go gambling and they suspend all sense of propriety," says the *Las Vegas Sun*'s McDarrah, about the people who will come to Sin City. "You expect to lose money. In what other activity do people come and say 'I'm only going to lose one thousand bucks.'" And, if you're self-appointed morality czar Bill Bennett, that figure could be $8 million. He's not without company. "Americans now spend more on gambling than on movies, videos and DVD's, music and books combined, and with an annual growth rate of about 9 percent since 1991," cites *New York Times* writer

Alex Berenson. "Gambling is growing substantially faster than the economy as a whole."[11]

Keep Your Eye on the Next Frontier

According to William Schmitt, gaming analyst at CIBC World Markets, the next frontier of gaming growth is Pennsylvania. Operators like Penn National would score from Pennsylvania.

LESSONS

- Know your politics. Governors are changing gaming legislation constantly. Know what they are up to because it could affect your investment.
- Visit casinos. I haven't seen much press about the cashless revolution of slot machines, but if you were to visit casinos you'd be up on that trend, which will benefit such companies as IGT.
- Pickaxes are it. In this industry, where it's unclear which company will get slammed by taxes, the best bets are the pickaxe companies like Multimedia Games, IGT, and Alliance.
- New and noteworthy. New hotels, like Atlantic City's Borgata, and new markets, like Macau, for MGM, can generate excitement, read: price increases, in a stock. Keep up with the news.
- Look for a dovetailing of vices. Vegas is doing well because people are also coming there to party it up. Throw in that the company is selling its share of booze, too. Argosy is doing well in part because people are smoking on its riverboats. Call it a perfect storm.

SHOPPING BAG

Alliance Gaming Corporation—AGI (NYSE)
www.ally.com

Alliance Gaming Corporation is an international gaming company that makes and distributes gaming machines and computerized monitoring systems for them. It also owns two casinos—the Rainbow Hotel Casino at Vicksburg, Mississippi, and the Rail City Casino near Reno, Nevada—and owns, operates, and services an installed base of slot and video gaming machines. The company makes its slots under the Bally name.

Price as of November 7:	$25.41
Price/Earnings:	18.28
52-Week Price Range:	$12.80–$25.61
Market Capitalization:	$1.27 billion
Trailing 12-Month Revenue:	$407.56 million

International Game Technology—IGT (NYSE)
www.igtonline.com/

International Game Technology develops and produces computerized gaming products. It also is involved in lottery systems developing, making, and selling of online lottery and pari-mutuel systems and related equipment.

Price as of November 7:	$33.43
Price/Earnings:	22.46
52-Week Price Range:	$17.84–34.75
Market Capitalization:	$11.54 billion
Total Revenue:	$1.85 billion

Argosy Gaming—AGY (NYSE)
www.argosycasinos.com

Argosy Gaming owns and operates six riverboat casinos in central United States.

Price as of November 7:	$25.32
Price/Earnings:	11.31
52-Week Price Range:	$15.21–$25.32
Market Capitalization:	$742.13 million
Trailing 12-Month Revenue:	$936.81 million

Station Casinos—STN (NYSE)
ww.stationcasinos.com

Station Casinos is a gaming and entertainment company that owns and operates eight major hotel/casino properties, each in the Las Vegas area, geared mainly toward area residents.

Price as of November 7:	$29.69
Price/Earnings:	17.18
52-Week Price Range:	$16.55–$33.50
Market Capitalization:	$1.73 billion
Trailing 12-Month Revenue:	$792.86 million

Multimedia Games—MGAM (Nasdaq: NM)
www.betnet.com

Multimedia Games supplies the Native American gaming market with interactive electronic games—including video lotteries—and the electronic player stations that play the games. The company also designs and develops software to create full systems for their customers.

Price as of November 7:	$41.45
Price/Earnings:	16.36
52-Week Price Range:	$15.37–$41.45
Market Capitalization:	$543.8 million
Trailing 12-Month Revenue:	$291.01 million

Shuffle Master, Inc.—SHFL (Nasdaq)
www.shufflemaster.com

Shuffle Master, Inc. makes and markets automatic card shufflers for card-based table games.

Price as of November 7:	$31.33
Price/Earnings:	24.71
52-Week Price Range:	$16.45–$32.81
Market Capitalization:	$519.45 million
Trailing 12-Month Revenue:	$56.13 million

Boyd Gaming Corporation—BYD (NYSE)
www.boydgaming.com

Boyd Gaming Corporation owns and operates 12 casinos, including Stardust and Sam's Town. One of the company's most high-profile properties is the Borgata in Atlantic City, Boyd's 2003 joint venture with MGM Mirage.

Price as of November 7:	$16.46
Price/Earnings:	$14.18
52-Week Price Range:	$11.13–$18.40

Market Capitalization: $1.05 billion
Trailing 12-Month Revenue: $1.36 billion

MGM Mirage—MGG (NYSE)
www.mgmmirage.com

MGM Mirage is an entertainment, hotel, and gaming company headquartered in Las Vegas, Nevada, which owns and/or operates 18 casino properties on three continents. Its properties include the Bellagio, a European-style luxury resort on the Las Vegas strip, as well as joint ownership, along with Boyd Entertainment, of the Borgata in Atlantic City.

Price as of November 7: $35.70
Price/Earnings: 19.58
52-Week Price Range: $24.09–$38.59
Market Capitalization: $5.17 billion
Trailing 12-Month Revenue: $4.46 billion

Scientific Games Corporation—SGMS (Nasdaq)
www.scientificgames.com

Scientific Games Corporation is really a tech company that provides services and products to the instant ticket lottery industry and the pari-mutuel wagering industry.

Price as of November 7: $13.45
Price/Earnings: 19.27
52-Week Price Range: $4.61–$13.88
Market Capitalization: $808.6 million
Trailing 12-Month Revenue: $455.25 million

CHAPTER

Weapons/Defense/War

Not Just Fly-by-War Kinds of Stocks

The U.S. gross domestic product (GDP) is not something to discuss at cocktail parties, and, unfortunately, it's not something investors get fired up about to investigate further. That's too bad, because if they did, they'd realize that lately it's being fueled by defense spending.

In the second quarter of 2003, the defense component of the GDP went up 44% from the previous quarter, which is the highest increase since the Korean War. However, nowadays, consumer spending makes up the bulk of the economy, accounting for two-thirds of GDP, whereas defense accounts for less than 5%. During WWII defense was about 40% of GDP.

However, defense is one powerful less-than-5% ingredient. "Without the defense spending increase, GDP growth would have been an underwhelming 0.7%," according to analyst Paul Nisbet of JSA Research. Instead it was up 2.4%, when analysts were only predicting a 1.6% increase.[1]

In turn, stocks popped up on the news at the end of July 2003, but nobody bothered to look at where the increase was coming from. Despite revenue gains from some of the biggest defense players their stocks haven't popped in lockstep. People aren't waking up and giving defense its proper due—yet.

Turn on CNN and you see bombs dropping, military strutting, and Pentagon officials smiling. Do you:

(A) Call your congressman?
(B) Call your hardware store for duct tape?
(C) Call your broker?

If you answered "C" you're a smart investor.

Defense spending is expected to rise sharply over the next 6 years. The Pentagon is planning on spending $240 billion on the military for what amounts to, simply put, a makeover. This in addition to the $2.3 trillion already budgeted for more routine military operations, like procurement. The 2003 procurement and R&D budget is up 20% from 2002. If you throw in the estimated $5 billion from Homeland Security, the increase is 25%, according to Citigroup Smith Barney's aerospace and defense analyst George D. Shapiro. Yet defense stocks are hovering near 8-year lows. Though shares surged from 2000 to 2002, the uptrend didn't last: As Pentagon spending for new weapons jumped, the shares fell when the likelihood of war became a reality.

At first this seems strange, but it makes sense if you take into account uncertainty. There's nothing the market hates more than uncertainty. There was uncertainty about when the war would start. Once it started, it was uncertain when it would end. Beyond that there's an uncertainty about how and where the government will focus our military spending. While we know they're going to be spending, it's still a question of where.

None of these stocks—or at least the ones I'll be talking about in this chapter—are just fly-by-war kinds of stocks. In other words the Iraq war isn't going to make or break any of them. Investing in the defense/weapons sector should be considered a long-term strategy.

Gipper-Time Redux?

"We're seeing a lot of money going into research and development and procurement at the same time," says Richard Sterk, a senior defense analyst at market research firm Forecast International. "Normally, it's one or the other."[2]

This smells a lot like Gipper-time. During the time of Star Wars and Cold War craziness there were 15%-plus annual rises in defense spending. Shares of contractors jumped, too.

Sounds dandy, right? However, these poor stocks have been at a low point, although there is a proposed 4% increase in the fiscal 2004 defense budget that just isn't good enough, considering that it was smaller than expected. However, it should be noted that much of the reason for the smaller increase was because of the larger increase the year before, when the defense budget went up 11%. Another reason the stocks aren't jumping is that many firms are involved in commercial aerospace, which, as a sector, has been a disappointment. See Figure 1.9 in Chapter 1 for the comparison of aerospace stocks to the S&P 500 as based on a study conducted by mutuals.com, parent of the Vice Fund.

The time when the sector really jumped was post Cold War, when there was a shakeout. Big players gobbled up the little ones, bidding their prices way up in the process. During the idyllic 1990s, the attitude became, "What, me worry?" Defense spending got chopped by half. Any upgrades were put on the back burner.

As a result, much of our equipment doesn't exactly have that new car smell anymore. According to *Smart Money* magazine, two-thirds of the Navy's aircraft are more than 15 years old and the average age of the Army's helicopters is more than 18 years. Decommissions will shrink the Navy's fleet to 291 vessels by 2006, a level not seen since 1916.[3]

That all means a lot of new orders and backlogs. Some analysts estimate that the defense budget should grow over 8% for the next few years–not bad, considering that in the 1990s that number was about 1.5% a year. Bush's fiscal defense budget for 2004 includes $380 billion in spending, or 3.4% of GDP. And that doesn't include extras like the war on terror and the conflict in Iraq. Homeland defense alone could account for $36 billion in fiscal 2004, according to the proposed budget.

These things take time, of course. That's why after September 11 stocks took a dive after a big runup: The government did not have the same immediate gratification need as investors. Defense contractors typically do well after conflict, but not while it is going on. So perhaps when you see bombs fly it's time to buy?

The folks at Smith Barney seem to think so. "As long as public support for increased defense spending stays above 40%, the defense budget will continue to grow as fast as GDP," according to analyst Shapiro. "We now believe the industry will shortly begin a several-year period of out-performance."[4]

Stockpiling Arms

Although defense and weapons aren't traditionally thought of as a vice, à la smoking, for example, many, link it with vice stocks because the socially responsible funds won't. The vice fund Ahrens owns Northrop Grumman (NOC), United Defense Industries (UDI), and L-3 Communications (LLL), among others.

Those three are part of a sector that is dominated by some major defense companies, such as Lockheed, that one must consider for this sector. Beyond that are some new players, which employ technology, that is another way to get at this sector. But first, the majors.

The Big Guns

The nation's second largest defense contractor, Northrop Grumman, has been acquiring everything that isn't nailed down. Litton, TRW—those big Cold War names are nothing but footnotes in the Northrop 10K now, and the company does about $20 billion in sales. It is virtually a pure-play defense company with over 95% of sales to the defense department or other government agencies. Northrop, however, is like the department store of defense companies—you can get everything here: services and solutions in systems integration, defense electronics, information technology, advanced aircraft, shipbuilding, and space technology. And it's exactly this diversity that will do a company good: Since it's got a toe (or really, in some cases, a leg) in so many different areas it will benefit from the broad government spending on our defense. One area to watch is shipbuilding. You may not realize it, but Northrop is the world's largest shipbuilder, and since Uncle Sam is now paying more attention and putting billions into this area, Northrop will get much of the action. Shipbuilding accounts for 20% of company sales and is a very high-cash-flow business. Some future headlines out of this company will be about unmanned drones, a key Northrop product, which we all heard a lot about during the Iraq war.

Regardless of how well positioned this company is, it still has some of the negatives of the defense sector. As I've pointed out, these companies suffer from a strange problem: fallen shares but rising sales and back orders.

General Dynamics (GD), the fifth-largest U.S. defense contractor, owes a debt of gratitude to the Navy. Anchors away, my friends: General Dynamics is now the Navy's number 1 supplier of combat vessels; in July 2003 it won a $287.6 million contract. The company expects full-year sales to reach approximately $15 billion in 2003, an 8% increase over the previous year. The company is not a one-military-branch kind of company, however. In June of 2003, General Dynamics was also awarded a contract worth up to $1.95 billion to support and maintain critical intelligence systems for the U.S. Air Force and another one worth up to $2 billion to provide software to defense department customers worldwide. Total backlog rose to $30.1 billion in 2003, up from $25.5 billion the year before.

Despite all this good news, the stock has been pummeled because of its ownership of Gulfstream—maker of the fancy business jets synonymous with CEO extravagance of the late '90s—which has been hit hard in the recession. Yet, though this stock isn't pretty, it's cheap, cheap, cheap. On a price-to-earnings basis it's the most attractive of its sector.

United Defense Industries is another company that has seen strong sales increases and stock going in the opposite direction. It's a big beneficiary of the military's makeover money. For example, Bradley Fighting Vehicle upgrades led the sales growth in defense systems, which also saw a pickup in development of an advanced naval gun system and deliveries of amphibious assault vehicles.

UDI is also benefiting from the high seas. It has some very lucrative contracts for maintenance and repair of Navy ships. Perhaps that ties into the fact that this company has some powerful friends. It was taken public by the Carlyle Group, the super-secret private equity group whose partners include former defense director, Frank Carlucci; Carlyle still has about a 25% stake in UDI.

One can't discuss defense stocks, or for that matter, own a basket of them, without including the old stalwart: Boeing (BA). Although Boeing does military work, it is really a commercial business. And it doesn't take an airplane engineer to realize that post 9/11 isn't the best time to be building airplanes–some analysts have concluded that it is "the early stage of earnings deterioration," but the company will always have its supporters.

Get Down to Tech

Considering that the war in Iraq has been the most technologically advanced of all of our fights thus far, it's not too strong a leap that many of the best future defense opportunities may be in technology. Many of those will be in the area of homeland defense.

The establishment of a Homeland Defense Agency in 2002, through a combination of 22 federal agencies, was certainly a big signal, as was the big budgeted and proposed spending. Our porous borders, for one, are a big problem. Uncle Sam has set aside nearly $400 million of the defense budget for an ID program and possibly $2 billion more to protect our borders. In total the money to protect them could go up to $15 billion in the next few years.

Since it doesn't look like terrorism is going away anytime soon these companies are piquing financiers' interests. Many of the companies are private right now, or just ideas in entrepreneurs' heads, but expect IPOs or spinoffs in the coming years.

"We've heard numbers as high as $1.2 billion for the amount of private equity invested in homeland security firms since 9/11," says Jack Mallon of Mallon & Associates, consultant and investment bankers.[5]

There are many funds with dedicated investments in the homeland security market. One, Laguna Research Partners in Irvine, California, for example, is one such company. It has an online site (www.LRPonline.net) offering data on homeland security companies for equity-research and venture-capital outfits. It has also created a Homeland Defense Industry index that tracks 18 Homeland Defense companies divided into "homefront" and "battlefield" sectors. They are a good, well-chosen group worth considering. The homefront segment includes Armor Holdings, AH (security products), Check Point Software Technologies, CHKP (digital security), CompuDyne, CDCY (attack protection), Identix, IDNY (biometrics–ID based on voice and retina), Internet Security Systems, ISSX (digital security), InVision Technologies, INVN (explosives detection), L-3 Communications, LLL (intelligence, surveillance and reconnaissance products), OSI Systems, OSIS (inspection products), Symantec, SYMC (digital security), Viisage Technology, VISG (biometrics), and Zebra Technologies, ZBRA (secure identification).

"The total operating performance of our index has remained consistently strong throughout the post-9/11 time-frame," says LRP's founder and senior homeland defense analyst Kevin B. Skislock. In the wake of 9/11, stocks shot way up only to come down to more reasonable valuations.[6]

Beyond the technology a big driver of defense companies is the idea of consolidation. That's certainly what drove them in the '90s. And it's that kind of activity in the middle-tier companies that will be driving things.

The prime candidate to do the acquiring is L-3, a company that seems to be on everybody's lips. L-3 itself has grown through serial acquisitions. It has become a major force as a government supplier of secure and specialized systems. It also makes flight recorders, display systems, and wireless telecom gear. The Pentagon and other government offices have snapped up L-3 products like secure telephone equipment and computer services for intelligence. The company has set aside about $200 million in cash for acquisitions. One smart purchase was PerkinElmer's detection-systems business: It's getting big contracts, and L-3's getting big money.

Not all of these acquisitions, for L-3 and others, will be done by good old American companies. Considering that we're the ones with the deep pockets–40% of global defense spending comes from the U.S. defense budget, and our spending beats out the next seven nations combined—companies based elsewhere want to get a piece of our action. Unfortunately for them, the only one to get lucky so far has been BAE Systems Plc (BAESY), the U.K.'s largest defense contractor, which has bought U.S. assets and even gets direct contracts from the Department of Defense via its wholly owned U.S. subsidiary, BAE Systems North America. Unfortunately, this is not the best option for conservative investing types since it trades on the Pink Sheets.

The Best Offense

The best offense for your portfolio may be a good defense, at least as long as terrorism continues to be a threat. The sector is on the upswing as the government's money is being deployed. From June 30, 2000 to June 30, 2003, according to research from the Vice Fund and mutuals.com, the stocks have risen 22.71% while the S&P has gone down 33.01% (see Figure 1.1). As long as our government remains hawkish and the world is a threatening place, keep looking for these stocks to do well.

LESSONS

- With the state of the world the way it is, defense manufacturers and security technology companies are going to continue to see great profits.
- Not only are governments beefing up, but so are consumers. The industry will profit further as security companies will be marketing their advances to the common Joe, much like what's happened with home and car alarm companies for years.
- Though stocks are at their 8-year lows, look for consolidation to drive the industry. Remember that old adage: "Buy low, sell high."
- Best investing bet: L-3.

SHOPPING BAG

Lockheed Martin—LMT (NYSE)
www.lockheedmartin.com

Lockheed Martin is a defense company working in the areas of systems integration, aeronautics, space, and technology services. As a lead systems integrator and information technology company, nearly 80% of Lockheed Martin's business is with the U.S. Department of Defense and the U.S. federal government agencies. Lockheed Martin is the largest provider of IT services, systems integration, and training to the U.S. government.

Price as of November 7:	$46.04
Price/Earnings:	17.58
52-Week Price Range:	$40.64–$58.95
Market Capitalization:	$20.76 billion
Trailing 12-Month Revenue:	$26.58 billion

General Dynamics Corporation—GD (NYSE)
www.generaldynamics.com

General Dynamics Corporation is a top supplier of defense systems to the United States and its allies. Among other products, it makes nuclear submarines. The company's aerospace group is the world's leading designer, developer, manufacturer, and marketer of mid-size and intercontinental business jet aircraft, and a major provider of maintenance and refurbishment services for a wide variety of business jets. Gulfstream, as in the Gulfstream jet, is one of its subsidiaries.

Price as of November 7:	$83.17
Price/Earnings:	14.57
52-Week Price Range:	$50.00–$87.45
Market Capitalization:	$16.45 billion
Trailing 12-Month Revenue:	$13.83 billion

Northrop Grumman Corporation—NOC (NYSE)

www.northgrum.com

Northrop Grumman Corporation is a global defense company providing products and services in the areas of defense electronics, systems integration, information technology, advanced aircraft, shipbuilding, and space technology.

Price as of November 7:	$89.05
Price/Earnings:	18.95
52-Week Price Range:	$78.27–$101.10
Market Capitalization:	$16.31 billion
Trailing 12-Month Revenue:	$17.21 billion

Boeing—BA (NYSE)

www.boeing.com

The Boeing Company is the world's leading aerospace company. It is the largest maker of satellites, commercial jetliners, and military aircraft. The company is also a global market leader in missile defense, human space flight and launch services. In terms of sales, Boeing is the largest U.S. exporter.

Price as of November 7:	$38.73
Price/Earnings:	20.01
52-Week Price Range:	$24.73–$38.73
Market Capitalization:	$30.99 billion
Trailing 12-Month Revenue:	$54.07 billion

Raytheon Company—RTN (NYSE)

www.raytheon.com

Raytheon Company is an industry leader in defense, government and commercial electronics; space; information technology; technical services; and business aviation and special mission aircraft.

Price as of November 7:	$26.97
Price/Earnings:	17.73
52-Week Price Range:	$24.31–$33.97
Market Capitalization:	$11.23 billion
Trailing 12-Month Revenue:	$16.76 billion

L-3 Communications Holdings, Inc.—LLL (NYSE)
www.l-3com.com

L-3 Communications Holdings, Inc. sells secure communications and intelligence systems, surveillance, and reconnaissance (ISR) systems; training, simulation, and support services; aviation products; and related specialized products.

Price as of November 7:	$48.20
Price/Earnings:	19.20
52-Week Price Range:	$34.23–$51.48
Market Capitalization:	$4.66 billion
Total Revenue:	$4.01 billion

United Defense Industries, Inc.—UDI (NYSE)
www.uniteddefense.com

United Defense Industries, Inc. designs and produces combat vehicles, artillery systems, naval guns, and missile launchers used by the U.S. Department of Defense and its allies worldwide. It is America's largest nonnuclear ship repair, modernization, overhaul, and conversion company.

Price as of November 7:	$33.90
Price/Earnings:	13.45
52-Week Price Range:	$20.06–$34.15
Market Capitalization:	$1.77 billion
Trailing 12-Month Revenue:	$1.73 billion

InVision Technologies, Inc.—INVN (Nasdaq NM)
www.invision-tech.com

InVision Technologies, Inc. is the leading provider of explosives detection systems for airplane security worldwide.

Price as of November 7:	$28.19
Price/Earnings:	15.95
52-Week Price Range:	$19.82–$30.30
Market Capitalization:	$476.7 million
Trailing 12-Month Revenue:	$439.13 million

CHAPTER

Booze

Sucker for a Pretty Case

Maybe it's because I spent a few years in San Francisco, with the day trips to Napa and Sonoma, or maybe it was too many lunches at Francis Ford Coppola's restaurant with its own delicious Merlot, but I developed an appreciation for wine. Before then wine to me was just for the wealthy connoisseur, but the city certainly educated me.

Wine was everywhere. Even my cute little corner deli, The Hollow Cow (I lived in a section called Cow Hollow), featured some of the best wines available and staff as knowledgeable about Chardonnay as they were about sandwiches. The place was always packed, with many of the customers buying wine, most of us in our 20s and 30s. San Francisco, of course, belies the fact that people in the 21 to 27-year age range are the smallest group of wine drinkers.

That may not be true for long. Back in New York, like so many other returned dot-com carpetbaggers, I've taken my appreciation of wine with me. Don't ask me what wines go with fish or meat or chicken—I don't have the faintest—but I do know that I'm drinking it more than other type of alcohol. My friends are doing the same.

Lately, I've become hooked on what should be called Bridget Jones Wine. It's an Australian wine called Alice White that I now ask for, instead of my former requests for "a nice red under $15." I'm clueless when it comes to whether I'd like Beringer or some Beaujolais, but I know I like the Alice White. Why? Because it's inexpensive, tastes good enough, and has a cute story on the back of its label–the serial adventures of a British woman named Alice traveling in nineteenth-century Australia. Recently, the brand introduced $1.99 single-serving–187-mL–versions of the product. They come with a catchy title, Lil' Joeys.

Maybe I'm a sucker for a clever package, but it looks like I'm not the only one. Alice White has quickly become one of this country's fastest-growing wine brands and is the fifth-ranking Australian brand in the U.S. in sales volume. It seems that smart marketing, branding, and innovations pay off in the slow-growth booze industry.

"I was off to drink you away."—Kid Rock

Mr. Rock's not alone in his methodology. Having a bad day? Get a drink. Having a good day? Make a toast. No matter what the motivation or the description, the action's still the same.

Where to go for some libations? Hit the bar. Or the liquor store. Or, these days, the supermarket, the drugstore, or the deli. Even the convenience stand at the theme park. Just about anywhere. This age-old panacea hasn't gone anywhere and yet it's gone everywhere. It seems there are few places where you can't buy booze and even fewer where your appetite won't get whetted for it. Turn on the television and you'll see more ads for booze than you would have a few years back. Open the magazines and you'll be inundated as well.

With more ads, there are more products too. New categories, like malternatives, or this generation's Zima (albeit a successful Zima), are springing up all the time. (Zima, for those who chose to put it out of their minds, was a spiked 7-Up type of drink marketed–and often mocked–in the early '90s.) As of late, however, it had a bit of a resurgence. (Blame nostalgia?) New and notable concoctions are fueling sales growth for the companies in this sector.

The result of all this boozing is that stocks in this category according to research done by the Vice Fund have gone up 32.05% from June 30, 2000 to June 30, 2003, versus a loss of –33.01% for the S&P (see Figure 1.5 in Chapter 1). In the 5-year period starting on June 30, 1998, alcohol stocks are even more impressive, posting gains of 46.02% while the S&P 500 lost 14.05% (see Figure 1.12).[1]

What Zima Wrought

The one to really kick off this generation was Diageo's (DEO) Smirnoff Ice, a malt liquor with a lemonade flavor, launched in January 2001. It remains the number 1 malternative seller in North America, representing one-third of all malternative sales here. As a result of the quick success, Smirnoff's competitors were quick to pile on with their own offerings. Notably, Anheuser-Busch (BUD) linked up with Bacardi to launch Bacardi Silver; SABMiller and Skyy Vodka did Skyy Blue; and SABMiller and Allied Domecq (AED) put out Stolichnaya Citrona and Sauza Diablo. (SABMiller, unfortunately, is not traded in the United States, and Bacardi and Skyy are privately held.) This is great for the spirits companies because the products increase brand awareness for their namesake hard liquors. Consumers seem happy too: Sales for the drinks reached $350 million in 2 years.

Trends that sweep in like that are something to watch out for because they can sweep out just as quickly. Single-handedly these fruity, fun drinks gave an adrenaline shot to an industry, which, although not moribund, certainly needed it. The malternatives' ads are immensely popular—and immensely risqué. (Maybe that's why they're so popular?) They are much racier than the traditional beer ads. One Bacardi Silver commercial that is drawing some attention shows a woman's hand reaching out from a shower to steal her boyfriend's Bacardi Silver; he follows the drink to join his gal in the shower. Skyy Blue offers tanned, buxom lovelies on fast boats holding bottles of the booze. In one year alone companies spent $450 million to promote malternatives.

Why so sexy? "It's a game of who gets the most attention, and one thing that gets people's attention is sex," says Tom Pirko, president of consulting firm BevMark. Perhaps their ads have gotten so ramped up because sales can only go up so much before fickle drinkers are on to the next cocktail. "Malternatives will never get half as far as their producers would like," says Pirko.[2]

Indeed, this trend seems to be on the wane, but on the wane after reaching a pretty high peak.

The group grew its retail sales by 30% in 2000, to $378 million, as compared with over twice that growth rate the year before. But even in a declining market numbers like that still spark interest, considering that the malternative category had the highest sales increase of all the beer categories of which it is classified as a part. Domestic premium beers grew sales only a bit above 5%, for example, while imports grew 6%. The inevitable shakeout is happening, though. Allied Domecq and SABMiller announced that they would stop producing Stolichnaya Citrona and Sauza Diablo. Diageo discontinued Captain Morgan Gold. Nonetheless, even at a declining growth rate these drinks are responsible for momentum in the spirits world, and they themselves are not over as a category. There are new entrants coming out. Diageo, for one, is still bullish on malternatives, and launched Smirnoff Ice Triple Black. Anheuser-Busch gave birth to Bacardi Silver 03, and Jack Daniel's Original Hard Cola, a cola-flavored malt beverage made with natural flavors was rolled out by Brown-Forman (BFB) and Miller Brewing Company. And there's still innovation in the category: The Jim Beam Brands unit of consumer products company Fortune Brands, Inc. (FO) rolled out Beam and Cola, a ready-to-drink beverage containing cola and real Jim Beam. This is different because it is using the named alcohol and not just its flavor. That's just the tip of the ice cube as far as innovation in concerned.

If you want to make money in malternatives, or for that matter, beer and alcohol in general, you need to watch for trends and see what's moving. In this case, it looks like Diageo's Smirnoff Ice is the winner. And though Diageo has its share of screw-ups, if you want to make one malternative bet, this is it.

Thin Is In

Alcohol companies follow trends closely—besides setting them every now and again—and as anyone worth his gym membership can tell you, it's all about fitness and health nowadays. Tight and toned is in, and although Americans may love their beer, few of us love what comes with it: the dreaded beer belly.

Beer producers are starting to get it. Enter the low-carb brews. If producers had their way, these would become what low-fat chocolate Power Bars are to chocolate brownies.

The gorilla entrant is Anheuser-Busch's Michelob Ultra, which has swallowed up 1.5% of the beer market in less than a year. The word-of-mouth campaign places it firmly in the grasp of the cult-like following of low-carb diets such as Atkins. In fact, it's actually known in some circles as the Atkins beer.

The beer tastes good enough to appeal to a wide audience. The consensus is that Ultra's motto—"Lose the carbs. Not the taste"—isn't too far off. Ads show a woman, mid-situp, with a six-pack (abs, not beer) that would make Arnold jealous. "We couldn't have anticipated the consumer demand," said Dave Peacock, vice president of high-end brands at A-B. "With the focus on low-carbohydrate diets today, we think it has a unique niche in the market."[3]

Well, maybe not so unique, but a smart idea nonetheless. In 1967, Gablinger's Diet Beer came out, bragging that it "didn't fill you up." Too bad that in addition to having no carbs, it had no taste; beer historians refer to it as the "Edsel of beer." There's also Boston Beer Co. Inc's (SAM) new entrant, Sam Adams Light, which has taken just under 0.5% of the market, but within a few months accounted for 20% of its company's volume. Other competitors bellying up to the low-carb bar include Labatt's Rock Green Light and Coor's (RKY) Aspen Edge.

Miller Lite has been around for 20 years and is comparable, both in calories and fat, to Michelob Ultra. The folks at Miller are playing up the low-carb angle, too. At 95 calories and 2.6 grams of fat, Ultra, however, has seven-tenths of a gram fewer carbs and one fewer calorie than Miller Lite. (But when counting carbs, everything makes a difference!) The carb count for both, however, is about one-half of what other light beers are serving up and about one-fifth of that of normal beers. They are priced about a dollar more than normal 12-ounce beers. There's concern about companies getting drunk on their own new developments, which cannibalize the sales of their predecessor products. Keep in mind that Anheuser-Busch, for example, owns Bud Light, the top selling beer in America, and Michelob Light. There's also its Bud Ice Light and Michelob Ultra. Nontheless, it all seems to be part of A-B's game plan. Juli Niemann, an analyst for RT Jones in St. Louis, attributes the success to smart marketing and understanding of the target audience. "What they're trying to do is promote their specialty things that have higher markup."[4]

Malternatives are also slimming down. Anheuser-Busch, for example, has reformulated its "Doc's" Hard Lemon brand, with fewer calories and carbohydrates than the original. Considering that most malt beverages have as many as 41 grams of carbohydrates per 12-ounce serving, the slimming is a good idea.

Other companies are tasting the slim opportunity. Thin Ice, made by Massachusetts-based Long Beach Brewing Company, promotes itself as the first no-sugar, low-calorie, and low-carbohydrate, flavored alcohol beverage on the market, with only 90 calories and 1 gram of carbohydrate per 12-ounce serving. Thin Ice contains the same amount of alcohol (4.2%) as the average light beer. Company president Mike Herbert says he wanted to jump on the opportunity. "When we sat back and looked at who's drinking the [flavored alcohol beverage] products, it's a lot of women and young guys who may not like the taste of beer, but are concerned with how many calories and carbohydrates they're consuming," he said. "I really don't think there are enough products that are low calorie and low carb that don't have a strict beer profile as far as taste. I thought if an alternative product was put together it might have some appeal."[5]

It seems that this spate of low-carb drinks is the beginning. It's always the case that one good idea spawns 50 others in this industry. To make money, the winner here is Anheuser-Busch. It looks like it will go from the company that promoted beer bellies to the one promoting belly shirts.

However, there certainly is demand. Morgan Stanley estimates that 19% of U.S. adults had tried a low-carb diet in 2003.

Legislate This

As with any industry, alcohol is one in which investors—and, hey, consumers, too—need to watch the law. It certainly does have a way of affecting things. As it stands, laws prohibit hard liquor from being advertised on television but allow beer commercials. That's because these malternatives are classified as malt beverages. And anyone above the age of 30 knows that malt liquor commercials are allowed on television. Remember smooth Billy Dee Williams going from playing Lando Calrissian in *Star Wars* to crooning, "Colt 45 . . . It works every time" surrounded by women in a bar?

However, it doesn't look like it's working every time for the liquor companies. The Alcohol and Tobacco Tax and Trade Bureau of the U.S. Treasury Department has proposed imposing tighter restrictions on the labeling and advertising of malternatives. Under the proposed rules, a malternative drink will be considered a beer product only if less than 0.5% of its volume is alcohol derived from distilled spirits. The proposed rules would treat malternatives as a beer product only if they meet a certain limit on the amount of distilled alcohol added. Not only that but they are considering changing the rules governing how flavored malt beverages are taxed. Industry experts warn that this could hurt the category's staying power. The proposed rules could spur producers to withdraw or slow the entry of new products, and if the liquor companies reformulate their products, the new tastes could really throw people off.

The Big Booze

If you're even thinking about investing in booze you have to consider Diageo and not just because it's the world largest spirits company. But that does count for a lot: It's responsible for such brands as Smirnoff, Johnnie Walker, Cuervo, and Tanqueray. Diageo now owns 10 of the top 20 spirits brands in the U.S. and holds a 23% market share, nearly two times its nearest U.S. rival.

This U.K.-based company had been weighted down with regulatory issues related to its acquisition of Seagram's brands in late 2001. However, that headache seems to be on the way out. And just as it was integrating the Seagram's business it was exiting its distracting food business—well, just about. It won regulatory clearance for the sale of Pillsbury to General Mills and got rid of Burger King.

However, despite the lusciousness of its hamburgers BK didn't fetch such a fetching price. Diageo lost about $2.2 billion on the sale of Burger King to a consortium of investors—Texas Pacific Group, Bain Capital Partners, and Goldman Sachs Capital Partners—for only $1.5 billion. That hangover will take a while for the company to shake.

Without having to divert its drinks focus onto food, however, the folks at Diageo have been better able to do what they do best: booze. Diageo's leading brands—Captain Morgan, Crown Royal, Seagram's 7, and Seagram's VO—are the company's backbone. In the first half of the most recent fiscal year, Diageo said premium drinks revenue was up 11% to $7.9 billion. Diageo's Smirnoff is the world's bestselling vodka, with more than 21 million cases sold each year. Johnnie Walker is the world's bestselling Scotch whisky, moving more than 10 million cases a year. With more than 5 million cases sold per year, Captain Morgan ranks as the No. 2-selling rum. Cuervo sells more than 4 million cases every year, making it the No. 1 tequila in the world. And rounding out the brands, Tanqueray is the No. 1 premium gin in the United States, selling nearly 2 million cases per year.

Diageo is an innovative little company, something that makes a difference in a slow-growth sector. It has 31 different malternatives in 39 markets. The *Wall Street Journal* even profiled Diageo's use of a new methodology to get its brands noticed: charm. The company got traction for its new $30-a-bottle "superpremium" vodka named Ciroc, distilled from French grapes instead of the traditional grain, available in fancy places like the Four Seasons in New York. Company representatives convinced the bartender there to create a vodka and champagne cocktail called Ciroc Rocks. This was no small accomplishment at a time of a glut of high-end vodkas, a lousy economy, and a backlash against French brands.

According to the *Journal*, Diageo representatives spent hours in the bar, holding tastings for the bartenders and buying drinks for customers. Ever since Prohibition spirits makers have been barred from selling directly to liquor stores, restaurants, and bars. Instead, they have to go through huge wholesale distributors, whom they can't control. The distributors' reps often sell Diageo brands along with a myriad of brands of their other clients, too. Now Diageo is playing hardball, using its leverage to sign 5-year contracts with its distributors. Under the pacts, distributors agree to create dedicated sales forces to get better shelf space, launch marketing campaigns for new premium products, and gather consumer feedback from retailers. Diageo is also naming just one distributor in each state to handle its goods. The company is training its distributors' sales forces in more sophisticated targeting techniques. The *Journal* points out how they specialize in the Hispanic community, differentiating between Dominican and Puerto Rican consumers in New York, for example. Salespeople dedicated to high-end establishments are being taught how to pitch products, for example, using in-room silver platters featuring Diageo brands.[6] This kind of targeted marketing is key, considering that the market for premium vodkas has been heating up. Since 2000, besides Ciroc, 147 new brands, including my favorite, Turi, have been launched. This into a market in which the top five brands—Absolut, Stolichnaya, Skyy, Grey Goose, and Ketel One—are practically household names.

Not all innovations catch on, however. The malternative Captain Morgan's Gold didn't spend much time on the shelves before it was pulled.

Nonetheless, while absorbing the Seagram's acquisition, the company is trying to increase sales faster than the industry average of 1–2% annual growth. Plus, the company has a 3.5% dividend and a valuation of roughly 10 times cash flow. If you want to buy some shares, keep in mind that they are traded overseas and that you will be buying the American Depository Receipt (ADR). Although

ADRs face the same currency and economic risks as the foreign shares they represent, considering that Diageo trades in the U.K., it should be fine.

Keep on Chugging

Well, you've just read about the world's largest spirits company. Now meet the world's largest brewer: $13.7 billion Anheuser-Busch. The company has been upping profits and volume like it's last call–sorry, I couldn't resist–while the beer industry as a whole is growing at a much slower rate.

A-B profits have climbed 13% per year from 1998 to 2003, even though sales rose just 4% annually. Part of what's driving the company is its strategic acquisitions–the company's products now account for 50% of the U.S. beer market. (Not bad, considering beer comprises 60% of all the alcohol Americans drink.) Also very important is the company's ability to raise prices. Few companies have this ability, called pricing power, but A-B definitely does. As a result it's able to get a higher revenue per barrel of beer. In the most recent financial report, the company announced that it was able to pull in 3.5% more in cash per barrel. As a result, in one quarter, net sales rose to $3.77 billion from $3.63 billion. The company earned $633 million, or 75 cents a share, up from $587 million, or 66 cents a share the prior year. The company liked the effect so much that it will raise prices further on select brands in certain markets.

It's not all beer funnels and roses at A-B, however. While profit growth is still phenomenal, it was about 1% slower in 2003 than in 2002. That is really from the overseas business; 2003 was the year of SARS. But one thing that might be something to consider is the perception of America throughout the world. This is important because Bud is indisputably an American brand.

And of course there are the theme parks, like Busch Gardens, which A-B owns. This one can garner a double whammy because not only is the theme park weather dependent–the summer of 2003 was practically one big monsoon on the East Coast—but while the rug rats are on the rides, parents are drinking Buds, wishing they were anywhere else. No kiddies in the park, no Buds sold.

There's no denying that A-B has its fans. Though the drinkers of what Anheuser-Busch offers may not be likely to party with the folks from *Kiplinger's Personal Finance*, it doesn't mean there's no love there. Well, at least the *Kiplinger's* folks are in love. They recommended the Bud stock, saying, "Its finances are as solid as the holdings in Fort Knox." They portray Bud as a conventional safety stock.[7] Well, bottoms up. The stock yields 1.5%, and the company raises the dividend regularly. In fact, it is in the twenty-seventh year in a row that it has upped its dividend. A-B's average annual dividend per share increase during the past 5 years was 8.4%, which represented top-quartile-dividend-per-share growth among S&P 500 companies. The company recently changed its dividend policy to make it even more widow and orphan friendly: It will increase dividends per share in line with the company's earnings-per-share growth, in constrast to a prior policy of increasing dividends per share somewhat less than the growth in earnings per share.

Drink and Be Alert

But as any club goer can attest, other drinks, nonalcoholic ones, are taking the beverage market by storm. The biggest of these is Red Bull, a potent combination of water, sugar, and caffeine that's leveraged hip athletes and extreme sports to grab the imagination— and dollars—of young drinkers worldwide.

The (unfortunately for investors, private) company called Red Bull was founded in 1984 by an Austrian, Dietrich Mateschitz, who saw the popularity of stimulating "tonic drinks" in Asia and decided to market them in Europe. In 1992 Red Bull entered its first foreign market, Hungary; today, it's in over 70 countries around the globe. More than 1.5 billion cans of Red Bull are consumed each year, making it the world's No. 1 energy drink. Mateschitz alone downs 10 cans a day. And it's not cheap either. It costs about 400% more then regular soft drinks.

The makers claim that Red Bull will "give you wings," or more specifically, increase physical endurance, concentration, and reaction speed and improve vigilance while stimulating metabolism. Not bad for a drink in a can that has the same amount of caffeine as a cup of coffee. A smart ad campaign featuring cartoon characters positions it as a quirky alternative to the big soda companies, and endorsements of athletes and competitions in such cool sports as motocross, surfing, skateboarding, BMX, basejumping, acrobatic flying, and kayaking have established Red Bull as the drink of choice for the young and edgy—or those who want to be. It's the trendy drink of choice among today's heartiest partiers who mix it with vodka.

The potent combination of caffeine, branding, and cool is working wonders for Red Bull. Red Bull has effectively created a new market—energy drinks—which is getting increasingly crowded as competitors like Rock star energy drink, Anheuser-Busch's 180, Pepsi's AMP, and Coke's KMX share shelf space. However, despite competition, Red Bull has 70% of the energy drink market. For 2002, the company said it grossed $1.2 billion in worldwide sales. Red Bull is the dominant brand and is likely to remain so for a long time.

Dietrich Mateschitz is now the richest man in Austria. He has another new drink derived from Asia, Kombucha, coming out, and it looks like his fortune will just increase. This fermented beverage, a combination of herbal tea, yeast culture, and lactic acid, is said to help digestion, improve skin tone, and reinforce the immune system.

Though the company is private at the moment, its products are creating new markets, which, as you can see from Pepsi, competitors are taking advantage of. How do you make money? Wait until Red Bull goes public, or follow a smart competitor to see who makes headway. Or take note if Red Bull or Kombucha starts to get mixed with one alcohol in particular, whose owner is a public company.

Wine and Rosy Stocks

A favorite of Vice Fund manager Dan Ahrens is New York-based Constellation Brands (STZ) (known at one time as Canandaigua), a big beer, wine, and liquor distributor. Its brands include Almaden, Inglenook, and Simi wines, and it also imports such beverages as Corona beer, Fleischmann's gin, and my favorite wine, the aforementioned Alice White. With over a dozen acquisitions in the past decade, the company recently completed its $1.4 billion acquisition of BLR Hardy, an Australian wine producer and distributor, making it the world's largest wine seller. A bonus: Australian wines are enjoying a wave of popularity in the U.S.

But as wine drinkers can tell you, there is a wine glut happening. Wine lovers are seeing the prices of their favorite California wines dropping because of overzealous planting. In 2002 there were 12% more grapes crushed, and 17% lower prices, compared to the year before. Many stock watchers were terrified that this dropping of prices would really hurt margins and companies. Indeed, some smaller players have gone out of business as a result.

However, there has been a silver lining. The low prices have brought new customers into the stores. Wines like Charles Shaw, aka "Two-Buck Chuck," the $1.99 wine sold only at Trader Joe's stores, now makes up 15% of all California wine sales. (California! This is the home of the United States wine country!) Customers who have traditionally stuck with lower-priced wines are being introduced to higher-quality goods, now at a discount.

Part of what's driving Constellation is cheap wine, and lots of it. *Forbes* writer Christopher Helman described it perfectly when he said that this was a company that "makes juice to suit winos and sommeliers alike."[8] It is a purveyor of jug wines, such as Almaden. Though Constellation knows from low-brow, it has also been buying and spinning out some higher-priced/more status-y wines, like Paul Masson brandy, which will garner higher margins. The Australian merger was very strategic, too, as this is a region whose wines are quickly growing in popularity. The widespread boycott of French wines leaves a big vacancy to be filled.

Americans are gulping down the vino. In 2002, consumption was up 5.2% compared with only a 1.3% rise for beer.

Constellation is among the companies embracing clever marketing—again, Alice White—including the screw-cap top, which is growing in popularity. It's easy to use—and once people forget the low-class image, they find that they appreciate it. But sometimes it's not too easy to wean people off the traditional cork and change people's habits in any way. Witness Prince Charles, "Quite why anyone should want to encounter a nasty plastic plug in the neck of a wine bottle is beyond me!"[9]

Corks or caps or plastic plugs aside, Stephen Roach, Morgan Stanley's famed gloomy chief economist, is very choosy about what he recommends, if anything, but he's recommending Constellation Brands. It's a good hedge against deflation because it's able to maintain its pricing power. For the 6 months ending on August 31, 2003, net sales rose 25% to $1.7 billion. Constellation has been a long term winner: The stock has gone up 621% in the past decade. Roach likes Constellation in large part because of the category it's in, consumer nondurables. This group, with the unsexy name, includes things like food, tobacco, and alcohol. Good in good times and even better in bad times.[10] Or, rather, needed in good times and even more needed and relied on in bad times—especially the alcohol.

LESSONS

- Like tobacco, alcohol can get the squeeze from legislation and public backlash. Higher taxes on alcohol and restrictions on advertising have long been obstacles for the industry. So, stay abreast of what's going on in the news and keep your eyes on judicial decisions that may affect this industry.
- Don't be fooled by trends alone. Despite what the girls of "Sex in the City" did for the Cosmopolitan, things that come in as a sudden trend can go out as a trend just as quickly. The exception is when the producers can innovate. Case in point: malternatives morphing into low-carb malternatives. Just look at Anheuser-Busch's reformulated Doc's Hard Lemon.

- Look for the innovative advertisers. I don't advocate sizzle over substance, but in this industry they have to have both. The smart company is the one that can effectively use advertising to separate itself from the rest of the pack.
- Look for companies with a deep bench. The company with a variety of types of alcohols and/or beers is the best positioned. When cheap wine is in, they're set. Australian wine the thing? They got it. (Hint: I'm talking about Constellation Brands.)

SHOPPING BAG

Diageo PLC—DEO (NYSE)
www.diageo.com

Diageo PLC is the world's largest spirits company, with brands including Smirnoff vodka, Johnnie Walker Scotch whiskey, Guinness stout, Bailey's Original Irish Cream liqueur, J&B Scotch whisky, Captain Morgan rum, and Tanqueray gin.

Price as of November 7:	$48.6
Price/Earnings:	13.5
52-Week Price Range:	$37.5–$48.9
Market Capitalization:	$39 billion
Trailing 12-Month Revenue:	$17.3 billion

Anheuser-Busch Companies, Inc.—BUD (NYSE)
www.anheuser-busch.com

Anheuser-Busch Companies, Inc. is the world's largest brewer. The outfit also holds an entertainment segment, with adventure park operations in addition to real estate development and transportation businesses.

Price as of November 7:	$51.30
Price/Earnings:	18.2
52-Week Price Range:	$45.30–$53.84

Market Capitalization: $41.8 billion
Trailing 12-Month Revenue: $16.6 billion

Allied Domecq PLC—AED (NYSE)
www.allieddomecq.com

Allied Domecq PLC is an international spirits and wine company, with brands such as Kahlua liqueur, Malibu rum, and Beefeater gin. The company also owns Quick Service Restaurants, which operates an international franchise business made up of Dunkin' Donuts, Baskin-Robbins, and Togo's, a sandwich chain.

Price as of November 7: $28.74
Price/Earnings: 12.1
52-Week Price Range: $17.14–$28.75
Market Capitalization: $7.95 billion
Trailing 12-Month Revenue: $5.2 billion

Brown-Forman Corporation—BFB (NYSE)
www.brown-forman.com

Brown-Forman Corporation makes and markets wine and spirits such as Jack Daniel's Tennessee Whiskey, Southern Comfort bourbon, and Finlandia vodka. Its portfolio also contains consumer durables, like fine China dinnerware, casual dinnerware, and stainless steel flatware produced under the Lenox and Gorham names.

Price as of November 7: $85.51
Price/Earnings: 18.2
52-Week Price Range: $60.25–$86.26
Market Capitalization: $5.19 billion
Fiscal 2003 Revenue: $2.4 billion

Fortune Brands, Inc.—FO (NYSE)
www.fortunebrands.com

Fortune Brands, Inc. is a holding company with such businesses as home products, office products, and wine and spirits, including Jim Beam bourbon.

Price as of November 7: $66.60
Price/Earnings: 16.0
52-Week Price Range: $40.60–$67.48
Market Capitalization: $9.67 billion
Trailing 12-Month Revenue: $5.68 billion

Boston Beer Company, Inc.—SAM (NYSE)
www.bostonbeer.com

The Boston Beer Company, Inc. is a craft brewer putting out favorites like the Samuel Adams Boston Lager, which makes up most of the company's sales.

Price as of November 7: $17.40
Price/Earnings: 22.0
52-Week Price Range: $10.10–$18.00
Market Capitalization: $240.43 million
Total Revenue: $215.36 million

Constellation Brands, Inc.—STZ (NYSE)
www.cbrands.com

Constellation Brands, Inc. is a producer and marketer of wine and spirits in America, Europe, and Australia. Brands include Almaden wine, Fleischmann's gin, and Corona beer.

Price as of November 7: $31.52
Price/Earnings: 11.45
52-Week Price Range: $21.90–$32.23
Market Capitalization: $3.31 billion
Trailing 12-Month Revenue: $2.73 billion

CHAPTER

Sex

Everybody Loves Hef

My trip to the Playboy mansion started out innocently enough. I agreed to help my friend Julie and her sister-in-law set up for her dinner-dance fundraiser for a hospital in Los Angeles. I figured that we'd be decorating a restaurant or a museum for the event; it never occurred to me that we'd be gussying up chez Hef. So, there we were, a group that looked more play date than playmate, a bunch of preppy girls putting out placecards, only steps away from the famous grotto.

So, what did I do? I snuck away from the gals and did some reconnaissance. I'm not so sure what I expected to see, considering it was 11 A.M., but never mind. First the grotto. It smelled like an hourly motel and made the pictures of honeymoon hideaways in the Poconos look romantic. Next I snuck into the gym—the house was off limits, darn—and it looked like it was done by the set decorator for the "Brady Bunch" house. Except I don't think I recall Alice labeling a receptacle for "soiled towels."

Besides one playmate-looking gal on the Stairmaster, I saw no bunnies running around and no bathrobe-clad Mr. Hefner. The only exotic thing I did see were peacocks walking free on the grounds and fun notepads labeled "The Playboy Mansion."

Even though the experience at the legendary place was less than transcendent, it didn't matter. That benefit was oversubscribed, with an unprecedented turnout. Everyone wanted to get a look at the mansion. It just goes to show that no matter who you are or how buttoned down your group is, sex sells.

Investing in Sex/Pornography: A Good Career Move?

Talking about sex in today's society is about as commonplace as breathing. The details of the Monica Lewinsky dress became breakfast conversation, and the question of Britney's virginity rivaled that of whether Saddam really had weapons of mass destruction.

In the *New York Times Magazine,* Frank Rich reported that pornography is bigger than any of the major league sports and possibly Hollywood. Porn is "no longer a sideshow to the mainstream . . . it is the mainstream."[1] *Newsweek* agrees: In its July 2, 2003 issue B.J. Sigesmund wrote, "pornography has gone mainstream all over America. From movies to television shows to music videos and magazines, porn stars and porn iconography are everywhere, pointing to a national comfort level that few would have predicted even a decade ago." He points to current examples like porn producer Seymore Butts (real name: Adam Glasser) acting in a Showtime reality show called "Family Business," Playboy playmates on "Fear Factor," and an episode of "Friends" in which the gang gets obsessed with an all-porn channel. Former underage porn star Traci Lords is promoting her autobiography, *Underneath It All.*[2]

The market for adult entertainment is enormous, and growing all the time. It's estimated that porn earns between $10 to $14 billion a year in the United States and $56 billion worldwide. In 2002, adult videos alone brought in over $4.04 billion in store rentals and sales, compared with $3.95 billion in 2001. Porn films accounted for almost half of Hollywood's over $8 billion in domestic box-office receipts in 2002. Another measure: that same year fewer than

500 traditional movie studio films were released—while there were over 20 times that in porno flicks released. And a lot of people watched them at home: Americans rented 800 million adult films on video or DVDs. And there are 260 million porn pages on the Internet—a hefty increase from the 14 million pages only five years ago. It's a practically recession-proof industry. "When people are feeling good they want to see sex, and when people are feeling bad they want to see sex," said Mark Kernes, senior editor of *Adult Video News*.[3] Or, as Larry Flynt put it, "I've always said that other than the desire for survival, the strongest desire we have is sex."[4]

Plenty of businesses are looking to cash in on that desire, much of them online. According to Web ratings services, about one in four regular Internet users visits one of the more than 60,000 sex sites on the Web at least once a month. More than 30 million people log on to porn sites every day. All these visits bring in about $1 billion.

Most of these are not tame fare either. But the crossover potential of porn stars into the mainstream has never been higher. Jenna Jameson, veteran of such classics as *Naughty in Nylons 1* and *On Her Back*, has made cameos on the prime-time network series "Mister Sterling" and hosted a program on E! Jameson, once known only to a niche audience, is now practically a household name. She has promoted Pony sneakers, Jackson guitars, and Abercrombie and Fitch. She has a two-book deal with HarperCollins, and counts Britney Spears, *during* her "I'm still a virgin" phase, as an admirer. Nowadays, having a porn past isn't a liability, it's an asset.

Unfortunately, the real secret to a successful porn Web site is the same thing that keeps many real investors away. Hard-core pornography is what people will pay for. After all, soft-core porn such as the net amateur site "Flash Your Rack," which encourages office gals to show their stuff to see what score they'd garner, are free all over the 'Net. There are also publications such as *Maxim* and *Stuff*, with their clothed-but-might-as-well-not-be-for all-we-can-see models both on line and in print.

But when a porn site is successful, it's *really* successful—35% profit margin successful.

Profitable Porn

The success of pornography began way before the Internet, of course, but as technology evolved, so did the ways to see a little skin. Before Sony put out the VCR in 1975, if you wanted to see a porno, you had to travel to some shady movie theater in a bad section of town. By 1985 about three-quarters of all U.S. households had a VCR, allowing many people to view their porn at home. The impact the VCR had on the porn industry was incredible: The porn classic *Deep Throat* alone has earned an estimated $100 million in sales, thanks in large part to the popularity of VCRs. Having a VCR made the viewing easier, but despite this huge change for the industry, there were still the obvious obstacles—namely having to walk up to the counter of your local video store and having to pay for renting *Debbie Does Dallas* while everyone around you has tamer fare like *The Godfather.*

That kind of embarrassment went away with pay-per-view television and the Internet (although I'm sure the cable billing and credit card company reps are smirking). One company that has been the beneficiary of view-at-home-porn is entertainment company Vivid Entertainment Group. The Van Nuys, California privately-held company makes hundreds of adult films and claims that it sells a million copies a month to cable, satellite, home video, and hotel retailers. Vivid, the employer of the aforementioned multitalented Miss Jameson, and its founders and principal owners Steven Hirsch and David James, are preparing for an IPO that could make them porn's first billionaires. It makes sense, since in 2002 their company sold $1 billion of products.

With the arrival of broadband Internet TV, Hirsch sees a completion of porn's evolution into prime time. According to Paul Keegan, who wrote about the company for *Business 2.0*: "The streaming of film over the Net is a breakthrough the entire entertainment industry is bracing for, but if the history of technology teaches us anything, it's that porn will lead the way." For Hirsch, this is the final step, when satellite and cable operators can be cut out of the picture and his studio's explicit sex films can be delivered at lightning speeds around the world, in many different languages, directly from Vivid's Web site.[5]

That's great, but as of this writing Vivid is still private, as are so many other companies in the porn industry. That's one of the biggest problems with investing in this industry—so many of the companies are small, arguably shady operations, shooting low-budget films in empty San Fernando Valley houses. Costs are low and profits are high, but there's little chance—unless you have friends on the inside—that you can get in on the (investing) action.

Women's Porn

Not all sex-related companies are the equivalent of Joe's Peep World in Times Square. There is a growing trend of woman getting more open about sex: sex toys, sex movies, and sex parties—all specifically geared to women. Yes, sex parties. The New York organization, Cake, profiled in *Vanity Fair*, among other places, throws underground, members-only parties where yuppie women feel "empowered" enough to let loose. And by "let loose" we mean orgy. So many are letting loose that the parties are packed with members paying $100, and the organization has expanded its empire to London. Imitators have sprung up across the country.

Woman-centric organizations like San Francisco's Good Vibrations have changed the way women think about sex. For nearly 30 years this company's been in business, selling a veritable buffet of different kinds of vibrators, sex toys, and movies—all geared toward women. Movies? Images? In one month alone, September 2003, nearly 10 million women downloaded Internet porn, according to Nielsen/NetRatings. To help "educate," Good Vibrations has a program that lets hostesses plan their own Pleasure Parties, a modern-day version of Tupperware coffee klatches. None of these companies, unfortunately, are publicly traded. The frustration continues.

Tough Shopping

Even the Vice Fund's Dan Ahrens—as much as he would love to invest in this sex sector—doesn't do it. The reason is in part that he has a $50 million market capitalization floor that he tries to stick to.

That's the same argument made by many of the funds, hence a reason for the lack of big institutional money in these companies. Plus, as Ahrens told me, "To be honest, there's not much in the way of good stocks to own." However, to that I say, that depends on where you look and how crafty you are at looking for what can be construed as sex investments.

Granted, the dedicated publicly traded porn companies have had a rough time of it in the stock market. New Frontier (NOOF), which is in the porn distribution business and controls one-fourth of its U.S. market, has seen its stock languish for years. The stock shot up, recently, however, after reports of profitable quarters. Nonetheless, the P/E ratio has traded at a fraction of the price of mainstream media companies, but Charles Kersh, an analyst with Denver brokerage firm Neidiger, Tucker, and Bruner, thinks that gap could narrow as satellite and digital cable proliferation grows.[6] Both satellite and digital cable supply service providers with room to grow by adding channels for mainstream and pornographic entertainment. Already, in a recent quarter, New Frontier increased the revenues from its cable/DBS/hotel services by 62%. (DBS stands for direct broadcast satellite.) Currently, its video-on-demand service, called TEN* On Demand, is distributed to 8 million cable households and 900,000 hotel rooms in North America.

Another porn biggie is Barcelona-based Private Media group (PRVI). The company doesn't produce original content but rather buys photos and movies and uses the images in various other media, including DVDs, videotapes, and magazines. Private Media's publications–including *Private*, which debuted in 1965 as the world's first full-color adult publication–are distributed in more than 35 countries. It's sort of like the international version of *Hustler*. The company also finances more than 100 films a year and has amassed the world's largest porn library. It recently launched its first branded TV channel in the U.S. called The Private Fantasy channel.

One critical driver for Private, and for other porn companies, is the explosion of the DVD market. Not only are DVDs cheaper to produce than videotapes, a single DVD can contain material in several languages, which is extremely attractive when selling in the European market. Increased DVD sales help to boost Private's bottom line. But this stock, too, has been getting roughed up in the market, hitting a 5-year low in early 2003, although the stock seems to be improving as of this writing.

Playboy (PLA), is of course, the *grande dame* (madame?) of the industry. One would think that it epitomizes true sex investing. Playboy Enterprises went public in 1961 and has a market cap of $462 million. The company estimates that almost 10 million Americans read *Playboy* every month, and the magazine's 3.25 million paid subscribers outnumber those of *Esquire, GQ*, and *Rolling Stone* combined. In addition, an estimated 5 million people read one of the magazine's 18 foreign editions, bringing *Playboy*'s global readership to almost 15 million.

Some 2,500 Playboy-branded products, like thongs, clocks, and pink rhinestone pendants are available in more than 100 countries, bringing in more than $250 million annually. Hugh's daughter, Christie Hefner, has been running the show since 1988 as chairman of the board and CEO. During her tenure, she has restructured operations, eliminated unprofitable businesses, and initiated the company's highly successful electronic and international expansion, forming global alliances that expanded the company's brand awareness and overseeing its highly successful Internet operations. She told Stephane Fitch of *Forbes*, "We're building a multimedia strategy so that more and more of them [readers] will see us on television or on line." By 2005, she vowed, profits from cable operations would help the stock jump to $40. "This is going to be a billion-dollar company or I'm gone," she says. On investing in a magazine for younger men, like *Maxim* and *Stuff*, Hefner said, "We could have invested in one, but we'd be getting back [only] a quarter of the return we're getting on our investments in [cable] entertainment."[7]

Sales have been flat for a couple of years, however, as growth in its entertainment group has been largely offset by a drop in its publishing business. Playboy has seen its business suffer as "lad mag" competitors nip away at its market share, not to mention the effect of online competitor sites. But *Playboy* is not alone. *Penthouse* has seen its publication decrease from 5 million copies per month at its peak in to a tenth of that. Even worse, from April of 2003 to July of

2003, it hadn't had an issue out in months. *Penthouse* founder Bob Guccone resigned as chairman and CEO in November, 2003. As of this writing, the publication is up for sale and its publisher, General Media, filed for Chapter 11 bankruptcy. (However, *Penthouse* may rise again—a bankruptcy reorganization plan has recently been filed.) Al Goldstein's *Screw* magazine is on hiatus and Goldstein, too, has filed for Chapter 11. *Playboy*, for what it's worth, is fighting back. The company hired James Kaminsky, the former editor of *Maxim*, to revamp the magazine by adding ethnic cover girls and features like video-game reviews and fashion coverage using professional male skateboarders and surfers as models. Kaminsky vowed to keep the magazine's famed good writing and to attract more Hollywood celebrities by allowing them to keep (some) clothes on. Nudity "is something we embrace," he said. "But there are different levels of nudity."[8] It seems his level is working out fine. In a recent six-month circulation report its newsstand sales were up 5%.

Nonetheless, Playboy's future growth lies not with its magazine but with cable and pay TV. With television, home videos, cable, and DVD distribution, Playboy is the largest provider of pay-per-view adult content. Its videos and movie channels are available in more than 113 million U.S. cable and direct-to-home satellite household units, and it has 20 more international Playboy networks with partners in 50 countries. Playboy's videos and DVDs are available in 200 countries, and they consistently rank, not surprisingly, among the top labels in *Billboard*'s yearly "Top Video Sales" rankings.

Three of the four adult cable channels in pay-per-view homes belong to Playboy. And those programs are getting a little more adult. The company had a soft-core focus until 1999, when it began a hard-core acquisition spree, starting with the Spice brand cable networks.

Gerard Klauer Mattison analyst Jeff Hoskins has high hopes for the purveyor of Playmates. He thinks the company will generate positive operating cash flow for the first time in a few years, and he expects operating income to double.[9]

Sounds intriguing, right? It can be argued the company has a great brand—Hef, the playmates, the mansion—they all scream sex appeal. (Just ask the fundraisers at the hospital benefit.) But this company's investment thesis seems to be a scene out of the movie

Groundhog Day, which had Bill Murray reliving the same day over again many times. We've heard it before, and before, and before. Still, this bunny seems to be bouncing along in the right direction, with a long track record. If you believe in the brand name and management's vision—and their ability to finally execute—then you should take a chance on *Playboy*. After all, at $16.85, it's not too far off its five-year low. But if you're not sold on the management and are concerned about competition, it's a pass.

Playboy is the biggest player in the fragmented adult industry, but even its revenue is just a tiny fraction of the sex industry. Selling porn in hotels, for example, is big business as we saw with New Frontier. According to *The New York Times* writer Timothy Egan, "40% of all hotel rooms in the nation have the equipment to show adult films and about half of all guests buy the films. For hotels, the sex that can be piped through television generates far more money than the beer, wine, and snacks sold from the rooms' mini-bars."[10]

His company helps hotels bill for in-room entainment. Over half of pay-per-view hotel sales are for porn films. All told, it's about a half billion in sales. And this kind of activity is accounting for about 70% of in-room profits.

Omni Hotels stopped showing porn pay-per-view movies in its nonfranchised hotels in 2000, losing some $4 million anually—$1 million in revenues and $3 million to replace televisions, which had been lent for nothing by their former provider. However, "we have had over 50,000 messages of support," said spokeswoman Kim Blackmon. One traveling businessman wrote: "Thanks for taking away the temptation."[11] Omni chairman Bob Rowling didn't think omni should profit from smut. "I'm a father of two boys," he said. "It wasn't the kind of thing we wanted offered at our hotels."[12]

Other chains aren't quite so full of morals. Marriott, Hilton, and Sheraton, show porn films in their hotel chains, despite increasing pressure from groups on the right like Citizens for Community Values and the American Family Association, both of which have pressured the Justice Department to go after hotels offering explicit fare. Across the country, perhaps unknowingly, "hotels are breaking the law. A lot of the material they sell opens them up to prosecution," said Bruce Taylor, a former prosecutor now president of the nonprofit National Law Center for Children and Families.[13] But the hotels are holding their ground. "We understand that there's a level of sensitivity and different feelings about this subject matter," Roger Conner, a Marriott spokesman, told *USA Today*. "We provide a wide range of choices and anyone can block (adult entertainment) out. No one has to see it."[14]

But the hotels certainly do see the profits, and they're not the only ones. The hotels share the money from the flicks with the providers of the in-room entertainment viewing equipment. The leader of that business, On Command (ONCO), is worth $400 million and its principal owner is Liberty Media, controlled by the well-respected cable industry visionary, John C. Malone. However, it trades as an over-the-counter-stock. As a general rule of thumb, I find that over-the-counter (OTC) stocks are a risky bet. Here's why: Stocks listed on exchanges, such as the New York Stock Exchange, are traded face to face at one location, in "trading pits." All others are OTC stocks, traded electronically via a network of dealers across the country. The Nasdaq market is the main OTC system in America, listing more than 5,000 companies. It encompasses a range of firms, from young, relatively unknown enterprises to behemoths such as Microsoft (MSFT) and Intel (INTC). Thousands of more obscure OTC companies that don't meet Nasdaq's listing requirements trade separately, often with their prices listed only once daily, on "Pink Sheets" or the OTC Bulletin Board. Often, little information is available about these companies, and they're frequently penny stocks typically traded at less than $1.00. (Penny stocks are usually best avoided, as they're frequently targets of fraud.) When I last checked, On Command shares were at $0.96.

The other player, Lodgenet (LNET), which offers on-demand entertainment in hotel rooms, is the more appealing investment. It does $180 million in annual business selling sex videos and other entertainment to hotels. It was trading at $18.78 in November 2003, with a market cap of $234 million. In the first 3 months of 2003 revenue rose 8% to $59.6 million.

The company provides broadband, interactive services, such as digital movies, to the hotel industry, and has the reach to let 260 million travelers a year use its products. For a while this company wasn't the best investment because it was mired in debt. However, it is managing to pull itself out, even having to take a financial penalty for paying off some of its debt early. It has been increasing revenue per room despite the reduction in occupancy in the hotel industry.

Digital TV services are also helping to raise revenues, because of their high prices and novelty. More and more hotels are installing this advanced technology. But the bottom line is this company is a good way to profit from perverts watching porn.

Porn in NYSE's Clothing

"Corporate giant AT&T, which is present in millions of households, has been providing The Hot Network, which features hard-core pornography, as well as the Playboy Channel and other soft-core porn channels for years." This from the Religious Alliance Against Pornography and the National Coalition for the Protection of Children & Families.[15] (The Web sites of these kinds of groups are terrific places to look for vice investment ideas—just find out what they're railing against. I figure if they weren't doing a successful job, then these groups wouldn't be bothering, right?) The merger of AT&T's broadband cable system and Comcast (CMCSA), shook things up, however.

In the merger, AT&T has spun off Liberty Media and its distribution of pornography in hotels and motels, as well as its broadband cable system (see page 142, first paragraph, re: On Command). And AT&T was soon to announce that it has ceased special billing for 900 numbers, ending its dial-a-porn business. This was a tough loss financially: AT&T was estimated to make hundreds a millions a year from dial-a-porn 900 numbers. On top of that, AT&T's income from cable porn was $10 to $20 million a month.[16]

Was public pressure the force that caused it to change? Not explicitly, but very, very likely. According to religious groups, Yahoo! is one such company that responded to public pressure and abruptly departed its 2-year-old online adult content business.

Comcast seems to bear little concern. In 2002, America's biggest cable company took in $50 million from porn.

Then there is that Detroit stalwart, that paragon of American virtues, the General Motors Corporation. Its 225-channel DirecTV satellite service includes adult channels that reportedly generated $150 million in revenue. DirecTV is part of Hughes Electronics (GMH), of which GM has been the main owner. Although religious organizations are trying to take some credit for pressuring for the divestiture to happen, the fact is that the only porn GM will be putting out now is of the auto variety, now that News Corp. (NWS) has finally acquired control of Hughes Electronics Corp. and its DirecTV service. Although no one is exactly forthcoming about how much they earn from porn, cable and satellite companies pull in some $1 billion a year from it.

So, yes, public pressure can be a risk. Companies profiting from porn may find their moral fiber and drop the business. However, it seems that the ones in the business now seem safe for the moment. Dropping porn from the company menu is no cause to short the stocks, but it's something to be aware of. Don't think because the church folks have overlooked a caught company's competitor that it is a good place to put money. More than likely, the company caught will also cite the competition as doing the same thing. On the flip side, if you think your favorite company is getting a little illicit porn profit on the side, search the annual report to do some more digging to find the pot of gold behind the pot of filth.

For Sex Purists

For you sex purists out there, there are other publicly traded companies that, well, trade in sex of some sort, more directly. You can't get much more direct than condoms.

"When things get tight in the economy, our products do seem to do better," says Adam Glickman, founder of retailer Condomania. "Whereas a night out can cost $50, here you are having fun for a couple of bucks." Glickman has seen condom sales pick up 8–10% in these recessionary times.

The easiest way to get a piece of Glickman's industry (his company is private) is by putting your money in Church & Dwight Co.,

Inc. (CHD). The well-respected consumer-goods maker best known for Arm & Hammer baking soda owns 50% of Trojan, which, with 65% of the condom market, is the top-selling brand in the United States. It has been aggressively marketing its condoms, encouraging safe sex for sexually active couples by using motivating advertising and giving away free samples at rock concerts and at popular spring-break destinations.

Trojan is boosting sales through the creation of more innovative products, like condoms with design features for mutual stimulation, and extra sensitivity. The sales pitch is no longer a fear campaign focusing on AIDS and pregnancy. Now, it's about fun, and, of course, protection, with increased pleasure as the hook. "People know that they should use condoms to help reduce the risk, but they feel condoms may detract from the experience," says Richard Kline, VP of marketing for Trojan, "but we're making the condom experience more pleasurable." With some of the biggest marketing muscle in the business behind it, newly launched condoms like Trojan He Pleasure and Trojan Twisted Pleasure, both with unique bulbous ends designed for extra stimulation, quickly became some of the top-selling brands in the category.

For the first nine months of 2003, the net income increased 26% over the results of the prior year. Unfortunately, however, condom sales account for less than 10% of Church & Dwight's earnings.[17] Thus, even if you're long on the growth of condom sales, that shouldn't be the only reason for buying Church & Dwight. Buy it because it's a good company.

Then there are the public strip clubs, like Rick's Cabaret International, the first publicly traded topless-bar chain (RICK). The company opened its first Rick's Cabaret in Houston in 1983 and went public with its IPO in 1995. Rick's now has six locations in Texas and in Minneapolis under the name Rick's Cabaret and XTL. In addition to the live dancing gals the company is ramping up its very profitable Internet auction model. Rick's has an auction site network under the name NaughtyBids.com, offering items like clothes worn in porn films. The company, however, has a market cap of less than $6.74 million and a trailing 12-month revenue of $15 million. So, while it may be a diamond in the rough, companies with very small caps are risky. They often trade very infrequently, and a big investor coming in to buy can swing things dramatically.

Recently, Hollywood madam Heidi Fleiss was hired to offer her unique business insight and ideas to the Daily Planet, an Australian brothel that became a publicly traded bordello in May of 2003. No ordinary whorehouse, the Daily Planet has 18 themed rooms in Melbourne with names like Venus and Xanadu; its Roman Room is decorated with marble columns and a giant spa. The Daily Planet raised $2.2 million in its IPO, and has plans to franchise its business in other Australian cities. These include building a "mega" brothel in Sydney, where, as in other parts of the country, prostitution has been decriminalized. Shares at the Daily Planet (DPL) were offered at 31 cents each on the Australian Stock Exchange (ASX), and debuted higher at 43 cents. By late trading on its opening day, shares were up 90% to 59 cents each. And, in late December, shares were even higher still—at 85 cents. There's a reason the world's oldest profession remains.

LESSONS

- Porn plays aren't always obvious. It doesn't have to be a company filming bored-housewife flicks in empty suburban houses in the San Fernando Valley. Other companies, like cable company Comcast and media conglomerate News Corp. have more stable, more accessible ways to make money from the business.
- Look at the more prudish of the skin peddlers. Magazines like *Maxim*, which are just this close to soft-core porn, are doing much better than their harder-core brethren. Consider this: *Playboy*'s new editor comes from *Maxim*, instead of, say, *Hustler*. And where porn goes mainstream—such as promoting Pony sneakers, or starring in network shows—is the sweet spot. For viewers and consumers it has the appeal of something that is still sort of taboo but all of a sudden within reach.
- As with any other industry, innovation counts. Especially in the formerly stodgy, medicinal condom market. Thanks to some savvy marketing folks, Trojan, which is part of Church & Dwight, has all sorts of new products, such as the extended pleasure concept, which are increasing sales for the brands.

- Technology is the driver and future of porn. Keep your eye on companies making tech advances. Vivid Entertainment Group comes to mind, but they're private—for now. However, as of this writing they have indicated that they intend to go public, so watch for it.
- Brands matter, even in porn. Vivid is getting a strong identity because it slaps the Vivid moniker on everything, especially their actresses. (The sentence "She's a Vivid girl" has its own connotation of a top-quality porn star.)
- Just because Playboy is THE porn company doesn't mean you have to invest in it. It's had a bumpy road in the past and although things are looking good, evaluate where the company really is when you're ready to part with your money. Don't make it a knee-jerk reaction to wanting to get into vice.

SHOPPING BAG

New Frontier Media, Inc.—NOOF (NasdaqNM)
www.noof.com

New Frontier Media, Inc. is an adult entertainment company that runs both an Internet group as well as a subscription/pay-per-view television group, which provides several 24-hour adult programming networks such as TeN, the erotic network; Pleasure; Extsy; and True Blue.

Price as of November 7:	$6.28
Price/Earnings:	N/A
52-Week Price Range:	$0.60–$6.52
Market Capitalization:	$122.03 million
Trailing 12-Month Revenue:	$36.75 million

Private Media Group Inc.—PRVT (NasdaqNM)
www.prvt.com

The Barcelona-based Private Media Group Inc. buys nudie pictures and blue flicks, which it then redistributes through its print publications, videotapes, DVDs, and the Internet.

Price as of November 7:	$2.12
Price/Earnings:	N/A

52-Week Price Range:	$1.07–$3.70
Market Capitalization:	$105.69 million
Total Revenue:	$41.05 million

Playboy Enterprises, Inc.—PLA (NYSE)
www.playboyenterprises.com

Playboy Enterprises, Inc., the company most associated with the word *adult*, sends its porn out to the world through its four business groups: entertainment, publishing, Playboy online, and licensing businesses.

Price as of November 7:	$16.85
Price/Earnings:	67–40
52-Week Price Range:	$7.92–$16.91
Market Capitalization:	$462.33 million
Trailing 12-Month Revenue:	$277.62 million

LodgeNet Entertainment Corporation—LNET (NasdaqNM)
www.lodgenet.com

LodgeNet Entertainment Corporation provides broadband, interactive television systems and services to hotels and casinos in North America as well as to some international markets.

Price as of November 7:	$18.78
Price/Earnings:	N/A
52-Week Price Range:	$6.03–$19.34
Market Capitalization:	$234.11 million
Trailing 12-Month Revenue:	$234.99 million

Comcast Corporation A—CMCSA (NasdaqNM)
www.comcast.com

Comcast Corporation is the county's largest cable company; it also provides high-speed Internet services and telephone services.

Price as of November 7:	$33.32
Price/Earnings:	119
52-Week Price Range:	$21.85–$34.85
Market Capitalization:	$75 billion
Trailing 12-Month Revenue:	$12.46 billion

Time Warner Inc.—TWX (NYSE)

www.timewarner.com

Time Warner Inc. is a media and entertainment company whose businesses include America Online, as well as movie, DVD, music, and publishing divisions. AOL owns HBO, purveyor of adult "documentaries," such as "Real Sex," as well as the hit series "Sex and the City."

Price as of November 7:	$15.83
Price/Earnings:	29.31
52-Week Price Range:	$9.90–$17.89
Market Capitalization:	$71.58 billion
Trailing 12-Month Revenue:	$40.96 billion

News Corporation Limited—NWS (NYSE)

www.newscorp.com

The News Corporation Limited is an international communications company that operates mainly in the areas of publications, movies, TV, satellite, and cable. It's vice-related mainly because it has acquired control of DirectTV, through Hughes Electronics, a big porn purveyor.

Price as of November 7:	$37.60
Price/Earnings:	28.06
52-Week Price Range:	$22.41–$37.80
Market Capitalization:	$50.08 billion
Trailing 12-Month Revenue:	$16.22 billion

Hughes Electronics Corporation—GMH (NYSE)

www.hughes.com

Hughes Electronics Corporation provides digital television entertainment services and broadband satellite networks. Through its DirecTV, it's a huge purveyor of porn.

Price as of November 7:	$16.65
Price/Earnings:	72.39
52-Week Price Range:	$9.40–$16.72
Market Capitalization:	$24.67 billion
Total Revenue:	N/A

Church & Dwight Co., Inc.—CHD (NYSE)
www.churchdwight.com

Church & Dwight Co., Inc. makes and markets consumer products. It is best known for the Arm & Hammer brand name, but has a huge portfolio including other brands such as Arrid, Brillo, and Trojan condoms.

Price as of November 7:	$38.81
Price/Earnings:	18.57
52-Week Price Range:	$27.59–$38.97
Market Capitalization:	$1.56 billion
Trailing 12-Month Revenue:	$1.05 billion

Rick's Cabaret International, Inc.—RICK (NasdaqSC)
www.rickscabaret.com

Rick's Cabaret International, Inc. owns and operates six adult nightclubs in Texas and Minneapolis, as well as Web sites, such as its NaughtyBids.com auction network.

Price as of November 7:	$1.82
Price/Earnings:	N/A
52-Week Price Range:	$1.06–$2.48
Market Capitalization:	$6.74 million
Trailing 12-Month Revenue:	$15.56 million

CHAPTER

Drugs

Marketing Phenomenon

Ask someone what he or she thinks is a vice stock, and the answer is usually "whoever makes Viagra." And the way its producer's marketing machine works, most times that is followed up with Pfizer.

Score two for Pfizer: One for the sale and one for the company identification.

What Pfizer (PFE) has done to the market for daddy's little helpers is akin to the renaming of all tissues as Kleenex. Viagra is now shorthand for any little pill that'll help his performance.

The word *Viagra* is in even in the *Oxford English Dictionary*.

The little blue pill has become a marketing phenomenon, which has in turn become part of pop culture. It has graced more magazine covers than many celebrities. It has become a punchline. More miraculous than what it does for its users, it has achieved the impossible: making celebrity pitchman Bob Dole seem virile. Sorry, Libby.

In addition, Pfizer deserves credit for busting the male impotence—which it quietly relabeled "erectile dysfunction" (ED)—market wide open. It made a subject that was rarely discussed between couples into dinner-party conversation. In so doing, it has created a huge new market for other sin stocks, not to mention for itself.

Its launch was highly successful. In the 12 months following the April 1998 introduction of Viagra, sales hit $1 billion. In 2002, sales were $1.7 billion and are moving closer to the $2 billion mark. The company expects to reach $2.5 billion in sales by 2006. Doctors have written more than 100 million prescriptions for the diamond-shaped wonder pill. There have been more than one billion tablets sold, with nine more sold every second. Its influence and popularity are so pervasive that it was reported that Saddam Hussein took it, at least according to his former mistress. (I guess Bob Dole is a better pitchman than he realized during his presidential run.)

Pfizer may have caught the attention of millions, but first it had to catch the attention of thousands of doctors. The company had to spread awareness not only that it was the first to develop a pill that could treat male impotence but that it actually worked. Drug reps courted physicians like heartsick lovers and inundated them with info about successful tests. Marketing to the providers—rather than going after the public first—did the trick. But the company hasn't stopped marketing. Even now its commercials urge potential users to speak to their doctors about whether they should use the drugs. Obviously, a patient needs to have a conversation with a doctor before any prescription gets written, but if the patient doesn't bring up the problem, often the problem doesn't get brought up. Though physicians may have an answer, they're not so likely to ask out of the blue if things aren't going so well in the bedroom. But people have become so open now about discussing sexual problems that general-care doctors—not specialists—now write 80% of the prescriptions.

Taking Off

Viagra has been enjoying a wide-open playing field for a few years now. Before Viagra came into the picture, the big choice for men with erectile dysfunction was a painful injection. Ouch! That's most people's reactions at the mere thought of it. As you can imagine, the treatment wasn't too popular. Consequently, sufferers just accepted their fate and wrote off their wild sex lives. There were other options, but considering that they consisted of implants or vacuum tubes, they weren't so enticing either.

Viagra has literally changed lives. Case in point: Hugh Hefner. The septuagenarian founder of the Playboy empire was resigned to leading a quiet life with his wife and kids. (The wife was a former Playmate of the Year, mind you, so it wasn't too tough.) Things changed when Viagra hit the market. Out went the wife and back in came the swinging. When asked if he could live without it, the admitted user Hefner said to 20/20's Elizabeth Vargas, "No. I've got four girlfriends."[1] And, mind you, these women aren't Bea Arthurs or the crew from the "Golden Girls." None of these ladies were even close to half his age, two of them were 21-year-old twins.

Hef wasn't only using the pill to correct a problem. "I think that Viagra is being undersold by Pfizer, because they are correctly touting it as an impotence drug. But it's a good deal more than that," Hef said. "It's a sexual enhancement drug. It's the best legal recreational drug out there."[2]

It's huge in some circles as a party drug. Sadly, it is not just used alone but in conjunction with illegal drugs, such as ecstasy, cocaine, and crystal methamphetamine. Obviously this is dangerous, but even more so than you'd think because the drugs can have dangerous interactions. Even worse is when Viagra is mixed with drugs called "poppers," which have nitrates in them; this can lead to a dangerous drop in blood pressure. Nitrates are also in heart medications. (More on this later.)

Because of its new party-hearty image it's not surprising that the drug is now a big black market hit. It's available over the Internet and in foreign countries, without a prescription, naturally.

Rivals for Your Affliction

Thanks to Viagra's pervasiveness the erectile dysfunction market is taking off. This means, however, that Viagra is getting some company but instead of just nipping away at its market share—though of course that's inevitable–this explosion should help raise awareness for the category. C. Anthony Butler, a Lehman Brothers pharmaceuticals analyst, expects the male impotence market to grow to $6 billion by 2008. About 32 million American men–that is, about half of men over age 40–have some trouble attaining or maintaining an erection sufficient for sexual intercourse. Despite the problem, only slightly more than one-third of those have tried Viagra, or any kind of treatment for that matter. Worldwide, the number of sufferers is 152 million, but here 9 out of every 10 men aren't doing anything about it. The ones who are doing something about it are younger, however, which only serves to keep moving the drug into the mainstream. When the drug was first released the common user was in his 60s; now he is in his 50s.

There certainly is room for competition with Viagra, considering that it has a 94% market share of the erectile dysfunction market. The most competitive drugs are called Levitra, Cialis, and Uprima. Levitra was introduced in the U.S. market in August 2003. Cialis was approved in November of 2003, and Uprima's not likely to be far behind. If you own a TV or radio, buy magazines, or surf the Internet, you're hearing those names a lot. The pharmaceutical companies will be continuing to pour on the publicity since they have to cut into the big brand's sales, but they also have to get the word out about why their products are better or more effective than Viagra. The user will wonder what pill X has or does that the little blue one doesn't. Currently Viagra has the monopoly on the market, but many people don't realize that it isn't perfect.

"Half the people who try Viagra don't try it again," says Merrill Lynch pharmaceutical analyst James Culverwell.[3] Doctors say they just don't refill their prescriptions. Indeed, Viagra is no universal panacea.

The drug works locally in the penis by blocking the chemical PDE-5, causing an erection by relaxing involuntary muscles in the penis to allow an increased volume of blood. It's supposed to take about an hour to kick in and lasts about 4 hours. So, as they say, timing is everything. Beyond making sure that you and your lucky friend are in the right place at the right time, Viagra poses some other, much bigger problems for its takers. There are common side effects, like headaches. Can you imagine the fights this must cause? After all the stress and frustration and waiting, the sexual partner may not be exactly buying the headache excuse ("After all we paid for that Viagra!").

Beyond the nuisances are more serious concerns. Viagra can fatally interact with nitrates used to prevent angina, which can cause a very dangerous drop in blood pressure. I've heard of instances in which some cardiologists are very wary of putting their patients on Viagra. Sadly, when one is of an age when ED is a problem, heart trouble is usually in the picture as well.

Enter Competition

Rival Cialis (the little yellow pill) was approved by the FDA in November of 2003 and is currently available in 45 other countries. Discovered by biotech firm ICOS (ICOS), and being co-developed by Eli Lilly (LLY), it is supposedly easier to use than Viagra. On top of that it goes to work faster, within 16 minutes–similar activation time to Levitra–it lasts longer than Viagra or Levitra, however, typically 15 to 28 hours. Dubbed the weekend drug, in France it's called *Le Weekend*, because users can take it on Friday night and have a fun-filled 48 hours.

Some argue that too much of a good thing may not be so good. Having a drug in your body for that long is questionable, considering that all drugs have side effects. "You want your drug to correspond to what it's being used for," says Carl Gordon, a general partner at OrbiMed Advisors.[4] Although some doctors believe that Cialis, like Viagra, could interact poorly with nitrates, Lehman Brothers analyst Anthony Butler disagrees. Cialis is also a PDE-5 inhibitor and works similarly to Viagra, he says, but it has yet to show any harmful interaction.

Cialis may be the biggest threat to Viagra because in the 8 months following its February 2003 launch in Europe and New Zealand, Cialis generated $109 million in sales, but Levitra shouldn't be counted out. Also known as vardenafil, this product is a joint venture between Bayer (BAY) and GlaxoSmithKline (GSK), and gained FDA approval in August of 2003. Like Viagra, it also works by blocking PDE-5 and has a similar duration. It must be taken about 25–60 minutes before sex and has worked within 15 minutes. Butler thinks that it should eventually bring in annual sales of $1 billion as the market–and the marketing–expands.

Levitra was released in Europe in early 2003 and was received very well. "We have a 14% share in Germany and 9% in Spain. But we've just started, so we're only up an up-curve," said chief executive Jean-Pierre Garnier.[5] After less than a month of availability in the United States, Levitra has garnered half of all new prescriptions written for erectile dysfunction drugs.

Cialis is already a big hit in Europe, although arguably not as big as expected. Lehman's Butler points out that the drug has done "a pretty good job of capturing some of the market in Europe, although not as much as it had initially planned for." It's more of a country-by-country preference, but in some countries it has a greater share of the market. Interesting to note is that Cialis has more market share in Germany than Levitra does, considering that Levitra is co-marketed by Bayer, a German company. "But I guess," says Butler, "people aren't seeing the distinction between Viagra and Levitra."

Ads Up

"A lot of people would think that because Viagra has been successful everybody must be satisfied . . . but that's not the reality," said David Pernock, senior vice president of marketing for Glaxo-SmithKline PLC, which is co-marketing Levitra. "It's one of the classic marketing battles shaping up."[6]

Indeed, *The New York Times* already dubbed Levitra's ad campaign "ribald" as it promotes the drug to healthy young men looking for sexual satisfaction beyond just being able to have sex. Levitra is shilled by the NFL. Its two parent companies have signed a 3-year sponsorship deal with the league and will sponsor an NFL "men's health education campaign."

For an industry that's trying to reach younger consumers, this is a great move. Among the faces for the campaign is former Chicago Bears coach Mike Ditka.

"A large part of the population we'd like to target are big NFL fans and big sports fans," according to Pernock. "The concept of heavy marketing during sports activities is a good thing. Guys watch sports a lot."[7]

That's what the folks at Pfizer are banking on as well; They have a deal with major league baseball. Texas Rangers' first baseman, 38-year-old Rafael Palmeiro, is a spokesman. "I take batting practice. I take infield practice. I take Viagra." Also pitching is NASCAR driver Mark Martin. I'm waiting to see President Clinton show up on the commercials.

Cialis is ponying up the marketing dollars as well. They sponsored the America's Cup in New Zealand in February of 2003. They also signed a deal in November 2003 to be the four-year sponsor of the PGA tour. So much for leaving your bedroom problems in the bedroom; now they're out on the golf course. Also rumored to be on deck as pitchman for Cialis is actor Paul Newman, who will undoubtedly get the ladies' attention.

It's Friday Night: Do You Know What Drug You're Going to Take?

When deciding which drug to take, it's important to know how you're going to take it. Cialis and Levitra can be taken with food, although Levitra doesn't do so well with some fatty foods. Cialis has an extra benefit in that you can also take it after meals.

Cost will be a factor too. Currently, in the United States, these drugs cost about $10 a pill. Many insurers cover the medication in their health care plans, but the supply they allow is very small. Still, users find the medicine too expensive, according to Butler.

Which to take? Besides the time-to-effectiveness differences, we don't know which is better. No reliable studies are being done to compare these drugs on an apples-to-apples basis to determine which is better; the only studies being done have questionable sources of funding. In other words, did the drug companies pay for the research?

And a Fourth

The fourth drug, Uprima, sold by TAP Pharmaceutical Products (a joint venture between Abbott Laboratories and Japan's Takeda Chemical Industries), could pose a unique threat. Though it's not in the top group, it will get lots of attention and a following, no doubt. In part, its groupies will like it because of how it functions: Instead of being a PDE-5 inhibitor, Uprima is a dopamine receptor antagonist. This means that the drug works by stimulating chemicals in the brain to increase the signals sent to the penis after sexual stimulation. While not as fast as some of the others, it definitely has gotten started before Viagra. It works within 18 minutes on average and hasn't shown any bad reactions to nitrates. However, keep in mind that it hasn't had as much of a chance to cause as many problems as Viagra, so interactions and side effects are still a possibility. One downside is that Uprima does not leave everyone with the best feeling. It causes nausea in 7–8% of users.

Uprima has been available in Europe since May 2001, but it has not been approved in the United States. Abbott (ABT) applied for FDA approval but withdrew its application because of concerns about dangerously low blood pressure.

Besides What to Put in Your Body, What to Put in Your Portfolio?

With Viagra, Pfizer is by far the marketing powerhouse in the business. Viagra will likely still maintain a 50% share of the ED market, especially if Pfizer introduces the quicker-onset version it is rumored to be developing. Nonetheless, although all the new drugs will drive investor sentiment for ED-related stocks, Pfizer will be playing defense: These shares are not the way to go if you're looking for a stock with a big impact. Plus, you have to figure that Viagra accounts for maybe 3% of Pfizer's overall sales. With a company this big–it had sales of $32 billion for 2002 and a current market cap of $73.6 billion–even 20–30% annual sales growth would have a minimal impact on overall sales and earnings. What it does do, of course, is bring a certain name brand recognition to Pfizer. So, for a big pharma company that's a nice, safe kind of stock for everyone to own, it's got mind share. Though that may not sound like a big thing, it is.

With the best general pipeline in the industry, Lilly has the most long-term investment potential. Lehman's Butler estimates that peak sales from the drug Cialis will be $2 billion, which it has to share with ICOS. The impact from Cialis on Lilly, however, with its $11 billion in 2002 revenues, will be relatively small. Nevertheless, Samuel Isaly, managing partner of OrbiMed Advisors, thinks that Lilly's share price could go up 25% on the drug if it were to hit big in a America.[8]

The Takeda and Abbott entrant, Uprima, has a long road ahead before it can be considered a serious competitor. This is really not the way to go to play the ED market, but of the two, Abbott is a better investment. Takeda is not easy for an American investor to trade.

The likely big winner, although the riskiest investment, is ICOS. The biotech company, which lost $161.6 million in 2002, is basically one big R&D lab, albeit a promising one. According to Andrew Heyward, analyst at Ragen MacKenzie, a division of Wells Fargo Investments, the value of Cialis alone is around $40 a share, based on discounted cash flow; the rest of the drugs in the pipeline are worth about another $20.[9] The stock is at $46.85, meaning that if all goes right shares could fly up.

Of course, it's not a rock-solid bet. This is a small company and just as it could be pushed in a good way by the success of Cialis, it could also be hurt in the process. In releasing second-quarter 2003 earnings the company said that the cost of marketing Cialis in the

U.S. will push it to a wider-than-expected loss in 2004 and that profitability won't come for 2–3 years.

If the marketing expenses have been rough so far—and the drug is only released internationally—consider that they will be even more brutal in the American market.

However, if you want to get the most leverage out of the ED market, it's through ICOS, says Lehman's Butler. "How much does this mean for ICOS? It's everything. From a revenue standpoint Cialis accounts for about 80-plus %. However, it's going to account for all the profits. If you want to be fully levered in ED it's through ICOS."

Viagra for Her?

"The Holy Grail in this area will be the drug to help female sexual dysfunction," said Butler. This market could be worth an estimated $1.5 billion. It's estimated that 43% of women have some kind of sexual dysfunction, but for most women it's psychological. And many of those women don't even realize they have a treatable problem. For those who do seek some kind of help, the ED drugs are out there. While they can use Viagra and the other drugs of its ilk, which increase blood flow to the genitals, it only works for about 1 in 4 women.

The issue is that the PDE-5 inhibitors work physiologically but not mentally, which is key for women. Although a lot of companies, including Pfizer, are trying to develop treatments, arguably the furthest along in the women's market is a tiny pharmaceutical company, Vivus (VVUS), which is also developing an ED drug. Both drugs are in too early a stage to consider Vivus as a good vice investment, however. For the 12 months ended December 31, 2002, the company reported a net loss of $10.6 million, compared with a net loss of $7.1 million for the same period in 2001. But keep an eye on it; in July it received two patents for its treatments of female sexual dysfunction.

There is also testosterone therapy. Proctor & Gamble (PG), for one is testing a testosterone patch to be worn near the navel. It is supposed to revive the libido. A concern with testosterone therapy, in general, is that it brings the potential of facial hair growth and worse side effects, such as a greater chance of heart attacks and breast cancer.

LESSONS

- First to dominate may be a good pick for the long haul. Pfizer's Viagra may have its share of competitors, but it's entrenched. The company whose product has become an icon has intangible value.
- Though pharmaceutical conglomerates can be huge, with market caps in the tens of billions, a blockbuster drug can make a difference to the top and bottom line. A single drug can create a buzz and excitement about the company.
- The new wave of erectile dysfunction drugs will all do well, for the most part. The likely big winner, though? Biotech company ICOS.
- Keep an eye out for the female sexual dysfunction market. Vivus, the industry leader, is on the right track, but it's not there. It may be in a few years, so bookmark this company's Web page.

SHOPPING BAG

Pfizer Inc.—PFE (NYSE)
www.pfizer.com

Pfizer Inc. is a global pharmaceutical company. It is perhaps best known for selling the ED drug Viagra.

Price as of November 7:	$31.94
Price/Earnings:	15.20
52-Week Price Range:	$27.90–$36.92
Market Capitalization:	$245.11 billion
Trailing 12-Month Revenue:	$32.37 billion

GlaxoSmithKline, PLC—GSK (NYSE)

www.gsk.com

GlaxoSmithKline PLC is a healthcare company that produces pharmaceutical products such as vaccines, over-the-counter medicines, and health-related consumer products. Their ED drug, vardenafil, known as Levitra, is a joint venture between Bayer and GlaxoSmithKline.

Price as of November 7:	$43.39
Price/Earnings:	15.91
52-Week Price Range:	$31.85–$44.25
Market Capitalization:	$131.15 billion
Trailing 12-Month Revenue:	$34.03 billion

Vivus, Inc.—VVUS (Nasdaq)

www.vivus.com

Vivus, Inc. is a pharmaceutical company that develops, acquires, and markets treatments for sexual dysfunction and urologic disorders in men and women.

Price as of November 7:	$3.81
Price/Earnings:	N/A
52-Week Price Range:	$3.11–$5.88
Market Capitalization:	$139.69 million
Trailing 12-Month Revenue:	$22.35 million

Proctor & Gamble Company—PG (NYSE)

www.pg.com

Proctor & Gamble Company makes and markets consumer products worldwide.

Price as of November 7:	$97.56
Price/Earnings:	19.36
52-Week Price Range:	$79.57–$98.59
Market Capitalization:	$124.49 billion
Trailing 12-Month Revenue:	$43.38 billion

Johnson & Johnson Inc.—JNJ (NYSE)

www.jnj.com

Johnson & Johnson Inc. makes and sells many diverse healthcare products in the following segments: consumer, pharmaceutical, and medical devices and diagnostics. In terms of vice, it is responsible for K-Y jelly.

Price as of November 7: $48.97
Price/Earnings: 16.55
52-Week Price Range: $48.05–$60.99
Market Capitalization: $144.63 billion
Trailing 12-Month Revenue: $36.30 billion

Abbott Laboratories—ABT (NYSE)
www.abbott.com

Abbott Laboratories makes healthcare products that bring in revenue through one of five revenue segments: pharmaceutical products, diagnostic products, hospital products, Ross products, and international. The ED drug Uprima is sold by TAP Pharmaceutical Products, a joint venture between Abbott Laboratories and Japan's Takeda Chemical Industries.

Price as of November 7: $42.33
Price/Earnings: 16.54
52-Week Price Range: $33.75–$46.94
Market Capitalization: $64.64 billion
Trailing 12-Month Revenue: $17.68 billion

Eli Lilly and Co.—LLY (NYSE)
www.lilly.com

Eli Lilly and Co. creates and delivers pharmaceutical products, including the ED drug Cialis, which was discovered by biotech firm ICOS and is being co-developed by Eli Lilly.

Price as of November 7: $66.46
Price/Earnings: 22.40
52-Week Price Range: $52.77–$71.40
Market Capitalization: $73.56 billion
Trailing 12-Month Revenue: $11.08 billion

ICOS CORPORATIOIN—ICOS (Nasdaq)
www.icos.com

ICOS Corporation is a Washington-based biotech company. The ED drug Cialis was discovered by biotech firm ICOS and is being co-developed by Eli Lilly.

Price as of November 7: $46.85
Price/Earnings: N/A

52-Week Price Range:	$15.45–$47.85
Market Capitalization:	$2.85 billion
Trailing 12-Month Revenue:	$92.88 million

Bayer AG—BAY (NYSE)

www.bayer.com

Bayer AG is a global company offering a wide range of products, including diagnostics, pharmaceuticals, and chemicals. Their ED drug vardenafil, known as Levitra, is a joint venture between Bayer and GlaxoSmithKline.

Price as of November 7:	$25.46
Price/Earnings:	13.42
52-Week Price Range:	$10.80–$25.99
Market Capitalization:	$18.66 billion
Trailing 12-Month Revenue:	$32.17 billion

CHAPTER 10

Vice in Sheep's Clothing

The Sex-Ed Issue

Booze you can understand. Porn companies, naturally. Gambling—that's another easy one. But who would think to look for vice investing in the mall? Or in your children's mail?

If you want to make money, you should.

Every generation of parents says kids are growing up faster in the current one, but there's little room to argue that this generation wins the race. I don't think there's ever been a generation of kids who have grown up more quickly.

If there is any doubt of that, just go and ask your kids what a threesome is. With any luck, they'll give you a blank stare.

However, if they shop at the retail store Abercrombie & Fitch, aimed at high school and college kids, they may know more than you'd like—especially if they get the company's catalogs. The Christmas 2003 issue with the words "Group Sex" on the cover caused such an uproar that it was consequently pulled from the shelves. But what I think was even more outrageous was the prior issue, the Back to School 2003 edition, also called the "Sex Ed Issue." Both publications are part of a series called the A&F Quarterly. Each costs $7–although the banned one fetches over $40 on eBay–and requires ID proving you're over 18 to buy. Its 280 pages are filled with pictures of lithe, nude, coeds frolicking.

The catalog comes in a brown paper wrapper, which is about the most appropriate thing about it, considering it doesn't just push the envelope. It gives the entire post office a shove.

I'm obviously not a puritan–after all, I'm writing a book advocating investing in vice–but this catalog practically defies description and sense. The Back to School 2003 is filled with pictures of naked coeds in threesomes. It's all T&A to the nth degree. With naked young bodies re-enacting scenes of privilege, such as studying in a musty old library, reading out on a bluff, and frolicking poolside on the stately grounds of a mansion, it's like a soft-core porn film come to life.

Of its 280 pages, the majority of pictures are naked pictorials shot by fashion photographer Bruce Weber: 100 other pages show clothes, and 50 pages are filled with articles. The articles aren't just the expected interviews with hot, young actresses like Amanda Bynes. But it's also Q&As with questions like "Who would you rather bone: Captain Kangaroo or Cap'n Crunch?" Over the years the quarterly magalog has published sex tips supplied by a porn star, group sex etiquette, drinking instructions called "Drinking 101." The latter went over really well with groups like Mothers Against Drunk Drivers, as you can well imagine.

To be fair, the company does also put out a regular catalog, which it sends out free, like every other catalog from L.L. Bean to Eddie Bauer, in case someone actually wants to see models in clothes. But it's these racier versions, called the quarterly magalog, that really defines this company. However, in December of 2003, Abercrombie said that it would discontinue the quarterly and unveil an "exciting campaign in the spring" of 2004. Jerry Falwell, start your engines.

Keep in mind that this company started out in 1892 as the Orvis of its day, supplying outdoor sporting goods and safari gear to aristos like Teddy Roosevelt and Ernest Hemingway. It certainly has pulled a 180. Just ask the American Decency Association that devotes *considerable* space to Abercrombie on its very colorful Web site. (The ADA Web site is fun reading and a great place to go for vice investing tips, by the way.) In between calling for the umpteen millionth boycott of the company, it offers some sermons (and tears) on the topic:

> As I perused A&F's Spring Quarterly 2003 today my heart was grieved as I thought about all the vulnerable, undiscerning, weak souls this catalog will draw in and wreak havoc upon. . . . A&F's latest catalog–just released–in my opinion, is vastly more de- structive than a *Playboy* magazine for varieties of reasons. One reason is that it's considered a catalog not a smut magazine. Pornography in the guise of a legitimate catalog. I know what young men will do with this catalog when they get it back into their bedrooms. And so does A&F.

Um, order the clothes online?

If (I mean, when) they do that, they'll find that the A&F Web site certainly doesn't do anything to veer from the company's image. Site visitors are greeted with nude, perfect-looking teens barely covering up their privates. Clothes for purchase are shown along the margins. It's pretty clear what's for sale.

The Fewer the Clothes, the Higher the Sales

Analyst Jeffrey Klinefelter from U.S. Bancorp thinks the sexy cata- log, Web site, and overall image goes a long way toward spreading the buzz that translates directly into fatter margins. In early April 2003, the research company Hoover's ranked Abercrombie third out of the 150 largest publicly traded retailers, with the largest net profit margins as averaged over the prior four quarters. With its 11.3% margins, it beat out companies like Tiffany, Bed Bath & Be- yond, and Talbot's, not to mention every single one of its (publicly traded) peers including American Eagle and Aeropostale. "When mall traffic is down," Klinefelter says, "they make sure they're maintaining mind share."[1] (Call me crazy, but catalogs showing naked, lithe teens engaging in threesomes tend to be memorable.)

The fewer the clothes, the higher the sales? It has looked that way. The edgy quarterly catalogs have been published since 1997 and are the brainchild of company CEO Mike Jeffries. When Abercrombie began selling the quarterly separately from its traditional catalog, annual net sales were $513 million. In 2003, they were $1.6 million.

Besides sex, what does the company sell? Mostly mundane, preppy sportswear, like the long-sleeve polo shirt for $29.50 and boxers for $14.50. There's occasionally stuff that matches the quarterly's tone, such as thongs for little girls as young as 10 years old. Those undies, with sayings like "Eye Candy" and "Wink Wink," quickly disappeared from the shelves when parents and religious groups went nuts. But the company seems to court controversy in all aspects. It offered a T-shirt that featured caricatures of Chinese laundrymen with the slogan "Wong Brothers Laundry Service–Two Wongs Can Make It White." Abercrombie recalled the shirts after thousands of students across the country called and e-mailed the company to complain about the racist and stereotypical images on the shirts. Hampton Carney, the Abercrombie spokesperson, reportedly said that the company did not know these shirts would be offensive to Asians. Instead, he said that the company thought that Asians would find these shirts funny.

Apparently not. Abercrombie isn't making friends with other ethnic groups so quickly either. In June of 2003, Abercrombie was sued in a case charging the company with cultivating an overwhelmingly white sales force. The lawsuit, filed by nine Hispanic and Asian plaintiffs, says that when minorities are hired they are channeled to stock room and overnight jobs. Other charges are that the company is biased against blacks, Hispanics, and Asians and that it requires the salesforce to show an all-white "A&F look."

The big risk with this company is that eventually, consumers will tire of its controversy-baiting gambits. Already the Quarterly gambit seems to have run its course: Even though one Christmas issue was on the shelves in November of 2003, monthly same store sales were down. However, longer term, the numbers are good: Abercrombie earned 5.51 cents a share in its fiscal third quarter ended in November 1, 2003, up 6% from the year before. Analysts expect the company to increase earnings 20–25% through 2007. Its shares, at a recent price of $28.22, trade at 11.96 times expected earnings. It seems that investors, not shoppers, are boycotting Abercrombie at the moment. They shouldn't be. Abercrombie shares, which deserve to trade at a multiple at least equal to their earnings growth, could double by the end of 2004. Nonetheless, the shares have outperformed the S&P, the Dow, and the Nasdaq from July 1998 through July 2003, not to mention that the company has had 30 consecutive quarters of earnings growth.

It's not just the oversexed Abercrombie & Fitch division, with its 651 stores, that's driving the overall company, mind you. Besides a kiddy chain, abercrombie, the company also has a chain Hollister, which caters to younger teens. That one continues to be a growth vehicle, with same-store sales up by a double-digit percentage consistently.

Not the Only Bad Thing in the Mall

Of course Abercrombie isn't the only retailer marketing sexy duds to your teenage daughter, but of all the competitors, it is best and most focused at it. In every galleria there seem to be the same competitors: Gadzooks (GAD) cute clothes but nothing for parents to lose sleep over, Pacific Sunwear (PSUN) nonthreatening California surfer wear and hip-hop clothes through its d.e.m.o chain, Hot Topic (HOTT) more Goth than anything else, with the exception of some thongs and T-shirts bearing Playboy logos, Aeropostale (ARO) and American Eagle Outfitters (AEOS) both more sporty than sexy. But none can hold a candle–g-string?–to Abercrombie's vice appeal.

The selling of mall-based sex isn't just about apparel, it also goes lower. To the feet. Just look at Pony. The footwear maker founded in 1972, worn by the likes of Wilt Chamberlain and Muhammad Ali, had lost its mojo by the 1980s. It wasn't until it started promoting itself in 2003 using porn stars–the ladies of

Vivid–that anyone gave it a second thought. However, the sad thing is that if the company didn't advertise that it was using blue-stars in its advertising, no one would know. Compared with Abercrombie's threesomes, these ladies appeared wholesome. Pony isn't publicly traded–but the retailers selling sneakers are.

High-End Sex Sells, Too

It's not just the low-end, mall kinds of stores that sell sex. These days people pay a lot of money to look cheap.

Witness the success of high-end retailers and couturiers. In today's culture there is such a thing as the red-carpet phenomenon. A retailer can be made or, if already made, get a huge spike in sales, if a famous actress sports its duds on the red carpet. But not just any little black dress will do–it better be pretty darn little. It seems like the less fabric, and the more skin, the better known the company becomes. Actress Elizabeth Hurley, in her dress featuring oversize safety pins holding the scant material together, and the green number Jennifer Lopez wore that was cut up to and down to *there*, gave Versace a household name. The company may claim it's a dressmaker, but it doesn't take a genius to figure out what it's selling.

Versace's print advertising also keeps the company in the public eye. Known for hiring celebrities to promote the brand, in 2003 it attached itself to self-professed "dirty girl" (or, in her vernacular, "drrty girl") Christina Aguilera, who was paid an estimated seven figures to promote the brand. Versace is a private company, but like many high-end clothiers, it quite possibly has dreams of going public one day.

But while you're sitting by the phone waiting for Donatella Versace to put down her champagne glass long enough to ask you to buy shares once they hit the NYSE, consider that this move may not be the best purchase. Not all publicly traded high-end retailers do well–not by a long shot. Though they may sell a lot, mismanagement isn't even the beginning of their story. As private companies, it's easy to excuse buying the nicest fabrics and working to the eleventh hour on fashion shows. Bottom lines pale in comparison to hemlines. Pretty much every top designer works from the same operations manual. But once the companies are public, those kinds of shenanigans never work. Donna Karan was typical. As a standalone public company it was a disaster. Now, it's part of conglomerate LVMH and has its act more together.

LVMH (which stands for Louis Vuitton Moet Hennessy) is one of a few luxury goods conglomerates and it's a good solid way to profit from vice. It channels the creativity of the big designers, pumps out fantastic numbers, and has professionals watching the financials. But, trust me, what they're selling is still as much of a vice as you'd ever want: The company owns brands such as Guerlain, Sephora, Givenchy, Christian Lacroix, and Dom Perignon, in a portfolio that includes everything from clothes to cosmetics.

The stock LVMH used to be easily available in the U.S., trading on the Nasdaq, until the company cancelled its American Depository Receipt program in October of 2002, apparently because it didn't want to deal with all the hassle of the regulations surrounding the Sarbanes-Oxley Act.

Though it doesn't have an ADR, it trades in Paris if you want to make the effort. However, things haven't been great as of late. Second-quarter sales in 2003 declined almost 15% mostly because of a decline in tourism. Since this company is so synonymous with France, I'd avoid it until all the bad feelings between the U.S. and France subside, if you want to see immediate upside. If you've got a long-term view, buy it when there are problems, because no matter what happens French goods will always be glamorous and sexy. When the Americans forgive the French, this stock will bounce back; it is so well run that it will survive fine through the bad times. Company head Bernaud Arnault is one of the best managers in the business.

Funny enough, though, the bright spots of the company are some of the most vice ridden. Marc Jacobs, the company made famous by Winona Ryder's court appearances in their clothes during her shoplifting trial, basked in even more of her reflected naughty glory when she starred in their campaign in early 2003. Perhaps at least partially as a result, the company had double-digit organic growth in the second quarter. It's en route to reaching an estimated $100 million in sales by the end of 2004.

The other star is Christian Dior, whose sales rose 10% in the first half of 2003 versus the same time period last year. According to Goldman Sachs analyst Jacques-Franck Dossin, the company is the second-fastest-growing luxury goods brand behind Coach.[2]

It's interesting to note that Christian Dior has had its own outrageous ad campaign. Before the company modified them, the ads for the perfume Addict ran the word *Addict* alone, with the tagline "Admit it" and an image of a bicep with a lipstick tattoo. Hey, kids, drugs are glamorous!

The initiator of crazy advertising, of course, was Calvin Klein. His "Nothing comes between me and my Calvin's" Brooke Shields ads in the '70s were a huge hit, as was his mid-nineties use of young-looking models, which brought on Justice Department wrath because of the child pornography nuance. The ads went, but revenues stayed and kept on staying. His jeans sales went up in the wake of the controversy.

Ads or Porn?

We're used to seeing naked women in advertising, but now men are getting their equal share and it just seems, I don't know, a little more dirty. YSL, part of the Gucci Group as of 1999, marketed its M7 fragrance with a hairy-chested, very naked, former martial arts champion Samuel de Cubber lying back relaxing. This did not go over well. Even the more adventurous folks in Europe and the U.K. threw a fit after the ad ran in October 2002. It was a historic moment—the first mainstream ad featuring a full-frontal male nude—but the protestor's didn't care. Because of the brouhaha the U.S. market was treated to a waist-up version.

Shock seems to come in abundance from the Gucci group. Its womens' perfume for YSL, called Opium, had some advertising so outrageous that it was banned in Britain. Model Sophie Dahl posed in the altogether to promote the fragrance, with her back arched so high it not so much suggested something sexual as a future trip to the chiropractor. Britain's Advertising Standards Authority (ASA) was not amused. The ad generated 730 complaints, practically a record for the ASA. Needless to say, the ad was pulled.

In a statement about his perfume ads, Gucci creative director Tom Ford simply said "Perfume is worn on the skin, so why hide the body?"

Well, if we're subscribing to his logic, everything he produces is worn on the skin.

Then there is the company's Boucheron division. Its Boucheron jewelry ad has a picture of a man's mouth that bears a bizarre intended resemblance to a woman's most private of parts.

And let's not forget that the Gucci Group's mainstay brand, Gucci, practically defined shock advertising. In 2003, it even one-upped itself (this being a company whose past ads included visible outlines of a penis). The Gucci ad in question featured a man kneeling beside a woman who was scantily clad, in a minidress, which opened to reveal quite the millennial twist on the bikini wax: the Gucci "G" logo shaved into her pubic hair. But shocking imagery is all part of Gucci's image, or at least the revived Gucci.

Gucci has been around for decades, known for most of its existence as a high-end leather goods house. The '80s were an absolute disaster for the company, financially and management-wise. But in 1990, little-known but well-respected American designer Tom Ford came on board. When he became creative director in 1994, he really sexed up the company's image. Overnight, it was a huge success. It became the label to own if you considered yourself a person with style.

Did the custom-made bikini-wax ad help sales?

"You couldn't put a meter on this particular ad and say, oh, wow, look at that [sales] spike that occurred because of that ad," said James Twitchell, professor of English and advertising at the University of Florida in Gainesville. "But this is what Gucci 'owns,' in advertising jargon. They are raunchy and edgy and slightly vulgar, which is an intriguing position for a luxury supplier to take."[3]

Though sex appeal is undeniable, when buying a stock based on that, watch out for an underlying desperation. In the first quarter of 2003, sales fell 6.7% versus the same time during the year before, and profits took a 97% nosedive. That's not to say its peers didn't get slammed too during that period. Earnings for the luxury goods group went down. SARS was a big factor.

But post-SARS shopping has shown pent-up charge cards. Retail sales went up in the summer months after the outbreak subsided.

Is Gucci a good buy? Despite bumps in the luxury goods road, the stock has held up just fine. It's more than doubled in the 5 years between July of 1998 and July of 2003, and it is practically back to its stock's highs in the beginning of 2000.

However, in November 2003, Chief executive Domenico De Sole and creative director Tom Ford, the geniuses behind the success, announced that they were leaving the company in April 2004. I think with them gone Gucci's new management will have to try even harder. (Surely, you can expect a plethora of nude ads doing who knows what.) Right now nearly 70% of the company is owned by Pinault-Printemps-Redoute (PPR), a French luxury goods company smart enough to try to keep Gucci on its already successful course.

The French Connection

The chain may not be as high end (read: expensive and worn on runways and red carpets) as some other brands. French Connection, though still not typical mall-crawler material, is a company that definitely uses sex to its advantage. It's not that its clothes are super-sexy, with skin exposed at every turn. The clothes, for teens and 20-something men and women, may be flirty, but it's really the branding that's off the charts here.

The company didn't spend much of its money on big advertising and promotional campaigns, either. It just changed its brand, in a subtle yet huge way. In 1997 the British clothier relaunched as FCUK, really just French Connection, UK. With that kind of name it's not as though a lot of money needs to be spent to get attention. The French Connection rebrand redefined the word success with one simple change. The company has sold 2 million (!) T-shirts that bear the logo, FCUK, in 2002 alone. In the wake of the relaunch there was a 27% jump in profits between 1998 and 1999.

It's been turning out impressive growth numbers ever since. In 2002 sales were up nearly 12.8%. Besides working on the infamous branding, the focus on wholesale retailing has helped push this company. The sizzle may have brought in consumers, but it's the effective management that ultimately keeps them. The strategy of the company is really to let third-party retailers and franchisees deal with sales while the folks at HQ spend their time looking after design and branding needs.

The company isn't just about T-shirts and flirty dresses. It's already enjoying a bit of a brand extension through licensing. The company has been attaching its brand to everything possible from cosmetics to condoms. One of its most outrageous marketing attempts was to attach its name to FCUK alcoholic drinks, in grapefruit and cranberry flavors, launched in 2001. Unfortunately, in May 2003, after a research study showed that the brand appealed most to young kids, it was last call for the short-lived drinks brand.

Those kinds of considerations aren't at play with the licensing of fragrances, toiletries, and cosmetics or at least until the fall of 2003 when the evangelical Christians turned their eyes to the company. It seems that the newly launched fragrances "Fcuk for Her" and "Fcuk for Him" aren't the eau of choice in the Bible Belt. Although some U.S. chains like Federated stopped selling the scents and some Fcuk merchandise, the effect is minimal and brand awareness has exploded.

If this kind of edgy company excites you, you've got good instincts. There is a problem, however. Though the company has stores all over the U.S., it is based in the U.K., and as of 2003 did not have an American Depository Receipt to make the stock purchase easier. But it's definitely a company whose growth just seems to keep going. It's scary to consider what they might do next.

Secret Stock

Though it may not seem as though there's much to be hidden, Victoria's Secret is very much a vice sheep in lamb's clothing. The lamb, of course, being Limited Brands, the Ohio-based retail holding company that owns Victoria's, as well as chains like Bath and Body Works, Express, White Barn Candle Company, and, of course, the Limited.

Victoria's Secret is probably the most easily identifiable and accessible vice company in America. Everyone seems to know the pink-and-white-striped shopping bag. Carrying it around raises eyebrows no matter how mundane the item inside may be (the store does sell pantyhose, even ones that aren't fishnet!). The chain has branded itself so well that when men are thinking of getting their ladies a little something for a big night in, it's straight to Victoria's Secret that they go.

The company is brilliant at creating brand recognition. On the sexy scale it rivals Playboy, yet it's done a great job at bringing in both men and women. The ads are so well done that no women are offended by the brand. Instead of being turned off by the T&A, they want to look like the models. And these aren't just any models, mind you, these are *supermodels*. These women are so well known that they go by only one name. Supermodel Giselle, for example, is known so well internationally that no last name is needed. These glamorous valkyries certainly carry a different message than that of Victoria's competitor, Frederick's of Hollywood. Cheap-looking clothes and cheap-looking women are part of what Frederick's, the original purveyor of lingerie, is known for. (Is Frederick's a good investment? Not exactly, considering that it's perpetually making a comeback and has been in and out of bankruptcy. It is a good idea to stay away until this company has proved itself for about 2 years.)

The models don't come cheap. Victoria's pays one of the highest fees in the business for a model endorsement.

One way Victoria's uses these models to its advantage and has set itself apart is through its attention-grabbing fashion show. It's risqué enough when any, ahem, clothing company decides to do a fashion show. Any attendee can tell you that it bears more than a little resemblance to a strip club. Think about it: Scantily clad women, often topless, are strutting around on a stage to pulsing music.

Now take that thought and realize that the product is sexy lingerie. In 2001 the show was so outrageous that it generated a slew of controversy and protests. Finally, after an investigation the Federal Communications Commission had to say that the content was protected under the First Amendment. It also generated a ton of viewers: 12 million people watched the show on NBC.

In the following year the company may have tamed the fare a little too much. Its fashion show came in third out of the three networks for the night it aired in November 2002, with only 10.5 million viewers. It came in behind the last episode of the "Bachelor II" (Aaron and Helene), which garnered 26 million viewers, and an episode of "West Wing," with 15 million viewers, in which Martin Sheen debates letting an Ayatollah-esque ruler's kid into the United States for surgery.

The show featured only about 13 minutes of models strutting around in lingerie. The rest of the time was taken up with segments about how models are picked and the like. The most outrageous moment in the show took place when fur protestors flipped out and took the stage when the aforementioned Giselle took the catwalk. (They hate Giselle because one of her other jobs is pushing the Blackglama fur company.) And, let's not forget the bizarre Heine Cam filming the models getting their rear ends ready for their close-up by a makeup artist. (There *are* limits.)

Perhaps Victoria's got the message that in its business prude doesn't pay. In 2003 it put out a limited-edition book, *Sexy,* with pictures that the company says were too racy for catalogs and advertisements. Unfortunately, the same thinking didn't go into the fashion show in 2003. One million fewer viewers tuned in versus the year before. With nude threesomes in our sights are we desensitized to girls in their skivvies?

No matter what the subtleties are of various years' collections, however, the company's clothes are undeniably sexy. With products like thongs, push-up bras, and garters, how could they not be? And the company even uses feathers and satin to add even more sex appeal. One of its most popular collections, the Very Sexy Collection, put out by the company in mid-2002, more than lived up to its name. It featured such items as a garter-thong skirt and something called a seamless merry widow. "It's one of the edgiest assortments they've had," says Jeff Klinefelter, a retail analyst at U.S. Bancorp Piper Jaffray. "It's taking their line up to another level." With that collection, the following quarter's sales were up 9% from the year before.

Victoria's has gone from a company with $150 million in sales in 1996 to $3.6 billion in 2002. Sales for 2003, as of November were up 7% over the same time period as the year before. It is the largest specialty retailer of women's fancy bras and panties and has 1,000 stores in the U.S. But perhaps what the company is most known for is its 395 million catalogs per year. (Are there 395 million fraternity members?)

Victoria's Secret accounts for over one-third of the sales for Limited Brands, which, at a recent price of $17.55, has a modest price-to-earnings ratio of 15.

It may not account for the majority of the Limited's sales, but there's no denying that Victoria's is a driver of the company. As long as it can maintain its sexy image—a lesson seems to be learned from the fashion show lose-out to Martin Sheen and Aaron Buerge—it is a company to own. After all, the clothes are inexpensive, especially compared to the costly French lingerie it resembles. No matter what the economy may bring, Victoria's is a company that doesn't seem to be able to really make a wrong move. And the sexier the collection, the more the upside potential sales and stock. So, read the fashion business section of your newspaper closely. If you see outrage about the styles, consider buying the goods and the stock–both may pay off.

LESSONS

- Pay attention to cultural trends. Who is using sex to sell its product today? It is a simple formula for selling to teens and adults alike? This doesn't mean that the company is well run, but you should note every really edgy ad or marketing campaign. Who is doing it? Any articles on how it is affecting sales? Which marketing is played out?
- See which companies are on the radar of groups like the American Decency Association; bookmark their Web site: www.americandecency.org. It's a virtual roadmap to who is using vice in their campaigns.
- If a company can extend its brand effectively, that's just one more avenue for bringing in sales. French Connection is giving its FCUK imprimatur to everything from condoms to cosmetics.

SHOPPING BAG

Abercrombie & Fitch Co.—ANF (NYSE)
www.abercrombie.com

Abercrombie & Fitch Co. sells casual clothes for men, women, and kids under the Abercrombie & Fitch, abercrombie, and Hollister Co. brands. One of the catalogues, the A&F Quarterly, could double as a porn mag; the nude shots are practically enough to make Hef blush.

Price as of November 7:	$28.22
Price/Earnings:	11.96
52-Week Price Range:	$18.95–$33.65
Market Capitalization:	$2.74 billion
Trailing 12-Month Revenue:	$1.60 billion

Hot Topic, Inc.—HOTT (Nasdaq NM)
www.hottopic.com

Hot Topic, Inc. is a mall-based clothing store that caters to teens; the clothes are often music-influenced.

Price as of November 7:	$28.00
Price/Earnings:	26
52-Week Price Range:	$13.60–$29.87
Market Capitalization:	$1.34 billion
Trailing 12-Month Revenue:	$443.25 million

Gadzooks, Inc.—GADZ (Nasdaq)
www.gadzooks.com

Gadzooks, Inc. is a mall-based retailer of casual clothes targeted at girls between 16 and 22.

Price as of November 7:	$6.50
Price/Earnings:	N/A
52-Week Price Range:	$2.03–$8.00
Market Capitalization:	$59.54 million
Trailing 12-Month Revenue:	$325.52 million

Pacific Sunwear of California, Inc.—PSUN (Nasdaq)
www.pacsun.com

Pacific Sunwear of California, Inc. sells casual clothes and shoes to teens and 20-somethings. It showcases the California lifestyle and also hip-hop through its d.e.m.o chain.

Price as of November 7:	$22.18
Price/Earnings:	18.53
52-Week Price Range:	$10.73–$24.56
Market Capitalization:	$1.67 billion
Trailing 12-Month Revenue:	$846.39 million

Aeropostale, Inc.—ARO (NYSE)
www.aeropostale.com

Aeropostale, Inc. is a mall-based store that sells casual clothes for kids from 11 to 20.

Price as of November 7:	$31.40
Price/Earnings:	17.65
52-Week Price Range:	$9.64–$34.70
Market Capitalization:	$1.16 billion
Trailing 12-Month Revenue:	$550.90 million

American Eagle Outfitters Inc.—AEOS (Nasdaq)
www.ae.com

American Eagle Outfitters Inc. sells casual clothes to kids and adults between 16 and 34.

Price as of November 7:	$16.51
Price/Earnings:	16.35
52-Week Price Range:	$12.54–$23.37
Market Capitalization:	$1.17 billion
Trailing 12-Month Revenue:	$1.46 billion

Limited Brands, Inc.—LTD (NYSE)
www.limited.com

Limited Brands, Inc., through various company names, including Limited, Express, and Victoria's Secret, sells clothes, toiletries, and intimate apparel.

Price as of November 7:	$17.55
Price/Earnings:	15.41
52-Week Price Range:	$10.88–$17.86
Market Capitalization:	$9.90 billion
Trailing 12-Month Revenue:	$8.44 billion

11

Pitfalls and Risk Management

So you're not Miss Cleo? Who of us is, besides the real Miss Cleo? (And, as history revealed, she really wasn't Miss Cleo anyway.) Without the aid of a 900-number fortune-teller there are ways to get a handle on, if not handicap, a potentially great investment.

A key to assessing risk and potential is to look at any investment in the context of history. It's useful to see how a stock, as well as an industry, has done over time. If you don't have access to a Bloomberg machine, you can do this easily via a Web site called BigCharts.com (see Box 11.1 for exact directions) to see how the shares have done over the long haul. This is especially important with shares that are sensitive to current events—some are more so than others. Many investors make the mistake of looking at shares in a vacuum, instead of how shares have done at times similar to current ones. On the brink of war? See how your favorite beer stock performed during similar time periods. Granted, it isn't the be-all-and-end-all guide, but it's useful information to have, nonetheless.

Some politicians are better for certain sectors than others. Before the election of 2000 it was big sport to figure out which candidate,

BOX 11.1

How to Draw Your Own Stock Charts

My favorite way to draw charts, both for comparing to other stocks and checking market indices, like the S&P 500 and the Russell 3000, is a Web site called BigCharts.com. It's free, by the way, and quite easy to use.

Once you're on the site enter the symbol of the stock you're most interested in. If you want to compare, say, Altria to its competitors, type in its symbol, MO, then click on the "Interactive Charting" button. On the left side you can choose whatever time frame you'd like.

From there, under the "Compare To" option, input the stocks you want to compare to (choose several at once to make an industry sampling) or also compare it to one of the various indices listed. Click "Draw Chart," and you've got a beautiful color-coded chart to let you know how your stock has done against its peers and a broader index. There you go—you've got context!

If you just want Altria's results, no problem. Follow most of the same steps as above, just don't bother putting in any other comparisons.

Bush or Gore, would do better for stocks in general. Many firms, such as Prudential Securities, Lehman Brothers, and Merrill Lynch made a pastime of putting out such lists. It seems that even pre-September 11 economists were speculating that George W. Bush would be a boost for the defense systems. They also said that he'd be better for tobacco, because a Republican White House would be less likely to go after the firms. Right on both counts.

A Gore win would supposedly have helped tech stocks—this was the candidate often checking his BlackBerry, after all. I should amend that to say that a Gore win would likely have helped tech stocks that are *not* Microsoft, considering how the Clinton administration felt about Microsoft—it was under siege from the Justice Department's antitrust suit. Who is to say if they were right, but under Bush after an initial rise Microsoft stock has essentially just plodded along. Gore supposedly would have been good for telecoms and broadband services, since he was probably our most educated leading figure in that area.

Bush was thought to be effective in trying to help seniors get drug and health coverage and in November 2003, Bush's medicare bill passed. With its prescription drug benefit, Bush was successful in getting medicare to pay for senior's prescription drugs. The wait for the bill to happen was tough: pharmaceutical stocks had declined 20% in the prior two years. With the passing of the drug benefit, drug stocks could do well, especially generic drug companies. In fact, one study estimated that this medicare prescription drug bill could result in $139 billion in profits to the pharmaceutical industry over the next eight years.

Pay attention, dear readers, to your politicians, boring as that may sound. But what if my politician, a local yokel, only reigns over backwater nowheresville, where I reside? Still pay attention to him or her. Even if it isn't a presidential election with issues of national importance, local politics are significant to investing. And if not your local politics, read someone else's local politics, especially if it pertains to the business in which you're invested.

Rolling the Dice

Gambling is a good example of how local politicians make a difference. Gambling has spread from Las Vegas and Atlantic City to jurisdictions throughout the country, on riverboats and Native American tribal lands, with local politics playing a big part. If one company, such as Argosy Gaming Company (AGY), is heavily concentrated in one region that is unexpectedly hit by a sizeable tax increase or an expansion in tribal casinos that are competitive, that could be a problem. Argosy, for example, was so pummeled from taxes affecting its Illinois riverboat casinos that its third quarter 2003 profits were down 14% from the prior year.

In the 2002 elections gambling was an issue in 23 gubernatorial races. Pro-gambling governors were elected in Maryland and

Pennsylvania, for example. (Maryland's governor ran on a campaign with a pledge to raise $400 million to $1 billion for schools by legalizing slots at the state's four racetracks. At the time the state was $1.7 billion in the hole.) This is noteworthy in part because both states are not far from Atlantic City. If gambling money is spent in Maryland and Pennsylvania instead, casinos and resorts in Atlantic City may no longer be as profitable. And what company makes much of its revenues and profits from Atlantic City? Trump Hotels & Casino Resorts (DJT), which operates three casinos in that one market, suffered a 15% decline in its gross operating profit for the first half of 2003 versus the year before.

Analyst Jason Ader, former head of gaming research for Bear Stearns, said that slot-making companies like Alliance Gaming Corp. (AGI) and International Game Technology (IGT) would benefit from the pro-gaming results.[1] He was right. But slots weren't the only significant thing about the election; lotteries also did well. As of November 2002, Tennessee, for example, became the 38th state to allow a state-run lottery. It's paying for college scholarships and school construction. The companies that would benefit from the lotteries are GTECH Corp. (GTK), Scientific Games (SGMS), and, again, IGT.

A single jurisdiction can matter, by the way. Ever heard the saying, monkey see, monkey do? It could be applicable here. After one state approves something, it often becomes easier to pass similar laws in another state. Part of the argument happening in Tennessee over legalizing lotteries was this: 37 other states, the District of Columbia, Puerto Rico, the U.S. Virgin Islands, all of Canada's provinces, and more than 100 other countries already had lotteries.

One way to handicap gambling stocks is to keep a close eye on the states' bottom line. Which states are deeply in debt? Are the governors at the point of murmuring about fixing the situation by increasing or allowing gaming or adding lotteries? Look for the obvious suppliers—see above—and get shopping.

On the flip side, those states that like to hike taxes can hurt gambling businesses, too, as we covered in Chapter 5. To that end, read the regional papers online. See Box 11.2 for Web sites and wires to watch for gaming news. That way you can be on the same page as the most astute analysts and ahead of the lazy ones.

BOX 11.2

Good Web Sites to Find Gaming Industry News

- biz.yahoo.com/ic/n/casino.html Yahoo's aggregation of industry news.
- www.gamblingpress.com Great for international news.
- www.casinowire.com Nice local stories pulled from regional papers.
- news.google.com/news?q=gambling+news&hl=en&lr=&ie=UTF-8&sa=N&tab=nn Google's news search engine pulls up articles from industry trade magazines.
- www.reviewjournal.com The *Las Vegas Review-Journal* always has good updates on the casino industry in Sin City.
- www.lasvegassun.com One of the *Las Vegas Sun's* columnists, Tim McDarrah, has a regular gossip column with great tidbits about the city and the gaming industry. (He's a former *New York Post* Page Six reporter so he knows from good gossip.)

Something Not to Bet On?

Unregulated Internet gambling sites made $4 billion in 2002 and are expected to make even more in 2003. (Combined with regulated ones, according to Bear Stearns, that number is more like $8 billion for 2002.) There are about 2,000 Internet gambling sites, located mostly in Costa Rica and 62 other offshore places. These places certainly do love the Americanistas: An estimated 60% of the revenues come from us.

Gambling from the convenience of one's own home sure is a lot easier and more savory than mixing and mingling with the gang over at the OTB. Plus, if one wants to gamble at 4 A.M., online is the "place" to do it.

While that may be good for the online sites, that's bad for the user, according to the government, especially according to Congressman Mike Oxley, chairman of the House Financial Services Committee, who co-sponsored legislation to outlaw the use of credit cards in online gambling. One reason gambling isn't so popular with our lawmakers is that much of it comes from Web sites operating outside the U.S., which are therefore not subject to our regulations. Plus, it's illegal in many states. If you bet online in a state that doesn't allow gambling, you're breaking the law. Moreover, even in states that allow gambling most of those that do, only allow users to bet on horse races. An estimated 80% of the online gambling in the U.S. isn't legal. Our legislators must reason that if you can't control the Web sites, you control the money flow. "Making those debts uncollectible will hit the Internet gambling business right where it hurts and that's in the their pocketbook," says Oxley.[2]

The house finally voted for a version of the legislation in June 2003, and it remains to be seen what will happen.

However, in 2002, similar legislation to prevent banks from funding Internet betting passed in the House but not in the Senate. Perhaps lobbyists from state lotteries and the tribal casinos were to blame. A bill (S-627) introduced by Senator John Kyl (R–Ariz), similar to the one in the House, promises not only to prohibit credit card payments, but to prosecute law-breaking companies. In October 2003 Kyl's bill had been placed on the senate's legislative calendar.

More likely the other one didn't go through because it was tacked onto an antiterrorist bill, as the FBI, among others, raised the specter that illegal gaming sites were a front for something more sinister. "The illegal Internet gambling industry must be stopped," said Bush administration economic adviser Lawrence Lindsey in a letter to then Senate majority leader Tom Daschle (D–S.D.). "Internet gambling offers a haven for money-laundering, organized crime and international terrorism." The bill passed but without any clauses related to gambling.

Nonetheless, in the wake of a settlement with two credit card companies that had loaned a woman money to bet online, companies like Citibank, Providian, Discover, MBNA, and American Express put the kibosh on dealing with payments from gaming sites. It certainly didn't hurt that the indefatigable Eliot Spitzer put the pressure on Citibank, which, mind you, is the world's largest credit card issuer. Spitzer talked to online payment service PayPal as well, now a part of EBay. As a result PayPal won't let New Yorkers use its ser-

vice to gamble over the Internet. In addition, over 400 banks, is-
suers of Visa and MasterCard, won't honor online bets.

All this has caused analysts to cut their revenue forecasts for Internet gambling sites by one-third. But of course the game, as it
were, isn't over. The smart companies will process transactions
right on their sites with your credit card. But it's unlikely that many
gamblers will be willing to give their credit card to some random
foreign Web site. Those based in Antigua or the Isle of Man are
supposed to be more reputable. Keep in mind that 95% of the foreign sites are credit card based. That's why prospective online gamblers could be more receptive to legit gambling companies stepping
in, like the Vegas brand-name casinos, although MGM Mirage
quickly shut down its U.K.-based online casino operations because
of uncertainty in the U.S. market. Anyway, offshore gambling is
supposedly only set up for those people living in a foreign country,
though smart online gamblers can figure ways around these rules,
not to mention smart operators. In the U.K. where online gaming is
heavily regulated, companies like Harrahs (HET) are starting to re-
ward gamblers with "prizes" instead of a direct cash payback.
They're trying it out first in England to see if it will work.

If our government finally decides to get serious about blocking
offshore gambling altogether, that would be a boon for legitimate
gambling operations, who are practically doing a jig thinking about
it. Remember, before the Internet, there was the old-fashioned way
of betting: If you wanted to do it legally, you had to go through
Nevada's sportsbook.

And That's Not the Only Sketchy Thing Out There

Researcher COM Score Media Metrix judges that illegal Web activity to be nearly $37 billion, almost as much as the $39.3 billion
in legal Web activity. And online gambling is only the eighth largest
business. Jeffrey Hunker, dean of the H. John Heinz III School of
Public Policy at Carnegie Mellon University, estimates that more
than 70% of all e-commerce is "based on some socially unaccept-
able if not outright illegal activity."[3]

Legalize It?

On the flip side what would happen if an illegal product, such as pot, were legalized? How would it affect other vice industries?

After years of clamoring for legislation–you should see the number of term papers arguing to legalize pot for sale on the Internet–it may be close to happening in Canada.

In Canada, it's already okay to take pot for medical reasons. In 2000, the Ontario Court of Appeals said that banning pot for medicinal uses violated the Charter of Rights. The House of Commons, the Canadian Senate, the justice minister, and the prime minister have shown endorsement for it. A business–Canada Medical Cannabis, Inc.–is planning to go public, making it the world's first publicly-traded marijuana company. This, on the heels of an October 2003 Canadian court ruling that businesses and individuals should be able to grow and supply large amounts of medical marijuana. It is estimated that 400,000 Canadians could need medical marijuana.

The question is how Canada's growing acceptance and possible legalization of marijuana will affect the U.S., considering that currently almost 95% of the pot grown in British Columbia heads south to our sunny shores–an estimated $2.5 billion worth is smuggled in each year. All told, it's a $4 billion annual industry.

There was a near miss in the United States, with Nevada in 2002, via an amendment on the ballot to make pot legal in that state. Had it gone through, a person 21 years or older could legally possess 3 ounces of cannabis. It didn't go through.

Since it was Nevada that begs the question of how it would affect the gambling industry, would people be too stoned to gamble? Who knows, but during the whole period leading up to the awards the gaming industry kept mum. A little too mum.

The debate still rages in the U.S. about the whether or not to make marijuana legal. In 1986 the U.S. Food and Drug Administration and the Drug Enforcement Agency approved tetrahydracannabinol (THC), the active ingredient in marijuana, in synthetic pill form. However, many doctors think the real thing is more effective. It was almost legal in California after voters approved Proposition 215, the Compassionate Use Act, in 1996, but the federal government ultimately gave it the kibosh. That hasn't stopped the growing of marijuana in California, though. It's estimated that the annual pot crop in California is worth about $4 billion a year– it's the state's top crop! In the whole country pot growers earn over $15 billion a year selling it wholesale.

If it were legalized, states would profit. It's estimated that in California alone it could pull in $300 million a year. That's about the amount that the federal government spends each year to fight it. Other estimates have come in based on $11 billion gross sales of marijuana nationally; the federal government could bring in $1 billion in income taxes a year.

Armchair Actuary?

If risks are your concern, could there be a bigger, riskier industry than tobacco? It would seem that you'd be hard pressed to find one. After all, it's an industry faced with lawsuits filled with numbers bigger than most people can fathom.

Unfortunately, it's not an industry where you can play armchair actuary to assess the risks. Morgan Stanley tobacco analyst David Adelman says the best way to handicap the risks in this industry is to look at history. This is a business that has been under fire from lawsuits for decades and it has been fighting them off, according to Adelman. "Look at the seriousness with which the industry takes the suits, the spending that they put in to defend themselves. There's no other industry in America that takes itself so seriously."

In the last 20 years, tobacco companies have spent about $2 billion defending themselves. In 2002 alone, Philip Morris spent $358 million. Now, due in part to many, many successful appeals (see Table 11.1) look at how little the plaintiffs have received. "In its entire history," according to Adelman, "the tobacco industry has paid out a total of $750, 000 from Brown & Williamson" (see Table 4.1 in Chapter 4).

Lastly, the laws seem to be on the industry's side. Adelman uses a peaches analogy: "If you found that peaches cause cancer and that all these years the peach manufacturer had been deceiving you,

TABLE 11.1   Punitive Damages Data in Outstanding Smoker Trial Losses

Case	Date	State	Compensatory Jury Award	Punitive Jury Award	Trial Judge Punitive Action	Current Punitive Compensatory Ratio	Intermediate Court Action
Carter	9/96	Florida	$0.75	$0.0	N/M	N/M	Upheld by FL Supreme Court
Henley	2/99	California	$1.5	$50.0	$25.0	N/M	Originally upheld by appellate court but the punitive damage verdict was vacated by the California Supreme Court in light of State Farm. On appeal to the California Supreme Court.
Williams-Branch	3/99	Oregon	$0.8	$79.5	$32.0	97 to 1	Original punitive dmg. award reinstated by Oregon Court of Appeals; Rehearing denied. Oregon Supreme Court denied review. On appeal to the US Supreme Court.

Whitely	3/00	California	$1.7	$20.0	$20.0	12 to 1	On Appeal
Jones	10/00	Florida	$0.2	$0.0	N/M	N/M	Re-trial ordered
Boeken	6/01	California	$5.5	$3,000	$100.0	18 to 1	On Appeal
Kenyon	12/01	Florida	$0.2	$0.0	N/M	N/M	On Appeal
Burton	2/02	Kansas	$0.2	Judge's discretion	$15.0	75 to 1	On Appeal
Schwarz	3/02	Oregon	$0.2	$150.0	$100.0	595 to 1	On Appeal
Bullock	10/02	California	$0.9	$28,000	$28.0	33 to 1	On Appeal
Boerner	5/02	Arkansas	$4.0	$15.0	$0	N/M	In response to B&W's post trial motion, the jury's $15 million punitive award was eliminated; On appeal

($) In millions. N/M = Not meaningful
Source: Morgan Stanley Research

then they'd have a problem. Tobacco isn't like that. No product has made users more aware of the risk."

Should that trend go the other way, it's highly unlikely tobacco companies will really suffer. It being lucrative for the government to keep them afloat, if there's a problem and more money is needed, tobacco companies have the ability to raise prices. Granted, it's not as easy now as it once was, but it exists; they have an above-average pricing power. One nickel in a price raise translates into $1 billion.

12

Your Vice's Future

Tech Sex

First there was regular sex, then as technology evolved, there were porn films. Then thanks to the development of the VCR both industries–porn films and the VCR business–boomed. Then phone sex evolved, as did corporations to capitalize on it with 900 numbers. And then, with a little help from Al Gore, the Internet was born. With it came chat rooms, where most of the talk was about sex. Companies like AOL harnessed all those desires and it's said that much of their growth came from that. It's also arguable that companies like Cisco and Sun Microsystems can attribute many of the sales of routers and servers to the large demand for the high bandwidth sex videos and images. And only time will tell how the Paris Hilton sex video–possibly the most downloaded ever, especially in New York media offices where real work came to a halt– has affected tech sales. But don't worry, it has.

Trend forecaster Faith Popcorn has a name for this kind of sex: ConSexion, that is, sexual relations of a kind without touching. "It could be phone sex, it could be Internet sex, it could be watching people have sex," according to Popcorn.[1] And it's growing.

But virtual reality sex, the Holy Grail of the industry, seems to be getting ever closer to becoming a reality.

In May of 2002 scientists reached a milestone: They felt the force of each other's touch across the Atlantic with a virtual reality handshake. Researchers in California, visiting from the Massachusetts Institute of Technology, and at the University College in London, each used a mechanical arm, a pen-shaped probe known as the PHANToM, to lift what looked like a black cube floating in a simulated room on a computer screen. As users manipulated the cube with the "pens," they felt as though the "pen" had hit something.

According to an article in Britain's *Sunday Mail,* which carries a long interview with noted futurist Ian Pearson:

> The goal is a computer-generated, three-dimensional world where you can see, touch and move objects as you would in reality. The idea researchers are edging toward is your entire body being encased in a tactile suit. Your eyes would look at two tiny monitors so that you would see the virtual world as if it was a real one. And when you raised your arm in the real world, sensors in the suit would mean it raises in the virtual one. But more than that, if someone gripped your arm in the virtual world, pressure pads in the suit would enable you to feel the grip on your body.
>
> You would be able to sit on a virtual chair and your suit would tense in the right way so you would hang, suspended on an invisible chair in reality.
>
> Inevitably, perhaps, the idea most spoken about is teledildonics [or cyberdildonics]—that is, virtual sex with imaginary partners, or real ones who are many thousands of miles away.[2]

This is how the Web site www.teledildonics.com describes the developments:

> Teledildonics [TD] is a virtual reality application that allows users to interactively have sex with other users who may be miles away, or across the globe. It is currently in its infancy, but poised to take the world by storm in the next few years. While eventually technology will allow for full-body suits that stimulate all five senses, the first generation of teledildonic devices will be much simpler.

The hardware currently being developed by several manufactures consists of a device that you would strap onto your pelvic region. The first TD devices will be automatic penis stimulators that connect to your computer via a cable so that software running on your machine can control the motions of the device. These will NOT be one of those penis pump devices that claim to enlarge your penis. These devices are designed solely to bring you to orgasm under external control. You slip the device over your penis (probably with a couple drops of lubricant), plug the control cable into your printer port, and the device slides up and down under control of the software you are running. This way you could be talking to a live girl on a Web site watching her, and she could remotely pleasure you. Or the device could be used while playing a game, mimicking the action you see on the screen. Naturally, a female version of the device would also be developed, although it's anyone's guess as to what kind of demand there will be. The possibilities are endless, while being the ultimate in safe sex. Now before you dismiss the whole idea as just a gimmick, let me point out there are many legitimate purposes for such a device. If you are with someone, but can't be together for extended periods of time because of a job or school, you can use one to remain faithful. If you are handicapped, normal sex might be physically impossible. If you have an incurable STD (like HIV or herpes) normal sex will carry a risk of transmission. If you are too shy around members of the opposite sex, you might prefer the anonymity that can be obtained with such a device. Whatever the reason, you can be assured that such devices are going to become available on the market in the near future.[3]

Once the industry has gotten all of this down, the hope is that next up will be machines that let people watch and talk to others on the Web while others, um, have their way with them.

Close, but Not Quite . . .

What has hit the market in this arena doesn't quite reach that ideal. A few companies put out products that were just glorified vibrators connected to a computer and then the Internet. They never really caught on.

The Virtual Sex Machine (VSM) is arguably the most advanced product available, but it seems like it has a long way to go. Essentially, it is a device that simulates the experience of oral sex via a condom-like machine that works in concert with a porno flick. It's hooked up to a computer and it mimics what the gal is doing on screen. If she moves up or down, so does the machine. An embarrassed *Salon* magazine writer tested it. His verdict: "My God, what have I become?"

But, guilt aside, he assured his girlfriend that the machine could never replace the real thing. "You have nothing to worry about."[4]

A few years ago, Vivid Entertainment attempted to create the dream of virtual reality futurists. The company produced a neoprene suit–the same material used in wetsuits. The getup sported 36 sensors attached to the chest and crotch set up to deliver five different sensations–tickle, pinprick, vibration, hot, and cold–to a specific part of the wearer's body. It worked this way: An electronic signal was sent to a DVD player, through the Internet, to the suit wearer's computer and finally to the suit itself, where it activated the appropriate sensor. Vivid spent about $180,000 to develop the suit, and it was supposed to sell for about $170. Initial results were poor and after rumors of concerns over the possible electrocution of pacemaker users, Vivid shelved the idea.[5]

These kinds of experiments are right up the alley of Ray Kurzweil, beloved by techies as the author of *The Age of Spiritual Machines*. Kurzweil has said that "sexbots," or software and hardware just for intimate encounters, will happen and the rendezvous can be tailored to the user's proclivities. Kurzweil takes the future sex thing one further: He thinks that people will be putting computer chips in their heads to have the brain increase the stimulation to a particular area during arousal. He also describes scenarios whereby a man could feel what a woman feels during sex and vice versa.[6] We're not there yet, but these are the types of developments to keep your eyes on. To keep up with Kurzweil, check his Web site www.kurzweilai.net.

The MIT/London cube/pen experience falls under the more scientific name of haptics. This is an exploding field. Researchers at the Virtual Reality Laboratory at the University of Buffalo are hard at work on it. They have created a system to transmit the sense of touch over the Internet using *sympathetic haptics*–the ability to feel what another person feels. The system uses a data glove to capture the hardness or softness of an object being felt by a person at a computer.

Though research is still ongoing, some uses are already being worked out for medicine, the military, and consumer electronics. Motorola, for example, is working on a way to have your phone simulate the feeling given when someone nudges you, instead of a ring or vibration. But knowing the proclivities of people, sex will be the area that drives money to the development of the commercial uses of the technology.

If all this sounds to you vaguely like the movie *The Matrix* you're not alone. The simulated world of the movie may be a reality for some. Dr. Nick Bostrum, author of *Taking the Red Pill: Science, Philosophy and Religion in the Matrix* and a philosophy professor at Oxford, argues that there is a 20% chance that most people today are really creations of software and living in a virtual reality. It's conceivable that technology could one day run lifelike simulation programs. Given that, how do you know that you really exist or are you just living in a simulation?

"That's a Wrap!"

Still in its infancy, but starting to take off, are pornography DVDs. They now make up more than 65% of the sales of all adult movies. This mainstream-seeming product is attracting a customer who normally wouldn't buy a porno film. As with most DVDs, they offer bonus features. In this industry, however, behind-the-scenes features include scenes of the gals getting ready to go on set or talking about their wildest sexual escapades. But one company is upping the ante on that and making it interactive, offering another feature reminiscent of the old "choose-your-own-adventure" books.

It's done by manipulating icons on the screen to make the porn star follow various scenarios: You make her a dirty talker or an innocent girl, vary her sexual positions, or ask her to strip. The viewer can become both director and participant.

The company responsible for this creativity is the 10-year old Digital Playground, which has always been on the interactive edge. It began by releasing interactive CD-ROMs. The company has 40% of the adult DVD market, including the interactive series "Virtual Sex with . . ." that has been described as a cross between a flick and a video game. That's a good market to have, considering that each Virtual Sex DVD costs $31.

Next up: Holograms? At least that's what Digital Playground hopes. It's not only preparing itself in case the technology ever makes it doable, it's also taking a hand in making the technology catch up. Besides working with a hologram company, it wants to sell a hologram machine compatible with the DVDs. It is shooting the performers against a black background so that once the technology is complete, the girl could appear to be a hologram in the viewer's bedroom or living room, as the case may be.

For regular digital cable subscribers, content providers such as Playboy are getting into the act on that front, but the offerings aren't yet as advanced as with DVDs.

Richard Gale, the head of marketing for Playboy TV UK, which broadcasts Playboy TV, Spice, and The Adult Channel, says that interactive TV will be key for the future but leaves detail vague: "Some of our plans stretch the existing iTV technology to the limits. Instead of an adult QVC, think more of what adult entertainment would be like in *The Matrix*."[7]

[Cell] Phone Sex

Whereas only about half of all Americans have cell phones, over 80% of Europeans do. And of the U.K.'s 56 million people, 50 million have mobile phones, meaning that some people are multiple mobile phone owners.

America is one of the most backward countries when it comes to cell phone technology advancements. Asia and Europe are way ahead of us. And, where there's technology advancement, vice will follow.

To make these kinds of things just a little clearer, it's helpful that companies like Nokia and Motorola are concurrently developing technology to make pictures and video clips more quickly downloadable.

Look out for an explosion of adult content coming soon to mobile phones or wireless providers. This is a lucrative proposition. Already, in Europe and Asia, 20% of their revenues come from services other than traditional calls. It is expected that this will jump to 50% by 2013.

Virgin mobile is developing its own mobile porn offering and the U.K. mobile phone operator Hutchinson has a deal with Playboy. It will offer the ability to download porn clips for about $4.25, while a two-minute soccer video should run about $.85.

German operator E-Plus has a deal with Playboy to supply its i-mode service with content. Finland's Wireless Entertainment Services (WES) announced in December 2002 that it had licensed Playboy content for distribution. Watch out Peoria: WES has signed a distribution agreement to bring graphics of Playboy playmates to U.S. cell phones.[8] And Private Media Group is planning on beaming pictures of its own lovely ladies to U.S. cell phone users, too.

In Italy, Telecom Italia Mobile, for example, already offers a pinup of the day and Wind Eureka, part of ItaliaOnLine, has a strip poker game. That means two vices in one: nudity and gaming. The latter could give wireless porn a run for its money. Irish Consultancy Alatto Technologies estimates that 4.5% of global mobile phone owners will gamble using a wireless device, which could generate an extra $683 million in revenue for the sector by 2006.[9]

However, Gartner Group, the industry research company, estimates that adult content over mobile phones was worth $87 million in 2002 and will generate $1.3 billion in revenues in western Europe alone in 2005, or about 5% of the total mobile data market.

And with a mobile phone the means for payment are much easier than over the 'Net; it's done through your phone bill.[10]

Porn is being out so quickly to mobile phone users in part because the mobile phone companies spent so much money—nearly 120 billion in Europe alone—on licenses to use 3G, the technology that allows for more applications needing higher bandwith at quicker rates. Porn profits help to pay off the bills.

Another example of current technology making a foray into porn is SMS, or short message service technology, also called text messaging. Private Media Group's adult reverse-billed SMS chat service signed up over 200,000 U.K. users in its first year.

On the tamer side, dating can be a big driver of things as well for SMS. The SMS market in the United States could reach an estimated 75 million users by 2007, who will send some 44 billion messages a month. Already 1.5 billion SMS messages are sent a month here.

Virgin offers a text message service called "Flirt Alert." According to Virgin Mobile's *Joy of Text* booklet, a "love poll" conducted by the company found that 50% of respondents regularly flirt using SMS [if they're teens make that 90%] while 53% say they have used SMS to ask someone out on a date because it was less embarrassing than a face-to-face or over-the-phone approach. Also, one in four felt that text messaging would help them "score" because it allowed them to be more forward than when talking directly to someone.

British wireless media company Carbon Partners has been hosting SMS flirting night parties for several years. The event has gotten so popular that on average 2,000 text messages are sent a night. Their biggest, in May of 2003, was billed as Europe's largest live dating event with more than 3,000 Londoners gathered at the party "Chemistry, Live Dating Event," for two nights of match-making. It worked like this:

> Upon purchasing their ticket for the Chemistry, each person selects a unique Chemistry identification name for the event. This i.d. name is the method by which all interaction takes place, online, through special calling cards distributed at the events and for

the text flirting. At the event itself, people can exchange text messages without revealing their mobile phone number, with all communication taking place by Chemistry i.d. Users have complete control of the system and can choose who they wish to flirt with, and when they are available to receive text flirts.[11]

Mobile Cupid

Bored on the way to work? Mundane errands got you down? Nowaways you can put that all in the past and multitask. No need to wait until you get home to see what loves may be awaiting you online.

Lycos UK is one of the many companies offering mobile chat rooms. Popular site Match.com began providing wireless dating, matchmaking, and communication capabilities to AT&T Wireless mMode customers in September 2003.[12]

BOX 12.1

Watch These Web Sites to Keep Up with Your Vice's Future

- www.teledildonics.com Chronicles the developments in teledildonics—that is, virtual sex with partners who are either imaginary or are not physically present.
- www.kurzweilai.com Web site of the futurist and predictor of sexbots, Ray Kurzweil.
- www.vrinnovations.com/company.htm Web site for Virtual Sex Machine company. Good links and press about it offers some good leads.
- www.avnonline.com Adult magazine site.
- www.techtv.com/wiredforsex "Wired for Sex" on TechTV is a new series that looks into the relationship between sex and technology. Check this site for show information.
- www.fleshbot.com Porn web magazine that links to adult material online of interest to its mainstream media-savvy readers. Fleshbot debuted with links to the Paris Hilton video.

In 2004 AOL expects its Love.com dating service, integrated with its instant messaging (AIM) capabilities, to be available on wireless phones. Instant messaging, cell phones, and dating service: how perfect for today's instant gratification society.

Internationally, the concept has been taken a step further. Mobile Entertainment Corp. (MEC), based in the U.K., launched Mobiledate-club.com, along with Dateclub, one of the world's largest dating agencies, to a big demand. It allows its over 85,000 members to view pictures of potential amours and with location-based technology to search for ones in the area. If members don't have a camera phone, MEC has deals with Nokia and Siemens to give them a good price on one. A product from Vodafone called live! is designed, among other things, to allow for the use of handsets with built-in cameras, letting would-be mates to check each other out before meeting.

There is a dangerous side to all this, of course: In Japan, underage prostitution, rapes, and murder have come from arranging dates from this new mobile phone technology. As a result the service by provider DoCoMo, for example, is highly regulated.

Japan is much more advanced than the U.S. and as result the more unsavory aspect of things has struck there first. One study reported that 77% of 20- to 40-year-old i-mode (Japanese wireless service allowing Web access and e-mail on mobile phones) users in Japan had received e-mail from porn sites. The porn and tech connection is so pervasive there that New York City's Japan Society put together a timely panel discussion: "Vices and Devices: How the Adult Entertainment Industry Is Driving Digital Innovation."[13]

CHAPTER 13

Afterglow

Vice Is Everywhere

By now you should have a pretty firm idea of classic vice stocks, but you should know that many other companies could be boosted by the same trends that push many of the stocks mentioned in this book. Sometimes it isn't apparent on first glance that they're vice stocks.

Take Abercrombie. Who'd have thought the clothier to aristocrats up and down the Eastern seaboard would be the company responsible for nude catalogs featuring threesomes—and I don't mean shirts, pants, and a vest—and thongs embroidered with "wink wink" for preteens. I would say that Messrs. Abercrombie and Fitch are spinning in their graves, but nowadays considering how well the company has done, they are likely in gilded mausoleums.

There are hidden vice stocks everywhere. To misquote Madonna, that paragon of sin, "Vice is where you find it." In fact, in this book I've just scratched the surface on vice. I didn't even really get into vanity. Actually, speaking of which, Estée Lauder has such a thing as a lipstick index that demonstrates that when times are tough, the tough go shopping—for lipstick.

The index is more anecdotal than anything, according to the company, and certainly not something they're planning on releasing.

But company spokeswoman Sally Sussman would tell me this: "We definitely see a spike in lipstick sales when the rest of the retail climate is challenged. It's the small luxuries that do well is what we learned from the index. Lipstick offers an easy pick-me-up or splash of color in an otherwise dreary moment." Any colors in particular? Just as I suspected: "The bolder colors do very well during these times," according to Ms. Sussman, who says company head Leonard Lauder most closely keeps track of the index.

If you don't consider lipstick a vice, just go to Lancaster, Pennsylvania to see many of the Amish gals are sporting red puckers. Believe me, you won't be confusing Mrs. Stoltzfuss with Paloma Picasso anytime soon.

(Apparently, the Estee Lauder folks are none too jazzed about being considered part of the vice camp. Said Ms. Sussman upon hearing what my book was about: "So, you're throwing us in that nasty lot?")

What Vice Is Hot Now?

When I read a paper I red-flag articles that look like they're propelled by vice in some way. You should be doing this, too. If you listen to Howard Stern, pay attention to what is being promoted both by the DJ himself and by the show's advertising. He seems to have a way of moving products. It is pretty uncontested that he essentially built the Snapple brand.

Today's find: A *Wall Street Journal* article about a Canadian ice cream maker CoolBrands. This was interesting to me, vice-wise, because they are making a killing in the newly expanding low-carb ice cream market.[1] Gluttony and vanity! People will always love their vices, but part of the investing trick on the shorter-term plays is to find out what vices people are loving NOW. (If the low-carb thing hits the skids, the company has experience, from working with Weight Watchers, to tailoring its products to different diets.)

The most important part of vice investing is to have fun. I know that this may sound silly, but think about it: You're buying these stocks based on people having fun. Right? So, if you're deadly serious about it, you might as well be putting your money into the semiconductor cycles. This is one of the few times you will be encouraged to go to Vegas and write it off as a business expense.

When you construct your own portfolio of vice, as I hope you do, be sure to have a healthy mix of industries, nature of the stocks (growth or value), domestic and international, and size. I've done my own model portfolio (see Appendix II) that you might want to take a look at. (Make that a long look—if you had been able to invest $1,000 on it five years ago, you'd have $1,418 to spend on your own vices. The S&P would have left you down $28.) Again, I'm not a financial planner but I put it together with one of the best professional money managers I know: Carter Crum, so I feel confident that you can benefit from reviewing it.

Returns of Socially Responsible Mutual Funds vs. All Other Mutual Funds as Well as the S&P

Social Criteria Funds

Fund Name	L Cls	Last Y-E 12/31/02 6/30/03 Cumulative Total Return	1 year 6/30/02 6/30/03 Cumulative Total Return	3 years 6/30/00 6/30/03 Annual Total Return	5 years 6/30/98 6/30/03 Annual Total Return	10 years 6/30/93 6/30/03 Annual Total Return	Latest Total Net Assets (Mil. $)
AB Funds:Cap Opptys;Ret	MLCE	10.38	1.37	N/A	N/A	N/A	821.8
AB Funds:Cap Opptys;Rtl	MLCE	10.24	1	N/A	N/A	N/A	11.1
AB Funds:Equity Idx;Inst	LCCE	11.74	0.13	N/A	N/A	N/A	6.1
AB Funds:Equity Idx;Ret	LCCE	11.55	-0.15	N/A	N/A	N/A	353
AB Funds:Equity Idx;Rtl	LCCE	11.58	-0.19	N/A	N/A	N/A	14.6
AB Funds:Glbl Eqty;Ret	GL	11.92	-2.41	N/A	N/A	N/A	685.4
AB Funds:Glbl Eqty;Rtl	GL	11.76	-2.64	N/A	N/A	N/A	14.7
AB Funds:Gro Eqty;Inst	LCGE	14.29	1.38	N/A	N/A	N/A	9.5
AB Funds:Gro Eqty;Ret	LCGE	14.34	1.34	N/A	N/A	N/A	1185.3
AB Funds:Gro Eqty;Rtl	LCGE	14.22	1.13	N/A	N/A	N/A	15
AB Funds:Gro&Inc;Ret	FX	8.71	4.84	N/A	N/A	N/A	1069.9
AB Funds:Gro&Inc;Rtl	FX	8.63	4.6	N/A	N/A	N/A	19.1
AB Funds:Intl Eqty;Inst	IF	8.96	-5.79	N/A	N/A	N/A	9.4
AB Funds:Intl Eqty;Ret	IF	8.9	-5.96	N/A	N/A	N/A	766.4
AB Funds:Intl Eqty;Rtl	IF	8.79	-6.06	N/A	N/A	N/A	15.6
AB Funds:Sm Cap Eq;Inst	SCCE	17.66	-3.74	N/A	N/A	N/A	6.9
AB Funds:Sm Cap Eq;Ret	SCCE	17.56	-3.83	N/A	N/A	N/A	277.5
AB Funds:Sm Cap Eq;Rtl	SCCE	17.37	-4.07	N/A	N/A	N/A	15.6
AB Funds:Value Eqty;Inst	MLVE	11.88	-2.84	N/A	N/A	N/A	10.3
AB Funds:Value Eqty;Ret	MLVE	11.76	-2.97	N/A	N/A	N/A	1036.1

Fund	Category							Net Assets
AB Funds:Value Eqty;Rtl	MLVE	11.59	-3.2	N/A	N/A	N/A		16.2
Alger Inst:Soc Resp Gr;I	MLGE	20	-7.61	N/A	N/A	N/A		1.3
Alger Inst:Soc Resp Gr;R	MLGE	N/A	N/A	N/A	N/A	N/A		0.1
Allied:Dow Islamic Idx;K	LCCE	11.13	0.96	-16.86	N/A	N/A		18.2
Allied:Dow Islamic Idx;M	LCCE	10.62	0.35	N/A	N/A	N/A		0.1
Amana:Growth Fund	MLCE	13.5	1.28	-12.47	6.45	N/A		22.7
Amana:Income Fund	EIEI	8.24	-3.54	-6.22	-1.85	6.16		19.7
American Tr Allegiance	MLCE	6.45	-6	-20.13	-2.02	N/A		19.9
Aquinas:Growth	MLGE	8.26	-7.37	-12.49	-1.54	N/A		53.6
Aquinas:SmCap	MCGE	11.64	-9.96	-11.17	-5.5	N/A		6
Aquinas:Value	LCVE	8.57	-6.77	-5.65	-4.47	N/A		36.7
Ariel:Appreciation	MCCE	13.25	0.3	11.67	7.7	13.45		1811.4
Ariel:Fund	SCCE	11.15	1.51	12.37	8.16	13.16		1713.9
ARK Fds:SI Bl Ch Eq;Inst	LCCE	10.42	1.72	N/A	N/A	N/A		0.8
ARK Fds:SI Cap Gro;Inst	MLCE	15.99	6.76	N/A	N/A	N/A		0.2
ARK Fds:SI SmCp Eq;Inst	SCGE	11.67	-10.31	N/A	N/A	N/A		0.7
Calvert Fd:N Vis SC;A	SCCE	8.2	-12.62	-3.32	1.89	N/A		141.8
Calvert Fd:N Vis SC;B	SCCE	7.66	-13.47	-4.27	0.78	N/A		17.2
Calvert Fd:N Vis SC;C	SCCE	7.69	-13.35	-4.13	1.01	N/A		17.1
Calvert Lg Cap Gro;A	MLGE	17.97	5.61	N/A	N/A	N/A		14.3
Calvert Lg Cap Gro;B	MLGE	17.31	4.57	N/A	N/A	N/A		3.8
Calvert Lg Cap Gro;C	MLGE	17.3	4.55	N/A	N/A	N/A		1.9
Calvert Lg Cap Gro;I	MLGE	18.25	6.23	-14.43	1.7	N/A		3.8
Calvert Soc Idx;A	LCCE	13.02	2.3	-14.46	N/A	N/A		25.5
Calvert Soc Idx;B	LCCE	12.53	1.32	-15.27	N/A	N/A		2.1

(continues)

Fund Name	L Cls	Last Y-E 12/31/02 6/30/03 Cumulative Total Return	1 year 6/30/02 6/30/03 Cumulative Total Return	3 years 6/30/00 6/30/03 Annual Total Return	5 years 6/30/98 6/30/03 Annual Total Return	10 years 6/30/93 6/30/03 Annual Total Return	Latest Total Net Assets (Mil. $)
Calvert Soc Idx;C	LCCE	12.55	1.32	-15.29	N/A	N/A	2.2
Calvert Soc Idx;I	LCCE	13.39	2.83	-14.09	N/A	N/A	4.4
Calvert Soc Inv:Bal;A	B	8.06	2.94	-5.17	-0.37	5.84	483.6
Calvert Soc Inv:Bal;B	B	7.49	1.84	-6.14	-1.44	N/A	18.5
Calvert Soc Inv:Bal;C	B	7.48	1.89	-6.14	-1.39	N/A	15.3
Calvert Soc Inv:E Eq;A	LCCE	9.66	1.99	-8.78	-0.12	N/A	37
Calvert Soc Inv:E Eq;B	LCCE	9.16	0.79	-9.78	-1.25	N/A	6.6
Calvert Soc Inv:E Eq;C	LCCE	9.13	0.79	-9.79	-1.27	N/A	4.1
Calvert Soc Inv:Eq;A	MLCE	9.36	1.57	-1.34	6.15	8.67	483.9
Calvert Soc Inv:Eq;B	MLCE	8.89	0.65	-2.25	5.09	N/A	64.9
Calvert Soc Inv:Eq;C	MLCE	8.94	0.73	-2.19	5.23	N/A	56.7
Calvert Soc Inv:Eq;I	MLCE	9.69	2.11	-0.91	N/A	N/A	34.4
Calvert Wrld:Cap Acc;A	MCGE	12.51	-0.11	-11.46	-2.57	N/A	99.4
Calvert Wrld:Cap Acc;B	MCGE	11.89	-1.05	-12.25	-3.44	N/A	13.9
Calvert Wrld:Cap Acc;C	MCGE	12.03	-0.97	-12.18	-3.35	N/A	10.3
Calvert Wrld:Intl Eq;A	IF	7.28	-4.6	-14.03	-5.25	3.06	151
Calvert Wrld:Intl Eq;B	IF	6.57	-5.91	-15.18	-6.46	N/A	5.4
Calvert Wrld:Intl Eq;C	IF	6.69	-5.59	-14.94	-6.22	N/A	8.8
Calvert Wrld:Intl Eq;I	IF	7.79	-3.58	-13.22		N/A	8.7
Capstone Serv:Intl;A	IF	3.05	-12.9	-16.22	N/A	N/A	8.3
Capstone Serv:Intl;C	IF	3.34	-12.5	-15.95	N/A	N/A	5.5

Capstone Serv:LC Eq;A	LCCE	10.74	-0.07	-11.53	N/A	N/A	N/A	44.2
Capstone Serv:LC Eq;C	LCCE	10.91	0.24	-11.27	N/A	N/A	N/A	29.3
Capstone Serv:SC Eq;A	SCCE	11.75	-4.22	1.44	N/A	N/A	N/A	14.2
Capstone Serv:SC Eq;C	SCCE	11.88	-3.82	1.75	N/A	N/A	N/A	7.9
Catholic:Equity;A	LCCE	11.25	-0.31	-9.85	N/A	N/A	N/A	4.5
Catholic:Equity;C	LCCE	11.3	-0.49	N/A	N/A	N/A	N/A	3
Catholic:Equity;I	LCCE	11.57	0.14	N/A	N/A	N/A	N/A	16.7
Citizens:Core Gr;Admin	LCCE	9.81	-1.36	-18.64	N/A		N/A	2.4
Citizens:Core Gr;Inst	LCCE	9.93	-1.1	-18.45	N/A	-3.95	N/A	63.6
Citizens:Core Gr;Std	LCCE	9.6	-1.73	-18.97	N/A	-4.61	N/A	285.3
Citizens:Emerg Gro;Admin	MCGE	12.91	-6.8	-24.05	N/A	N/A	N/A	8.6
Citizens:Emerg Gro;Inst	MCGE	13.09	-6.57	-23.84	N/A	N/A	N/A	5.4
Citizens:Emerg Gro;Std	MCGE	12.64	-7.28	-24.31	N/A	1.45	N/A	157.9
Citizens:Glbl Eq;Admin	GL	5.05	-5.52	-21.23	N/A	N/A	N/A	2.1
Citizens:Glbl Eq;Inst	GL	5.24	-5.21	-21.01	N/A	N/A	N/A	6.7
Citizens:Glbl Eq;Std	GL	4.94	-5.84	-21.44	N/A	-1.88	N/A	101.8
Citizens:SC Core Gr;Stnd	SCGE	14.08	-5.56	-8.21	N/A	N/A	N/A	17.8
Citizens:Value	LCVE	14.44	-1.14	-8.33	N/A	0.4	N/A	16.2
Delaware Soc Aware;A	MLCE	13.51	0.82	-11.32	N/A	-4.42	N/A	18.4
Delaware Soc Aware;B	MLCE	13.04	0.12	-11.96	N/A	-5.13	N/A	21.7
Delaware Soc Aware;C	MLCE	13.04	0	-11.96	N/A	-5.13	N/A	5.6
Delaware Soc Aware;Inst	MLCE	13.69	1.04	-11.08	N/A	-4.18	N/A	0.6
Domini Inst:Social Eqty	LCCE	11.29	0.83	-12.05	N/A	-1.56	N/A	185.3
Domini Soc:Equity Fund	LCCE	10.96	0.2	-12.49	N/A	-2.11	9.53	1068.4
Dominion:Shep Lg Cp Gro	MLGE	12.59	-3.22	-35.13	N/A	-10.13	2.37	3.8

(continues)

Fund Name	L Cls	Last Y-E 12/31/02 6/30/03 Cumulative Total Return	1 year 6/30/02 6/30/03 Cumulative Total Return	3 years 6/30/00 6/30/03 Annual Total Return	5 years 6/30/98 6/30/03 Annual Total Return	10 years 6/30/93 6/30/03 Annual Total Return	Latest Total Net Assets (Mil. $)
Dreyfus Prem Third;A	LCCE	9.9	-5.88	-20.31	N/A	N/A	14.1
Dreyfus Prem Third;B	LCCE	9.51	-6.57	-20.96	N/A	N/A	16.9
Dreyfus Prem Third;C	LCCE	9.51	-6.57	-20.98	N/A	N/A	3.7
Dreyfus Prem Third;R	LCCE	10.27	-5.29	-20.01	N/A	N/A	25.1
Dreyfus Prem Third;T	LCCE	9.79	-6.14	-20.68	N/A	N/A	0.6
Dreyfus Prem Third;Z	LCCE	10.16	-5.58	-20.2	-5.82	6.44	532.3
Enterprise:Glbl Soc;A	GL	9.17	-4.09	N/A	N/A	N/A	2.7
Enterprise:Glbl Soc;B	GL	8.86	-4.51	N/A	N/A	N/A	1.3
Enterprise:Glbl Soc;C	GL	8.87	-4.64	N/A	N/A	N/A	0.8
Enterprise:Glbl Soc;Y	GL	9.34	-3.57	N/A	N/A	N/A	0.2
Forum:Winslow Green Gro	SCGE	52.86	21.1	N/A	N/A	N/A	30.9
GMO:Tobacco-Fr Core;III	MLCE	10.71	0.04	-7.26	0.79	11.78	198.7
GMO:Tobacco-Fr Core;IV	MLCE	10.61	0	N/A	N/A	N/A	374.9
Green Century:Balanced	B	34.69	14.36	-13.17	5.21	8.53	50.8
Green Century:Equity	LCCE	10.57	-0.44	-13	-2.66	N/A	28.4
MMA Praxis:Core Stk;A	LCCE	6.13	-4.55	-8.04	N/A	N/A	32.2
MMA Praxis:Core Stock;B	LCCE	5.77	-5.18	-8.61	-2.57	N/A	115.7
MMA Praxis:Intl;A	IF	4.95	-11.45	-18.51	N/A	N/A	76.5
MMA Praxis:Intl;B	IF	4.7	-11.97	-18.97	N/A	N/A	17.7
MMA Praxis:Value Idx;A	LCVE	12.27	-0.94	N/A	N/A	N/A	20.5
MMA Praxis:Value Idx;B	LCVE	12.03	-1.44	N/A	N/A	N/A	4

Fund	Type									
Morg Stan KLD Soc Ix;A	LCCE	11.97	0.84	N/A		N/A		N/A		1.1
Morg Stan KLD Soc Ix;B	LCCE	11.39	0.03	N/A		N/A		N/A		6.4
Morg Stan KLD Soc Ix;C	LCCE	11.42	0.04	N/A		N/A		N/A		1.2
Morg Stan KLD Soc Ix;D	LCCE	11.95	1.03	N/A		N/A		N/A		1.4
Neuberger Soc Resp;Inv	MLCE	16.1	6.66		0.28		1.36	N/A		163
Neuberger Soc Resp;Tr	MLCE	15.98	6.3		0.02		1.1	N/A		28.6
New Alternatives Fund	S	7.27	-9.41		-8.65		-0.84		3.85	39.8
New Covenant:Bal Gro	B	7.6	3.1		-2.67	N/A		N/A		272.4
New Covenant:Bal Inc	B	5.91	6		2.13	N/A		N/A		122.6
New Covenant:Growth	MLCE	10.29	-2.16		-10.83	N/A		N/A		709
Noah Inv:Large-Cap Gro	MLGE	11.91	-1.09		-22.39		-5.83	N/A		9.1
Parnassus Fund	MLCE	14.97	2.89		-10.44		8.03		9.46	351
Parnassus:Equity Income	EIEI	8	9.39		3.02		10.26		10.47	475.5
Pax World Balanced Fd	B	6.96	3.07		-2.66		4.18		9.59	1107.6
Pax World Growth	MLGE	18.73	5.38		-15.17		-3.67		32.3	
Portfolio 21	MLCE	8.99	-3.8	N/A	-9.7	N/A		N/A		20.4
Rainbow Fund	MCVE	-5.18	-16.78		-8.82		-11.52		-1.84	0.6
Schwartz Inv:Cthlc Vl	MCCE	12.14	-2.93	N/A		N/A		N/A		114.4
Security Eq:Soc Awar;A	LCCE	10.16	0.69		-13.41		-2.85	N/A		8.9
Security Eq:Soc Awar;B	LCCE	9.76	-0.06		-14.21		-3.82	N/A		6.4
Security Eq:Soc Awar;C	LCCE	9.67	-0.12		-14.19	N/A		N/A		1.5
Sm Barney:Soc Aw;A	FX	9.79	2.29		-5.33		0.92		8.08	261
Sm Barney:Soc Aw;B	FX	9.37	1.5		-6.09		0.14		7.25	104
Sm Barney:Soc Aw;L	FX	9.34	1.52		-6.03		0.17		7.29	20.1
Summit:T Soc Impact	LCCE	11.4	-0.07	N/A		N/A		N/A		3.8

(continues)

Fund Name	L Cls	Last Y-E 12/31/02 6/30/03 Cumulative Total Return	1 year 6/30/02 6/30/03 Cumulative Total Return	3 years 6/30/00 6/30/03 Annual Total Return	5 years 6/30/98 6/30/03 Annual Total Return	10 years 6/30/93 6/30/03 Annual Total Return	Latest Total Net Assets (Mil. $)
TIAA–CREF:Social Chce Eq	LCCE	12.83	2.17	–10.4	N/A	N/A	80.7
Timothy Plan:Aggr Gr;A	MCGE	19.96	–1.08	N/A	N/A	N/A	6.5
Timothy Plan:Aggr Gr;B	MCGE	19.64	–1.83	N/A	N/A	N/A	0.8
Timothy Plan:Csv Gr;A	MLCE	7.8	–0.9	N/A	N/A	N/A	11.3
Timothy Plan:Csv Gr;B	MLCE	7.32	–1.7	N/A	N/A	N/A	9.6
Timothy Plan:Lg/MCG;A	LCGE	6.42	–3.87	N/A	N/A	N/A	16.3
Timothy Plan:Lg/MCG;B	LCGE	6.13	–4.62	N/A	N/A	N/A	1.8
Timothy Plan:Lg/MCV;A	MLVE	10.87	–4.45	2.24	N/A	N/A	21.3
Timothy Plan:Lg/MCV;B	MLVE	10.49	–5.09	1.42	N/A	N/A	4.2
Timothy Plan:SmCp Vl;A	SCCE	10.51	–9.38	3.94	4.07	N/A	25.8
Timothy Plan:SmCp Vl;B	SCCE	10.1	–10.06	3.11	3.22	N/A	15.2
Timothy Plan:Str Gr;A	MLCE	10.43	–5.79	N/A	N/A	N/A	9.2
Timothy Plan:Str Gr;B	MLCE	9.76	–6.66	N/A	N/A	N/A	12.1
Walden Social Balanced	FX	5.27	3.67	–0.99	N/A	N/A	20.8
Walden Social Equity	MLCE	8.39	2.2	–3.24	N/A	N/A	31
Womens Equity Mutual Fd	LCCE	7.21	–1.26	–3.72	1.37	N/A	15
Average/Total		11.04	–1.67	–10.42	–0.83	7.53	19598.3
Non-Social Criteria Funds		12.41	–0.54	–9.05	–0.04	7.6	3057723.8
S&P 500 Daily Reinv	XI	11.76	0.25	–11.2	–1.61	10.04	N/A

Source: Lipper, A Reuters company

APPENDIX

Stocking Up on SINDEX

69 Stocks Representative of Vice, Avarice, and Social Irresponsibility

BOOZE

Company Name	Stock Symbol	11/7/03 Closing Stock Price	Shares Outstanding ($ Millions)	Market Cap ($ Millions)	Weight in Index	Beta	Fair Value	Notes
Allied Domecq PLC	AED	$28.74	281.657	$8,095	0.66%	0.35	$25–$27	Maker's Mark, Kahlua, Beefeater Gin, Baskin-Robbins, Dunkin' Donuts
Anheuser-Busch	BUD	$51.30	814.760	$41,797	3.41%	0.12	$65–$68	Parent Company of world's largest brewer
Compania Cervecerias	CU	$20.09	60.932	$1,224	0.10%	0.76	$10–$12	Beer and wine products in Chile and Argentina
Diageo PLC	DEO	$48.60	805.540	$39,149	3.20%	0.12	$40–$43	London-based producer and distributor of spirits
Fortune Brands	FO	$66.60	145.870	$9,715	0.79%	0.77	$60–$65	Jim Beam, DeKuyper cordials, Gilbey's gin, Cointreau
Heineken	HINKY	$36.85	392.000	$14,445	1.18%	1.00	$38–$41	Dutch brewer of Heineken, Amstel
Kirin Brewery	KNBWY	$8.18	967.000	$7,910	0.65%	0.47	$7–$9	Premier brewer in Japan
Robert Mondavi Corp.	MOND	$35.75	16.357	$585	0.05%	0.91	$40–$43	California wine producer
Adolph Coors Co.	RKY	$56.01	36.402	$2,039	0.17%	0.35	$83–$87	Coors, Killian's Red, Keystone, Zima
Boston Beer Co. 'A'	SAM	$17.40	13.817	$240	0.02%	0.71	$18–$20	Largest craft brewer in U.S.; 5th largest overall
SABMiller PLC	SBMRY	$8.95	999.000	$8,941	0.73%	0.90	$9–$10	Recent merger between South African Breweries and Miller

Constellation Brands	STZ	$31.52	105.147	$3,314	0.27%	0.42	$63–$67	Global beer and wine importer

CASINOS AND GAMES

Alliance Gaming	AGI	$25.85	49.689	$1,284	0.10%	-0.24	$27–$30	Making gaming systems
Argosy Gaming	AGY	$25.32	29.313	$742	0.06%	0.68	$50–$55	Riverboat casinos
Boyd Gaming	BYD	$16.46	64.038	$1,054	0.09%	0.74	$14–$17	Casinos in Vegas and in other states
GTECH	GTK	$47.46	64.500	$3,061	0.25%	-0.08	$65–$70	Leader in online lottery products
Harrah's Entertainment	HET	$45.78	110.465	$5,057	0.41%	0.57	$50–$55	Harrah's, showboat, Rio
International Game Technology	IGT	$33.43	345.063	$11,535	0.94%	0.36	$30–$35	Gaming software, machines
Isle of Capri Casinos	ISLE	$22.16	29.250	$648	0.05%	0.85	$50–$55	Owns land and riverboat casinos
Mandalay Resort Club	MBG	$40.85	61.493	$2,512	0.21%	0.81	$47–$50	Operates 16 gaming properties
MGM Mirage	MGG	$35.70	149.698	$5,344	0.44%	0.68	$30–$33	Casinos in Vegas, Detroit, Australia
Multimedia Gaming	MGAM	$41.45	13.125	$544	0.04%	1.47	$61–$65	Supplies both elctronic games and the player stations
Park Place Entertainment	PPE	$10.18	301.974	$3,074	0.25%	1.20	$7–$9	12 to 15 equity interests in 20+ gaming projects

(continues)

Company Name	Stock Symbol	11/7/03 Closing Stock Price	Shares Outstanding ($ Millions)	Market Cap ($ Millions)	Weight in Index	Beta	Fair Value	Notes
Penn National	PENN	$23.60	39.566	$934	0.08%	0.76	$20–$24	Owns gaming properties, horse race tracks
Scientific Gaming	SGMS	$13.45	60.118	$809	0.07%	1.20	$25–$39	Parimutual game systems
Shuffle Master	SHFL	$31.33	16.576	$519	0.04%	0.55	$14–$15	Card shufflers
Station Casinos	STN	$29.85	58.189	$1,737	0.14%	0.88	$40–$45	Owns eight Vegas theme hotels
Wynn Resorts	WYNN	$20.00	82.352	$1,647	0.13%	1.00	$10 –$12	Building the $2.4 billion La Reve hotel
DEFENSE INDUSTRY								
Alliant Techsystems	ATK	$51.80	38.623	$2,001	0.16%	-0.15	$65–$70	Pentagon's largest ammo supplier
Boeing Co.	BA	$38.90	800.216	$31,128	2.54%	0.72	$33–$38	Largest commercial jet and satellite maker
Rockwell Collins	COL	$28.02	179.312	$5,024	0.41%	1.00	$25–$28	Military aircraft cockpit controls
Cubic Corp	CUB	$29.75	26.72	$795	0.06%	0.25	$17–$20	High tech electronics for defense market
Curtiss-Wright	CW	$76.48	10.318	$789	0.06%	-0.12	$97–$102	Motion control components that make bomb doors open
Elbit Systems	ESLT	$18.88	38.796	$732	0.06%	0.31	$16–$18	High performance electro-optics components
General Dynamics	GD	$83.17	197.737	$16,446	1.34%	0.44	$94–$97	One of the largest defense contractors

Company	Ticker	Price					Range	Description
Goodrich Corp	GR	$27.53	117.665	$3,239	0.26%	1.24	$23–$25	Loading gear evacuation slides for large jets
Honeywell	HON	$30.47	862.051	$26,267	2.14%	1.27	$25–$27	Largest maker of cockpit controls, small jet engines
L-3 Communications	LLL	$48.20	96.392	$4,646	0.38%	0.31	$55–$60	Sophisticated surveillance & recon suppliers
Lockheed Martin	LMT	$46.04	450.875	$20,758	1.69%	-0.16	$50–$55	World's largest military weapons manufacturer
Northrop Grumman	NOC	$89.05	186.629	$16,619	1.36%	-0.03	$122–$125	Second largest, recently bought TRW's satellite and electronics
Raytheon	RTN	$26.97	413.988	$11,165	0.91%	0.39	$30–$35	High tech missiles and electronics
United Technologies	UTX	$86.68	470.559	$40,788	3.33%	1.20	$70–$75	Pratt & Whitney jet engines, Sikorsky helicopters
Fast Food								
McDonald's	MCD	$26.01	1269.164	$33,011	2.69%	0.86	$33–$35	Ronald McDonald and friends
Wendy's International	WEN	$39.50	113.469	$4,482	0.37%	0.37	$30–$33	Biggies and Frosties
YUM! Brands	YUM	$34.30	294.153	$10,089	0.82%	0.30	$29–$31	Taco Bell, Pizza Hut, KFC
TOBACCO								
Loews Cp-Carolina Group	CG	$24.44	39.910	$975	0.08%	1.00	$20–$22	Newport, Kent, True

(continues)

11/7/03

Company Name	Stock Symbol	Closing Stock Price	Shares Outstanding ($ Millions)	Market Cap ($ Millions)	Weight in Index	Beta	Fair Value	Notes
British American Tobacco	BTI	$23.93	1098.00	$26,299	2.15%	0.10	$45–$50	Over 300 brands
Gallaher Group ADS	GLH	$40.50	163.800	$6,634	0.27%	-0.28	$40–$43	Cigs, cigars sold in UK
Altria Group	MO	$49.51	2029.498	$100,480	8.20%	0.33	$70–$75	Marlboro (largest), Kraft Foods
R.J. Reynolds Tobacco	RJR	$49.96	84.313	$4,212	0.34%	0.84	$45–$50	Second largest—Winston
Imperial Tobacco Group	ITY	$33.19	375.000	$12,473	1.02%	-0.01	$23–$25	UK maker
U.S Tobacco	UST	$34.97	166.479	$5,822	0.48%	0.89	$33–$36	Smokeless Tobacco; Skoal
SEX DRUGS								
Pfizer	PFE	$34.08	7631.523	$260,082	21.23%	0.53	$37–$40	Viagra
Eli Lilly	LLY	$65.85	1122.904	$73,943	6.04%	0.89	$34–$38	Zyprexa, Cialis (U.S.)
Johnson and Johnson	JNJ	$48.81	2968.143	$144,875	11.83%	0.79	$60–$63	K-Y jelly
ICOS	ICOS	$46.70	62.900	$2,937	0.24%	1.68	$1–$2	Cialis—sexual dysfunction drug in Europe
AmerisourceBergen	ABC	$61.07	111.900	$6,834	0.56%	-0.02	$95–$105	Drug Distributor

MISCELLANEOUS VICE

Name	Ticker	Price	Shares	Market Value	Weight	Beta	Price Range	Description
Abercrombie and Fitch	ANF	$28.22	96.697	$2,729	0.22%	1.58	$35–$40	Clothing
Cadbury Schweppes	CSG	$26.19	522.874	$13,694	1.12%	0.08	$35–$40	Chocolate
Church & Dwight	CHD	$38.81	40.289	$1,564	0.13%	0.44	$38–$40	Trojan condoms
Gucci Group	GUC	$85.09	100.723	$8,571	0.70%	0.99	$50–$55	Vanity galore
Hershey	HSY	$76.94	130.117	$10,011	0.82%	−0.35	$80–$85	Leading US producer of chocolate and confectionery
Limited Brands	LTD	$17.65	517.985	$9,142	0.75%	1.45	$17–$20	Victoria's Secret
Nestle PLC ADS	NSRGY	$55.85	1543.854	$86,224	7.04%	0.16	$55–60	Chocolate
Playboy Enterprises	PLA	$16.85	22.574	$380	0.03%	1.25	$12–$13	Playboy empire
Private Media	PRVT	$2.12	44.905	$95	0.01%	0.74	$4–$5	Adult magazines, videos
Rick's Cabaret	RICK	$1.81	3.707	$7	0.00%	0.79	$12–$13	Strip clubs, adult Web sites
Sara Lee	SLE	$19.86	794.468	$15,778	1.29%	0.30	$23–$24	Junk food, bras
UniLever ADS	UL	$34.82	736.180	$25,634	2.09%	0.21	$55–$60	Petroleum jelly, ice cream
Summary Statistics			32083.754	$1,225,072	99.73%	0.5303		
SINDEX 69 Value	**$38.18**							

Source: Carter Crum, CFA, and Caroline Waxler. Note that data will be updated and revised on the Web site www.stockinguponsin.com on a routine basis.

The SIN-69 Stock Index

The reasons for creating the Stocking Up on SINDEX are three-fold. First to establish a benchmark that can be used to measure the return and risk of vice stocks and vice mutual funds. Second, we'll see that the Index can stand as a portfolio in its own right, should you wish to do so—it has performed rather well on both an absolute and risk adjusted return basis. Finally, it will establish the universe of stocks from which we will pick our own short list of favorite vices, called the titillating twenty.

Good managers measure themselves against the *appropriate* index, and the most ethical professional managers are even moving toward developing customized blends of indexes to better reflect their styles or style combinations (i.e. "our fund measures itself against a custom index blend comprised of 60% S&P 500 and 40% Russell 2000 Value Index because 60% of our portfolio is in large cap growth stocks and 40% of our portfolio is in small cap value stocks.") Interestingly though, as we believe vice investings is a style unto itself, which will become increasingly more studied, there are no customized indexes to measure vice investors against. The Stocking Up on SINDEX is an Index of stocks that seeks to remedy this problem!

(For more information go to www.stockinguponsin.com)

APPENDIX

III

The Titillating 20

Of all the vice stocks, these are the ones that are the most undervalued relative to the other vice stocks.

Company Name	Stock Symbol	11/7/03 Closing Stock Price	Shares Outstanding ($ Millions)	Market Cap ($ Millions)	Weight in Index	Beta	Fair Value	Notes
BOOZE								
Anheuser-Busch	BUD	$51.30	814.760	$41,797	6.44%	0.12	$65–$68	Parent company of world's largest brewer
Diageo PLC	DEO	$48.60	805.540	$39,149	6.03%	0.12	$45–$50	London-based producer and distributor of spirits
Fortune Brands	FO	$66.60	145.870	$9,715	1.50%	0.77	$60–$65	Jim Beam, DeKuyper cordials, Gilbey's gin, Cointreau
Constellation Brands	STZ	$31.52	105.147	$3,314	0.51%	0.42	$46–$48	Global beer/wine importer, Franciscan, Simi, Corona
Adolph Coors Co.	RKY	$56.01	36.402	$2,039	0.31%	0.35	$83–$87	Coors, Killian's Red, Keystone, Zima
CASINOS AND GAMES								
Argosy Gaming	AGY	$25.32	29.313	$742	0.11%	0.98	$50–$55	Riverboat gambling casinos in Midwest
International Game Technology	IGT	$33.43	345.063	$11,535	1.78%	0.53	$30–$35	Worldwide leader of gaming machines and software
Multimedia Gaming	MGAM	$41.45	13.125	$544	0.08%	1.82	$61–$65	Supplies both electronic games and the player stations

GUNS AND AMMO

Alliant Techsystems	ATK	$51.80	38.623	0.31%	-0.15	$65–$70	Pentagon's largest ammo supplier, solid rocket fuel
L-3 Communications	LLL	$48.20	96.392	0.72%	0.31	$70–$75	Supplier of secure communications systems and specialized communications
Lockheed Martin	LMT	$46.04	450.875	3.20%	-0.16	$58–$63	World's largest military weapons manufacturer

FAST FOOD

McDonald's	MCD	$26.01	1269.164	5.08%	0.86	$33–$35	Ronald McDonald and friends
YUM! Brands	YUM	$34.30	294.153	1.55%	0.30	$25–$27	Taco Bell, Pizza Hut, KFC

TOBACCO

Altria Group	MO	$49.51	2029.498	15.48%	0.33	$70–$75	Marlboro, Kraft Foods

DRUGS

Pfizer	PFE	$34.08	7631.523	40.06%	0.53	$37–$40	Viagra
AmerisourceBergen	ABC	$61.07	111.900	1.05%	-0.02	$95–$105	Drug distributor
Eli Lilly	LLY	$65.85	1122.904	11.39%	0.89	$55–$60	Cialis, Prozac

MISCELLANEOUS VICE

Abercrombie and Fitch	ANF	$28.22	96.697	0.42%	1.58	$35–$40	Clothing

(continues)

Company Name	Stock Symbol	11/7/03 Closing Stock Price	Shares Outstanding ($ Millions)	Market Cap ($ Millions)	Weight in Index	Beta	Fair Value	Notes
Hershey	HSY	$76.94	130.117	$10,011	1.54%	-0.35	$80–$85	Leading U.S. producer of chocolate and confectionery
Sara Lee	SLE	$19.86	794.468	$15,778	2.43%	0.30	$23–$24	Junk food, bras
Shares outstanding (Millions)			16361.53					
Portfolio Beta			0.4580					
Portfolio Market Cap			$649,199					
Value of Index			**$39.68**					

Source: Carter Crum, CFA, and Caroline Waxler. Note that data will be updated and revised on the Web site www.stockinguponsin.com on a routine basis.

20 Sin Stocks for the Next Five Years

Our rules:

1. Buy low and hold.
2. Avoid the value trap.
3. Management is important.

Our first criterion is that we want to buy stocks when they are cheap, that is, when they are selling at a large discount to intrinsic value. Our estimate of intrinsic value is the price a buyer would be willing to pay today, in cash, to own the whole company. Then we only buy the stock if it is selling at less than 60% of that number.

Our second criterion is that business value must grow as time passes. One of the most frequently experienced problems of a value investing approach is that it leads many value managers to own the statistically cheapest companies that are often also the most structurally disadvantaged companies.

Our third and final investment criterion is to invest only in companies that we believe management is smart, honest, and economically aligned with shareholders.

Put it all together and the end result is a selection of Twenty Stocks in which are our favorites from the original pool of 69. If we are right, we should outperform the SINDEX 69 over the course of the next five years, and, we hope, outperform the other market indexes as well.

Thinking of our investments in minimum terms of five years at a stretch, as we have been saying all along, many just in and of itself give us the edge over our peers because of reduced transaction costs and taxes. Combined with a solid fundamental stock picking approach, as described above, in industries that never go out of style, we are confident about the future. As they say in Vegas, best of luck! (For more details go to www.stockinguponsin.com)

Notes

Chapter 1

1. Dixon Murray, Teresa. "Fund invests in vice, but, so far, sin doesn't pay." Cleveland, OH: *The Plain Dealer*, March 9, 2003.
2. Earle, Julie, and Florian Gimbel. "Vice squad puts the pressure on ethical investors." U.K.: *Financial Times*, September 29, 2002.
3. Leerskov, Meghan. "Vice is nice: The underbelly of the investment world isn't such a bad place to be. [Editorial]." *Buyside*, January 1, 2003.

Chapter 2

1. *Merriam-Webster's Collegiate Dictionary*, 10th ed., Springfield, MA: Merriam-Webster, 1999.
2. Fernandez, Bob. "Exploiting the Profits of Vice: Investors Come Out Smoking, Roll the Dice with 'Irresponsible' Mutual Fund." *The Houston Chronicle*, October 14, 2002.
3. *Ibid.*
4. Johnston, Jo-ann. "Investors Search for Ethical Investments." *The Tampa Tribune*, August 18, 2002.
5. Taken from the PBS Web site description of its movie, *Andrew Carnegie*, as part of their American Experience Series. www.pbs.org/wgbh/amex/carnegie/filmmore/description.html.
6. Middleton, Timothy. "Mutual Funds Feel-Good Investing? I'd Rather Make Money." MSN Money Web site, Posted 8/19/03, http://money central.msn.com.
7. Hulbert, Mark. "Strategies: Good for Your Conscience, If Not Your Wallet." *The New York Times*, July 20, 2003.

Chapter 3

1. PBS Web site, *Betting the Market*: http://www.pbs.org/wgbh/pages/frontline/shows/betting/pros/lynch.html.
2. Harris, Lynn. "Makeover for aging sex symbol: K-Y Jelly, the old-fashioned 'personal lubricant,' gets an image revamp to appeal to younger set." *The Toronto Star*, May 23, 2003.
3. Strasburg, Jenny. "Gap's sales fall 2%; Drop is improvement for retailer as industry suffers from slump." *The San Francisco Chronicle*, September 6, 2002.

Chapter 4

1. "Cigarettes: Anatomy of an Industry from Seed to Smoke [book review]." *Publishers Weekly,* January 1, 2001.
2. Sellers, Patricia, and Julia Boorstin, and Christopher Tkaczyk. "Altria's Perfect Storm; Hit by cut-rate competitors, taxes, and most of all, litigation, the company that owns Philip Morris faces its worst crisis in years." *Fortune*, April 28, 2003.
3. "Lorillard Launches Ad Campaign Targeting Cigarette Excise Taxes– 'No Tax . . . No Crime' Initiative." PR Newswire. May 8, 2003.
4. *Ibid.*
5. From British American Tobacco's Web site, www.bat.com, via The Vice Fund's Web site, www.vicefund.com.
6. Kemp, Kenny. "Cash from Ash." U.K.: *Sunday Herald,* July 13, 2003.
7. Dreman, David. "Tunnel Vision." *Forbes*, March 17, 2003.

Chapter 5

1. www.gamblingphd.com.
2. *Ibid.*
3. Gorman, Tom. "Topless Shows Put the 'Sin' Back in Sin City," *LA Times,* June 17, 2001.
4. 20/20 Downtown (10:00 PM ET)–ABC, April 24, 2002, Las Vegas, Nevada, abandons family theme and reverts back to earlier adult-oriented image
5. *Ibid.*
6. Smith, Rod. "Growth foreseen for slot machine sales." *Las Vegas Review-Journal,* September 26, 2002.
7. *Ibid.*

8. Jones, Chris. "MGM Mirage to shut Web gambling site: Legal, political doubts plagued effort." *Las Vegas Review-Journal,* June 05, 2003.
9. Smith, Rod. "Sluggish Economy, Higher Taxes Take Toll on Gambling Operators." *Las Vegas Review-Journal,* June 4, 2003.
10. Dehaven, Judy. "Still Gambling–Borgata, taxes and competition will shape Atlantic City's future." *The Star-Ledger*, May 15, 2003.
11. Berenson, Alex. "The States Bet More on Betting." *The New York Times*, May 18, 2003.

Chapter 6

1. Staff. "What's Ahead in Aerospace Defense Played Big Role in Second-Quarter GDP Growth, Analyst Says." *Aerospace Daily*, August 4, 2003.
2. Laise, Eleanor. "Beyond Iraq." *SmartMoney*, May 1, 2003.
3. *Ibid.*
4. Peltz, James. "Defense stocks not booming in wartime Iraq: Fighting not factor, analysts say. Shares pricey." *Los Angeles Times*, March 23, 2003.
5. Martin, Neil A. "Secure investments: The Homeland Security Act has given investors some potentially attractive opportunities." *Barron's*, June 16, 2003.
6. *Ibid.*

Chapter 7

1. English, Simon. "The Vice Fund aims for rewards in this life." UK: *The Daily Telegraph*, August 27, 2002.
2. Waxler, Caroline. "Sex Appeal." *Worth*, November 2002.
3. Kirk, Jim. "Wait nearly over for U.S. rollout of low-carb beer." *Chicago Tribune*, May, 2, 2002.
4. Salter, Jim. "Anheuser-Busch Claims Half of Beer Market." Associated Press, April 24, 2003.
5. Todd, Heather. "Breaking the Ice: New malternative beverage 'thin' on calories and carbohydrates." *Beverage World,* April 15, 2003.
6. Lawton, Christopher, and Deborah Ball. "Diageo Mixes It Up–Liquor Giant Targets System Dating to End of Prohibition; Following the Beer Model?" *The Wall Street Journal,* May 8, 2003.
7. Kosnett, Jeffrey R. "Simple and Safe." *Kiplinger's Personal Finance,* July 1, 2003.

8. Helman, Christoper. "Seeing stars; No. 2 winery Constellation Brands makes juice to suit winos and sommeliers alike." *Forbes Global,* January 6, 2003.
9. "Prince warns of GM crop 'threat'." U.K., BBC News, June 11, 2002.
10. Freedman, Michael. "That Sinking Feeling; Could deflation happen here? A gloomy Stephen Roach says it may well be on its way." *Forbes,* July 7, 2003.

Chapter 8 Notes

1. Rich, Frank. "Naked Capitalists: There's No Business Like Porn Business." *New York Times Magazine,* May 18, 2003.
2. Sigesmund, B.J. "XXX-ceptable porn has gone mainstream. Today's adult-film stars are writing books, making movie cameos and hitting prime time. When did America get so comfortable with hardcore?" *Newsweek,* July 2, 2003.
3. Pondel, Evan. "Mainstream Move Adult Film Company Advertises with Snowboards and Athletic Shoes." *Los Angeles Daily News,* May 9, 2003.
4. Egan, Timothy. "Erotic Inc.–A special report. Technology Sent Wall Street Into Market for Pornography." *The New York Times,* October 23, 2000.
5. Keegan, Paul. "Prime Time Porn." San Francisco, *Business 2.0,* June 2003.
6. Waxler, Caroline. "Sex Appeal." *Worth,* November 2002.
7. Fitch, Stephane. "The Unhappy Hawker." *Forbes,* January, 21, 2002.
8. Barrera Diaz, Cynthia. "The Naked Truth." Australia: *The Gold Coast Bulletin,* May 27, 2003.
9. Waxler, *op. cit.*
10. Egan, *op. cit.*
11. Bean Yancey, Kitty. "Coalition wants to change hotel porn channels." *USA Today,* September 24, 2002.
12. Bean Yancey, Kitty. "Omni turning off porn at some hotels. Chain removes 'temptation,' at a loss of more than $4 million." *USA Today,* February 4, 2000.
13. Bean Yancey, Kitty. *op. cit.,* September, 24, 2002.
14. *Ibid.*
15. "Religious Leaders Launch Petition Drive Aimed at Getting Fortune 500 Companies Out of the Pornography Business." PR Newswire, December 17, 2002.

16. LaRue, Jan. "AT&T Getting the Porn Ring Out of Its Collar." Concerned Women of America Web site (www.cwfa.org.), March 20, 2003.
17. Waxler, *op. cit.*

Chapter 9

1. Fink, Mitchell, with Lauren Rubin. *New York Daily News*, November 4, 1999.
2. *Ibid.*
3. Lloyd, Linda. "Two pills look to topple Viagra's reign in market, Levitra expects approval next month, Cialis later this year." *The Philadelphia Inquirer*, July 6, 2003.
4. Waxler, Caroline. "Sex sells." *Worth*, November, 2003.
5. "Glaxo says Levitra doing 'fairly well' in Europe." Reuters. News. July 23, 2003.
6. Japsen, Bruce. "Drug Companies Take on Pfizer for Share of Viagra Market." *Chicago Tribune*, July 13, 2003.
7. Lloyd, *op. cit.*
8. Waxler, *op. cit.*
9. *Ibid*

Chapter 10

1. Waxler, Caroline. "Sex Sells." New York, *Worth*, November 2002.
2. Kapner, Suzanne. "Dior Bucks Trend With 10% Sales Gain." *The New York Post*, July 18, 2003.
3. Navratil, Wendy. "Oo-la-la! Is Gucci ad simply gratuitous?" *Chicago Tribune*, March 9, 2003.
4. Waxler, Caroline, *op. cit.*

Chapter 11

1. Smith, Roc. "Gambling Industry: Gambling supporters succeed. *The Las Vegas Review-Journal*, November 7, 2002.
2. Ryssdal, Kai. "Profile: Bill to curb Internet gambling." Minnesota Public Radio: Marketplace Morning Report , May 8, 2003.
3. Sager, Ira, Ben Elgin, Peter Elstrom, Faith Keenan, and Pallavi Gogoi. "The Underground Web." *BusinessWeek*, September 2, 2002.

Chapter 12

1. Aktar, Alex. "The New Reality after a Year of Economic and Religious Scandal, Faith Popcorn Predicts 2003 Will Be about Food, Family and Vanity." New York: *New York Daily News,* January 1, 2003.
2. Passmore, Daryl. "Our brave new world." U.K.: *Sunday Mail,* January 12, 2003.
3. www.teledildonics.com.
4. Phillips, Mike. "My date with the Virtual Sex Machine." Salon.com, February 5, 2003.
5. Spark, David. "Make Love to Your Computer." TechTV, Wired for Sex Web site. Posted April 24, 2003 and Modified June 27, 2003.
6. Maheu, Marlene M., "Future of Cyber-Sex and Relationship Fidelity," SelfhelpMagazine.com Web site: www.selfhelpmagazine.com/booklet/future.html
7. "MA/iTV–Porn providers let the viewers join in." U.K.: *New Media Age,* August 8, 2002.
8. "Growth Looks Limited for Wireless Adult Content." U.K.: *Wireless Data News,* April 23, 2002.
9. Skeldon, Paul, "Sex and the city." U.K.: *Communications International,* October 1, 2002.
10. Harvey, Fiona. "Welcome to 3G–girls, games and gambling." U.K.: *Financial Times,* February 25, 2003.
11. Lowe, Sue. "News and Features–Text and the city." Australia, *The Sydney Morning Herald,* March 3, 2002.
12. "Dating evolution." U.K.: *New Media Age,* May 29, 2003.
13. Hochbaum, Leah. "High-tech Japanese adult fare guiding TV trend." *Video Age International,* May 1, 2003.

Chapter 13

1. Cherney, Elana. "CoolBrands: Low-Carb Bet–Canadian Company Scoops Out a Trendy Ice-Cream Strategy." *The Wall Street Journal,* August 18, 2003.

Index